Surprised by Grace

Surprised by Grace

A Spiritual Journey from West to East and Back

Kevin Patrick Joyce

The Crossroad Publishing Company
New York

The Crossroad Publishing Company
www.crossroadpublishing.com

Copyright @ 2024 Kevin Patrick Joyce

Crossroad, Herder & Herder, and the crossed C logo/colophon are registered trademarks of The Crossroad Publishing Company.

All rights reserved. No part of this book may be copied, scanned, reproduced in any way, or stored in a retrieval system, or transmitted, in any form or by any means, electronic, mechanical, photocopying, recording, or otherwise, without the written permission of The Crossroad Publishing Company. For permission please write to rights@crossroadpublishing.com.

In continuation of our 200-year tradition of independent publishing, The Crossroad Publishing Company proudly offers a variety of books with strong, original voices and diverse perspectives. The viewpoints expressed in our books are not necessarily those of The Crossroad Publishing Company, any of its imprints or of its employees, executives, or owners. Although the author and publisher have made every effort to ensure that the information in this book was correct at press time, the author and publisher do not assume and hereby disclaim any liability to any party for any loss, damage, or disruption caused by errors or omissions, whether such errors or omissions result from negligence, accident, or any other cause. No claims are made or responsibility assumed for any health or other benefits.

Cover image: Labyrinth of Chartes, wikimedia commons

Library of Congress Cataloging-in-Publication Data
available from the Library of Congress.

| ISBN | 9780824597085 | BC-Paperback/softback |
| ISBN | 9780824598327 | EA-Digital |

Books published by The Crossroad Publishing Company may be purchased at special quantity discount rates for classes and institutional use. For information, please e-mail sales@crossroadpublishing.com.

*To my mother, Margie Joyce (1929–2022)
My best editor and cheerleader*

Contents

ACKNOWLEDGMENTS	XIII
PREFACE	XV

1. BEGINNINGS ... 1
   Family
   My First Love
   Pursuing a Priestly Vocation

2. HIGH SCHOOL SEMINARY ... 11
   Heartbreak
   Facing Family Alcoholism
   Spiritual Friendship
   Tragic Death of Uncle Dave
   Relationships with Women
   A New Meditation Practice: *Lectio Divina*

3. UNSETTLED COLLEGE YEARS AND AN AWAKENING ... 24
   Turbulence after the "Summer of Love"
   A Spiritual Awakening
   An Auspicious Journey to Mexico
   Exposure to Transcendental Meditation in a Factory
   Father Dunstan, a Modern-Day Desert Father

4. VOCATIONAL CRISIS IN MEXICO ... 36
   Arrival in Mexico
   Father Donald Hessler and *el Nuevo Guadalupanismo*
   An Undeclared Romance
   A New Host Family
   Vocational Crisis

Contents

5. **SIMONE WEIL, MEDITATION, AND JUNG** — 46
   Simone Weil
   Transcendental Meditation
   Senior Year: Return to a Spiritual Routine
   The Psychology of Carl Jung
   Herman Hesse's *Narcissus and Goldmund*

6. **ENCOUNTER WITH CHRISTIAN MYSTICISM: MEISTER ECKHART** — 56
   Eckhart's "Talks of Instruction"
   Eckhart's Experience of God
   The Unity of God and Human Beings

7. **ENCOUNTER WITH AN EASTERN TRADITION** — 64
   Encountering Maharishi Mahesh Yogi
   Maharishi's Religious and Philosophical Tradition
   Spiritual Practices during the Course
   Aftereffects of the Course
   Processing with Father Dunstan

8. **GRADUATE SEMINARY AND A LIFE-CHANGING DECISION** — 74
   Arrival at St. Patrick's Seminary
   Dogma
   Faith
   Jesus and the Avatars
   Decision to Leave the Seminary

9. **BREAKING THE NEWS** — 83
   Challenged by Father Don McDonnell,
     Cesar Chavez's Mentor
   Breaking the News in Mexico

10. **SEEKING A NEW DIRECTION IN SPAIN** — 89
    An Emotional Departure
    The East-West Dialogue Resumes
    Getting Serious about the Faith Again
    A Unique Christmas
    Bill Gibson Enters my Life
    The End of the Course

11. **European Odyssey**   102
   Tension with Old Friends
   A Providential Encounter
   Holy Week in Rome
   Encountering the Spirit of St. Francis
   Breathing the Spiritual Air of Assisi
   Synchronicity in Zurich

12. **A Crisis Brews during the Odyssey**   149
   Synchronicity or Divine Providence?
   Study at the C. G. Jung Institute
   Connecting with My Swiss Family in the Alps
   Retreating to the Monastery of Taizé
   A Crisis Brews in Paris

13. **Breakthrough**   122
   Breakdown and Breakthrough during
     Brother Sun, Sister Moon
   Return to Taizé
   The Universal Value of Monasticism

14. **The Final Weeks of the Odyssey**   133
   The Monastery of la Pierre-qui-Vire
   Revelations
   Farewell to Pierre-qui-Vire and Leo
   A Surprise Trip to Mont Saint-Michel
   The World-Famous Monastery of Solesme
   The Last Week in Paris
   The Last Day: Chartres Cathedral

15. **Forging a New Path in California**   148
   Back with Family in Alameda
   Full Time at the School of Music
   A Spiritual Experiment That Failed
   A Prophetic Dream
   Withdrawing from the SJSU School of Music
   Painting Our Way to Hawaii

Contents

16 Encountering Buddhism in Hawaii — 160
  The Catholic Approach to Interreligious Dialogue
  Fundamental Buddhist Teachings
  Salvation in Buddhism and Christianity
  Understandings of Jesus Christ
  God and the Afterlife
  Meditation Practices
  The Fruit of the Hawaiian Experience

17 Teaching Meditation during the "Boom" — 176
  Six Weeks on Cobb Mountain
  Teaching Meditation
  A Six-Month Advanced Meditation Course in Switzerland

18 Seeking Enlightenment in Switzerland — 182
  Serious Asceticism in the Alps
  St. Teresa of Avila's *Interior Castle*
  The Vocation Question
  Breakthrough

19 A Rough Landing Back in the Seminary — 193
  Deflation
  A Supernatural Intervention
  Ma's Death
  A Master's Thesis and a Ph.D. Dissertation

20 St. Teresa of Avila, Spiritual Master — 204
  The Carmelites
  St. Teresa's Life as a Carmelite
  St. Teresa's Method of Meditation
  St. Teresa's Legacy
  Comparing St. Teresa and Maharishi

21 Ordination — 214
  Language Study and Reconciliation in Mexico
  Internship
  Getting Ready for the Big Day
  The Big Day

22 **Celebrations and a Surprise Assignment**   224
    First Mass and Reception
    More Celebrations
    Two Weeks in Mexico
    Climbing the Oaxaca Mountains
    A Surprise Assignment

23 **Divine Providence is Real**   231

About the Author   236

Acknowledgments

THE IDEA FOR THIS BOOK CAME FROM A PUBLISHED AUTHOR and good friend, Jack Forem. He talked me out of my original plan, which was to write a book about the spiritual masters and mentors who have impacted my spiritual journey. Jack said, "There are innumerable books about gurus and spiritual masters. People want to read a story. Tell your story and how those masters touched your life."

I accepted Jack's counsel and spent three summers writing in a hermitage at the New Camaldoli Monastery in Big Sur, California. I am exceedingly grateful to the Camaldolese monks for their generous hospitality and encouragement of my project.

Throughout the course of my writing, many people graciously read my manuscript and offered valuable recommendations: Roberta Forem, Gina Bence, Robert Rodd, Father Manuel Sousa, Justin Kim, Father Gerardo Menchaca, Dennis Stradford, Kevin Friel, John Bright, Steven Ellison, Rev. Anita Warner, and Cesar Molina, M.D.

I am very grateful to those who offered their endorsements found on the back cover of this book: Paula Huston, Dr. Adrian Walker, Dr. Anthony Lilles, Dr. Mario Starc, and Dr. Gerald Gonzales. Special thanks to my mother, Margie Joyce, who read most of the manuscript out loud with me before her death in 2022. Her insights and collaboration were priceless.

I wish to express my deepest gratitude to Gwendolin Herder, publisher of The Crossroad Publishing Company, for her enthusiastic support throughout the publishing process. Finally, I want to express my appreciation to my eagle-eyed copyeditor, Maurya Horgan.

Preface

For centuries, spiritual seekers have profited from reading accounts of people's spiritual journeys. Well-known examples include Augustine of Hippo's *Confessions*, Teresa of Avila's *Story of Her Life*, Thomas Merton's *Seven Storey Mountain*, and M. K. Gandhi's *Story of My Life*. Reading spiritual autobiographies has provided me with light for my own journey and has helped me correct course when I have veered off the path.

For several decades remarkable spiritual masters—both contemporary and from the distant past—have come into my path. These masters have provided me with reliable and wise guidance for the spiritual journey. One purpose of this book is to share how these masters and mentors have provided me with inspiration and direction and how they may help readers of this book. A second objective is to analyze and compare two paths that have most influenced my life: the Christian and the Vedic tradition from ancient India.

When I completed the book, another theme emerged—"Divine Providence"—which refers to Divine interventions in the course of our spiritual growth. These interventions are manifestations of "grace," the gratuitous gift that God makes to us of his own life, infused by the Holy Spirit into our soul to heal it and to sanctify it.

I hope that my story and reflections will support those already on a spiritual journey and encourage skeptics and nonbelievers to take a gamble on God.

1
Beginnings

Family ▸

IN 1949 I WAS BORN IN ALAMEDA, CALIFORNIA, THE ONLY island city in the San Francisco Bay and an architect's paradise. Alameda boasts about three thousand Victorian-era homes from the late 1800s, as well as plenty of gorgeous examples of other styles: Tudor-Revival, Mission Revival, Italianate, and bayside villas.

If you stroll down the tree-lined streets of Alameda today, you can see that the town has not changed much from one hundred years ago, the time when many of the houses were built. The island was then known as the City of Homes and Beaches.[1] For the first four years of my life, I was raised in a large, handsome Tudor Revival house that my maternal grandparents, John and Mabel Thoeni, bought in 1934 in the middle of the Great Depression for $14,000. They owned the most popular bakery on the island, the Bonaire. My grandfather died when I was four. Although I was only a young child, I remember him with great fondness. He used to take me on rides in his 1940 Buick along the Alameda Gold Coast to gaze at the bay and the bayside villas.

My parents, Pat and Margie Joyce, married young and didn't have much money, so we shared my grandparents' home along with my uncle, Dave Thoeni, and my great-grandmother, Anna Helena Culver (Gran Gran), who was born in 1868 in Benicia, the capitol of California from 1853 to 1854. I spent my early

---

1. *Alameda Magazine*, January-February, 2008 (Internet search).

years listening enthusiastically to her stories of the distant past. It amazed me to think that she was born just three years after the end of the Civil War. She died at the age of ninety-three when I was eleven. I was blessed with all these terrific babysitters, including my dad's sister, Catherine Ann Joyce, who was only eleven when I was born. She would beg my parents to schedule date nights so she could take care of me. When I was seven, she married Jerry Schoenbachler and they eventually had four children. But during my first years of life, I was happily the recipient of her early maternal instincts.

My Uncle Dave was a genius who graduated from the University of California at Berkeley and later worked at the Lawrence Livermore National Laboratory; he became an inventor of cutting-edge instruments for eye treatments. Prior to his impressive professional career, he built hot-rods and motorcycles. When I was about three years old, he used to put me on the handlebars of his motorcycle and take me on exhilarating trips around Alameda. My parents would have been horrified had they known! But I'm glad they never knew because Uncle Dave provided me with some of the most exciting experiences of my early life.

Although she did not live with us, my mother's sister, Catherine Jeanne Thoeni, enriched my early life. She joined the Sisters of the Holy Names of Jesus and Mary in 1942 and took the name of Sister Catherine Irene. In those days, the sisters were allowed to visit their homes only once a year, although we could visit them monthly in their convents. I remember her home visits vividly. She was very loving and a lot of fun. She was quite a fine pianist and would play the piano for me. I was enthralled watching her play. She inspired me to start inventing melodies on the piano, a habit that led me to beg for piano lessons at the age of eight. My parents did not have sufficient income to pay for the lessons, so my grandmother offered to pay—which she did every month until I entered high school.

In 1952 my brother Brian came along. My parents bought a small postwar house across the street from Edison Elementary School, which I attended through fourth grade. In many ways my early life in Alameda was idyllic. Lots of kids lived nearby, and we rode our bikes to the many parks and beaches without fear. At the same time, our family faced a major challenge. My parents and I noticed that Brian began to exhibit bruises. My parents took him for tests and discovered that he had hemophilia (a blood clotting disorder). Whenever he played too hard or had a fall, he would bleed internally. Throughout his childhood, our parents often had to take him to Children's Hospital in Oakland for blood transfusions followed by days of recovery in the hospital. His condition contributed to a very deep bond between me and Brian. Witnessing his periodic suffering elicited heartfelt empathy in me and led me to take on the role of protector.

Despite his physical affliction, Brian developed a great sense of humor and exhibited brilliance. Throughout his eight years at St. Philip Neri School, he received the annual scholarship merit pin given to the best student in the class. He was also an impressive artist and a natural athlete despite the limitations of hemophilia.

In 1960 we moved to a large shingle Craftsman home built in 1909 in a turn-of-the century neighborhood near the east shore. Brian and I were used to a small three-bedroom, one-bath house. Our new home was two stories with a full basement where our parents set up ping-pong and pool tables. They also gave us the big master bedroom and placed there a large play-table for our board games. To our further delight they designated the adjacent bedroom as our "playroom" which had a spacious walk-in closet where we stored our toys, games, and mountains of comic books. Brian and I could not believe our good fortune—nor could the many friends who regularly came over to share in our windfall.

Even though Brian was three and a half years younger than I, we became the best of friends. We played lots of ping pong and board games together, and every night before bed I would read him Hardy Boys novels and other kids' adventure stories. We also developed a spiritual relationship when I trained him to be an altar boy. For me it was a special joy to serve Mass with Brian.

The new house was ideally situated. Our parish church, St. Philip Neri, was a block away. My grandparents' house was a six blocks' walk. Half a block up the street was Lincoln School, a large public middle school that I entered in fifth grade.

One day the fifth grade teacher, Miss Milligan, invited us to tell the class what we wanted to be when we grew up. One by one, each student shared his or her dream. When it was my turn to speak, a few students murmured "Oh, we know Kevin wants to be a doctor." Since first grade I had told people that I wanted to be a doctor, inspired by Brian's frequent trips to the hospital.

In response to Miss Milligan's question, I responded "When I grow up, I would like to be a doctor or [long pause] a priest." A collective gasp erupted from most of my classmates. In that public school where Catholics were a minority, my Protestant and Jewish classmates were shocked by my statement. Immediately they began peppering me with comments such as, "But you always said you wanted to be a doctor! Priests can't get married! You won't be able to have a family!" I was so taken aback by their intense disapproval that I decided then and there that I would keep my desire to become a priest private for the foreseeable future.

What motivated eleven-year-old Kevin Joyce to seriously consider becoming a Catholic priest? The answer has much to do with my family, my religious formation, and an extraordinary experience of the Divine when I was seven years old.

My family was strongly Catholic. We attended Sunday Mass every week even though we usually arrived at the last minute (my parents liked to sleep in on Sundays). We prayed a blessing at every meal and had religious images displayed around the house. Contributing further to our Catholic identity, my dad worked as athletic director of the Catholic Youth Organization (CYO) for the Archdiocese of San Francisco from 1958 to 1974. His work brought him into contact with priests from all over the Bay Area, and I was intrigued by his priest stories, such as his story about visiting Father John Heaney, chaplain of Sacred Heart High School in San Francisco. Both men were fine athletes, and one day they were challenged by students to engage in a wrestling match. My dad took off his tie and Father Heaney took off his clerical collar. The two of them proceeded to duke it out on the wrestling mat. My dad told me many other entertaining stories about the priests he worked with in CYO. These accounts led me to see the priesthood as a happy, "normal" life in which a man could make a difference in the lives of young people.

My dad's CYO job brought him into contact with the Golden State Warriors and the San Francisco Giants. Periodically, the Warriors asked my dad to provide water boys. My brother and I eagerly volunteered for the job, along with a bunch of our friends. Those were the days of the

Warriors' first "dream team." It was a thrill to bring water to legends such as Wilt Chamberlain, Al Attles, Nate Thurmond, and Guy Rodgers.

Being involved with the Church also provided opportunities for exciting experiences with the Giants. Once a year the Giants' organization hosted the CYO youth at Candlestick Park. My dad organized the event and had access to the Giants' dugout. One of the most amazing moments in our young lives was to accompany my dad to the dugout and shake hands with great stars like Willie Mays, Orlando Cepeda, and Willie McCovey.

Other key influences in my spiritual formation included the example of my parents' care for my often-infirm brother. Brian missed up to thirty days of school each year because of internal bleeding episodes—some of which required hospitalization. Mom would spend hours with Brian during his hospitalizations even though she was working part-time for an insurance company. During those hospitalizations, my dad would always stop at the hospital on his way home from work and play cards with Brian. Once Dad even arranged for Willie Mays to visit Brian—an unbelievable thrill for Brian, who was a huge Giants fan.

My mom served as Den Mother for my Cub Scout den and made my friends feel more than welcome in our home. She also introduced me to the world of classical music, which had a major impact on my future avocation as a musician. When I was about five years old, she invited me to listen to a recording of Arthur Rubinstein playing two Beethoven piano sonatas—the "Pathetique" and the "Appassionata." I was mesmerized by their beauty and power, and I began to listen to classical music in earnest. Once I began taking piano lessons at the age of eight I never stopped playing.

My mom was a columnist for the local newspaper, the *Alameda Times Star*. The paper offered complimentary issues to new residents of Alameda. She interviewed new residents by phone gleaning grist for vignettes with the hope that they would become subscribers. The den where she worked at home was soon wallpapered by copies of her column. Later she was promoted by the editor to write feature stories.

My Irish-born paternal grandmother, Delia Joyce (Nana), was a catechist in her Oakland parish. She died when I was seven years old, but by then she had strongly impacted my religious sensibilities. Periodically

I would spend a weekend with her and my grandfather. During breakfast she would explain to me the questions and answers contained in the *Baltimore Catechism*, the official 1950s teaching guide of the Catholic Church in the United States. She made that rather dry question-and-answer presentation of Catholic doctrine come alive—so much so that, as soon as we would sit down to eat breakfast I would say, "Nana, teach me the catechism!" Even today, decades later, I remember some of the questions and answers that she explained to me, such as:

> Question: Why did God make you?
> Answer: God made me to know Him, to love Him, and serve Him in this world and to be happy with Him forever in heaven.

I could feel her love for the Lord, the Church, and the teachings that she shared with me. She would take me to Mass and Benediction, and I felt moved by the devotional atmosphere and the sense of mystery in the Latin services. I sensed the peace and joy that the Catholic faith brought her.

My maternal grandmother (Ma) also strongly impacted my spiritual development. My parents and I lived in her house until I was four years old. Ma was a second mother to me. After my parents and I moved to Edison Court, I went to Ma's house after school each day because my mother worked part-time. Ma would always have freshly baked cookies waiting for me and piles of comic books from the 1950s. (If we had kept those comics, selling them years later could have financed my parents' retirement!) She also had an old upright piano which I played daily, thanks to her financing my piano lessons. Like Nana, Ma had a transparent spirituality and the gift of hospitality. I would often invite friends over to play Monopoly. They came not only for board games but also to enjoy Ma's cookies. As they left the house she always said, "Please come again!" As the years passed, I would often hear people make the same comment about Ma and Nana: "Kevin's grandmothers are saints."

The most transformational experience of my childhood occurred when I was seven years old. In those days, most children from observant Catholic families prepared to receive their First Holy Communion in the second grade. Sister Austin, the teacher responsible for preparing us second graders in 1956, belonged to a religious order called the Sisters of the Holy Family. She had the ways of an affectionate grandmother, and she communicated to us children such great love for God and the sacrament of the Holy Eucharist that I could hardly wait for the day of my First Communion celebration.

When the big day arrived, the children processed into the church with hands folded and sat in the front pews. When the moment arrived to receive Holy Communion, the gates of the altar rail were opened (lay people were rarely allowed into the sanctuary in those days), which for me felt like entering into a celestial sacred space. We climbed the steps leading to the altar two by two and received the Sacred Host on our tongues as the priest said in Latin, "May the Body of our Lord Jesus Christ guard your soul unto Eternal Life."

After receiving Holy Communion, I felt something entirely new. All those sessions sitting at Nana's breakfast table listening to her share her faith, and all those compelling teachings of Sister Austin had created a deep-seated desire in me to receive Christ in Holy Communion. I was not disappointed. On the contrary, when we processed out of the church and waited to greet our families, I felt a quiet, exquisite joy that was more palpable than any happiness I had ever before experienced. I thought to myself, "This is so awesome. Why don't people receive Holy Communion every day?" At that moment I decided that I would attend daily Mass, beginning the next morning. No one had ever suggested such a practice to me, and I didn't share my intentions with anyone—not even with my parents.

The following morning, I woke up early, rode my bike a half mile to the parish church, and arrived early for the 7:30 Mass. The church was mostly empty. I walked up to the front pew, knelt, and began praying the Rosary. Soon about thirty parishioners had arrived and Father O'Brien, the pastor, began the Mass, which was celebrated entirely in Latin, much of it inaudibly. Most of us had a bilingual Mass book (an English-Latin "Missal") in order to follow the prayers and biblical readings. The atmosphere was profoundly peaceful and uplifting.

For a few months I sat alone in that front pew for daily Mass, but then my friend Dave Tebow joined me. The following year another friend, Mike Cole, joined us. The spiritual companionship added a new dimension to my experience of attending daily Mass. Eventually, Dave and I joined the altar boys, which intensified my experience of a small

Christian community and brought me into a close relationship with the parish priests.

From second through eighth grade, I continued to attend daily Mass and began to find myself drawn to the priesthood. I admired how priests of my parish served the parishioners and led us in worship. Consequently, when Miss Milligan asked the fifth-grade students what we wanted to be when we grew up, I already had found my vocational aspirations shifting from becoming a doctor to becoming a priest.

My First Love

The fact that I would have to make a promise of celibacy in order to become a priest was not an issue for me in the fifth grade. I had never been in love. But soon thereafter, I developed a crush on a vivacious and beautiful northern Italian girl in my class named Vicki Simi. It was "puppy love" at first, but gradually developed into full-blown adolescent infatuation. By seventh grade the romantic interest was mutual, and we became a "couple." We were in the same homeroom and used the opportunity to speak excitedly with each other whenever the teacher was not looking. At the monthly seventh grade dances, I danced every dance with Vicki, during which I felt enchanted.

The seventh-grade romance taught me a lesson about sexuality and chastity. One day after school, Vicki invited me to her house to listen to music. When we arrived no one else was home. We went into the family room and Vicki put on a record with my favorite pop song: "Theme from a Summer Place." We danced to the slow, romantic tempo, and I felt utterly entranced. When the song ended, we just looked at each other silently. The satisfaction we felt at that moment was complete. The healthy boundaries we learned in our Catholic homes for maintaining a chaste relationship in the midst of strong romantic attraction enabled both of us to appreciate a subtle, tender erotic interaction in a modest, restrained way.

The intense romance ended after about three months, probably because I had no previous experience in the boyfriend role. My communication skills in such a relationship were undeveloped. I was better dancing with her than conversing. Without speaking about it, we stopped seeing each other and soon she started going with another guy. I was crushed. Gradually I recovered and refocused on my vocational plans. The feelings I had for Vicki morphed into a close but nonromantic friendship.

Pursuing a Priestly Vocation

At the beginning of the eighth grade, I took the entrance exam for St. Joseph's High School Seminary in Mountain View, California, along with about four hundred other young men from around the San Francisco Bay Area. We were told that only one hundred would be accepted into the freshman class. For several weeks I lived in a heightened state of anxiety, but then received the happy news that I had been accepted. I began telling my friends. Most of them thought I was crazy. Ironically, the only close friend who supported my decision was Tom Barni, who had recently stopped practicing his Catholic faith. We have remained lifelong friends.

Even my mother opposed my going to the seminary so young. She went crying to the pastor begging him to convince me to wait until I completed high school. Father O'Brien assured her that I would be just fine in the seminary. She thereafter gave me her full support as did my father. However, soon there were to be two further tests, both involving Vicki.

One Saturday I was mowing the lawn in front of our house and Vicki arrived with two of her girlfriends. She said, "Kevin, we don't want you to leave for the seminary. We want you to stay in Alameda. The three of us have decided that if you change your crazy plan and instead attend St. Joe's (the local Catholic high school in Alameda), we will give up our plans to attend Alameda High and we will go with you to St. Joe's." I could not believe what I was hearing. Here was the girl with whom I had been infatuated for four years telling me that she and her two friends were willing to change their high school plans to keep me in Alameda. I was amazed by how much they cared for me. I thanked them for their concern and assured them that I really wanted to be a priest and I would be happy in the seminary.

The second test occurred the week prior to my entering the seminary. My oldest friend from kindergarten, Robert Rodd, hosted a farewell party for me in his back yard on a warm summer evening. A large group of our middle school friends were in attendance, including Vicki and her new boyfriend. At the party we were all dancing late into the evening. Finally, I had the guts to ask Vicki to dance. Her boyfriend could not exactly object since the party was in my honor, so Vicki and I had our last dance together. As we were dancing, I was overwhelmed by the reality of what I would have to give up to become a priest. I felt more attracted to Vicki than ever before. The stars were out, the music was romantic, Vicki looked beautiful. I asked her if I could kiss her (I had never *really* kissed a girl before). She looked into my eyes with desire and said yes. So, we kissed . . . a short but very sweet kiss. I was in bliss! I thought to myself, "Kevin, are you crazy? Are you sure you want to become a priest?"

The next day, when I had recovered from the romantic intoxication, I reflected on the question, Are you sure you want to become a priest? Are you willing to give up the possibility of marriage? I looked into my heart and into my personal history. On a deep, intuitive level, I knew that the closeness and joy in my relationship with Christ that I periodically experienced, especially during daily Mass, was what I most wanted in life. Throughout elementary and middle school, I underwent the inevitable, normal struggles and dramas of childhood and adolescence. The one constant anchor was the daily Mass. It helped me to turn over my life to the care of God. That connection and the desire to share it are what inspired me to leave everyone I knew and set off for St. Joseph's High School Seminary at the age of fourteen.

2

High School Seminary

In September 1963, my family, Tom Barni, Robert Rodd, and Jim Ready (my best friends from middle school) drove me to St. Joseph's High School Seminary in Mountain View, where I joined about four hundred young men who shared my dream of becoming a priest. St. Joseph's was called a "minor seminary"; it was operated by the Priests of San Sulpice (the Sulpicians) and provided four years of high school and two years of college. Graduates then transferred to St. Patrick's Seminary in Menlo Park, the "major seminary," for another six years of education—two years of philosophy and four years of theology. St. Joseph's was out in the country on a thousand acres in the foothills of Los Altos, California. It was noted for superior academics, an array of sports programs, spiritual training, and ample extracurricular activities. I engaged in drama, journalism, sports, and served as student liturgical music director. I made good friends, and threw myself into a ton of new activities. Eventually I ended up on the tennis, swimming, and track teams.

    I paid a price, however, by leaving home so young. My life in Alameda had been happy and fulfilling. I had a close relationship with my parents, brother, grandmother, and a host of good friends. I felt loved and appreciated despite the predictable adolescent insecurities and drama. I attended excellent schools and was closely connected to my parish. Entering the seminary would mean separating myself for extended periods of time from the people I loved and the world I knew. My life at the seminary would be cloistered. In those days, seminarians were allowed to go home only during the major vacations: Thanksgiving, Christmas, Easter, and summer, although our families could visit us once a month on "Visiting Sunday."

Despite the pain of separation and entering a community where I knew only one person (Dave Tebow from my parish), I profited a great deal from the seminary formation and grew to enjoy my new life. The four hundred students gathered for community prayer, meditation, and Mass every morning. We also prayed the Rosary together in the evening while walking in silence around a spacious monastic-style courtyard in which were planted dozens of mock-orange trees that filled the courtyard with an unforgettable fragrance.

The most captivating spiritual experience for me upon arrival was the Sunday Solemn High Mass. In my home parish I had never experienced this most ceremony-rich form of the Mass because it requires a deacon and a subdeacon in addition to the priest-celebrant, a well-trained choir capable of singing Gregorian chant, and several skilled acolytes. As the Mass began, the four hundred students and twenty priests (all dressed in cassock and surplice) began singing an ancient chant, "*Asperges Me*," supported by a thirty-voice choir, accompanied by a grand pipe organ, and led by a world-class music director, Father John Olivier. As we chanted, the ministers processed up the main aisle dressed in elaborate vestments led by an incense-bearer.

As the celebration continued, I felt so overwhelmed by its beauty and transcendence that I said to myself, "How could anyone leave this place?!" I experienced what Catholic liturgy at its best is supposed to engender: a reflection of the heavenly liturgy as described in the Book of Revelation.[1]

That first Solemn High Mass in the seminary did seem heavenly to me. But it wasn't an entirely new experience. It was a more ritually and symbolically rich celebration of the quiet, intimate daily Masses of my childhood.

Heartbreak ▸

My new life as a seminarian began as an exciting adventure: an entirely new community of four hundred idealistic young men, inspiring priests,

---

1. See references to the Mass in Revelation 15:3–4 (the Gloria), 19:1–6 (the Alleluia), 4:8 (the Sanctus).

stimulating classes, a highly competitive sports program, and a more intense spiritual life. However, just a few months after my arrival at the seminary the most painful experience of my high school years occurred. The event brought me considerable guilt and remorse that would not heal for many years.

Once I arrived at the seminary, Vicki and I began corresponding every few weeks. The letters were an innocent and delightful way to continue our middle school friendship, but without romance or drama. At the same time, periodically I would hear faculty members indicate that seminarians should not continue relationships with girls back home. Even though I did not feel I was doing anything wrong by writing Vicki, I checked it out with my spiritual director. He suggested that the relationship could harm my priestly vocation. Because I was trying to give a hundred percent to my new life as a seminarian, I didn't listen to my heart, and I wrote a letter to Vicki in which I said that I had to break off the relationship. When I mailed the letter, I immediately regretted my decision. The next day I mailed a second letter negating the contents of the previous letter saying that I was looking forward to seeing her during the upcoming Thanksgiving vacation.

When I arrived home for Thanksgiving break, I went to visit Vicki, who greeted me coldly. We sat down for an extremely uncomfortable conversation. She was deeply hurt by my two letters. The first letter devastated her because it implied that she was a threat to my vocation even though she had done nothing to deserve the insinuation. On the contrary, she simply wanted to maintain what had become a life-giving friendship that had matured over the four years of middle school. The second letter confused her as much as the first letter, and she concluded that she wanted nothing more to do with a young man who was so unstable in his emotional life.

I didn't know what to say. Like most fourteen-year-old young men, I didn't know how to express my feelings clearly, and didn't know how to integrate a relationship with a close female friend into my new world as a candidate for the celibate priesthood. I left Vicki's home feeling ashamed, guilty, and utterly confused. We did not speak again for twenty-three years.

For the next two decades, whenever Vicki came to mind, I felt regret and guilt over how I had ruined a beautiful friendship.

[*Fast forward*: At the age of thirty-seven, I decided it was time to seek reconciliation. That year, I received an invitation to the twentieth reunion of Alameda High School's class of 1967. Even though I didn't attend AHS, I had kept in touch with some of my middle school friends who went on to AHS. They included me on the invitation list.

As soon as I read the invitation, I thought, "I must go! Vicki Simi will probably be there. I need to seek her forgiveness."

The reunion was held at the clubhouse of Alameda Municipal Golf Course. I entered the clubhouse and worked my way through the crowd asking people if they had seen Vicki Simi. After half an hour, I felt someone tap me on the shoulder. It was Vicki. She gave me a big hug and appeared very happy to see me. Throughout the evening, we shared excitedly what had happened to us over the past many years.

As I drove home, I couldn't contain my jubilation. After holding on to regret and guilt for so many years, the reconciliation happened almost effortlessly. In fact, during our conversations, it didn't occur to either of us to bring up the painful separation from twenty-three years earlier. We were absorbed in the joy of recovering one of the most special relationships of our adolescence. At that moment of elation, I never dreamed that, twenty five years later, I would be the priest to accompany Vicki as she battled stage four cancer.]

Facing Family Alcoholism ▸

Another painful challenge during my high school years was facing the alcoholism of my mother, Margie. I am including this story at her request.

When I was in seventh grade, I noticed that my mom began to periodically abuse alcohol. She would go out drinking with girlfriends and return with a glazed look in her eyes. It didn't happen every day, and when she did drink, she continued to carry out her responsibilities in the home. But my dad, my brother, and I became increasingly concerned about her. The drinking continued for several years.

The problem was compounded because my father had a problem with alcohol as well. I never saw him drunk, but when he did have more than a couple of drinks he became surly. It was a very sad situation. My parents clearly loved each other and us boys. They consistently supported and encouraged us in our education and personal growth. When they were sober, we had very happy times as a family. But when they drank, the atmosphere around the house became tense. The situation continued throughout my years at the high school seminary and a few years beyond.

The breakthrough occurred when a family friend who was a recovering alcoholic convinced my mom to attend an Alcoholics Anonymous (A.A.) meeting. She took to the A.A. program immediately. She had been trying to control her drinking but, like most alcoholics, was trying to do so through will power—a sure recipe for failure. When she informed me that she had begun to attend A.A. meetings, I was overjoyed. At the same time, my dad began participating in Al-Anon meetings—a recovery program for family members of alcoholics.

Brian and I would have profited from entering into the Al-Anon program or its sister program for adolescents, Alateen. Alcoholism is a family disease. Everyone is affected and acts out different roles. By the time I was fifteen I had taken on the "rescuer" role because of my position as family seminarian. Periodically, I would reproach my mom for her drinking and would attempt to counsel my dad about how he ought to handle the situation. However, I was powerless to change my mother or the family dynamics.

Some years later I began to attend Al-Anon meetings. The program enabled me to connect the predicable effects of alcoholism with my emotional and psychological struggles. A quote from one of the Al-Anon books described my problematic reactions to the family alcoholism:

> We who have been affected by someone else's drinking find ourselves inexplicably haunted by insecurity, fear, guilt, obsession with others, or an overwhelming need to control every person and situation we encounter.[2]

The Al-Anon program and literature gave me hope for my own recovery:

---

2. Al-Anon Family Groups, *How Al-Anon Works for Families & Friends of Alcoholics* (Virginia Beach, VA: Al-Anon Family Group Headquarters, 1995), 6.

It is possible for us to find contentment and even happiness, whether the alcoholic is still drinking or not.[3]

Al-Anon helps us to stop wasting time trying to change the things over which we have no control and to put our efforts to work where we do have some power—over our own lives.[4]

I thank God for A.A. and Al-Anon. The fact that my mom entered into recovery was an immeasurable blessing for our family. As a family we continued to struggle with the effects of the family disease, but the Twelve-Step program gave us tools for recovery from a very painful period in our family history. The tools also enabled us to reach out to other families afflicted with addiction. Over the years my mom has served as a sponsor for other alcoholics. In her fifties she became a marriage and family therapist. Her own experience as a recovering alcoholic gave her skills to help those suffering from addictions beyond what formal academic training can offer.

Spiritual Friendship ▸

A transformative experience for me in high school involved friendship. In middle school I had good friends, but no experience of "spiritual friendship." My first day in the seminary I met Dave Neuner, whose bedroom was directly across the hall from mine. Dave quickly became quite popular and was elected class president. He stood out as one of the best athletes in the seminary and the nicest guy you would ever want to meet. We soon became best friends. Not only did we share our most personal thoughts and experiences with each other, but we prayed together. He developed a special affection for my brother, and we would go to the chapel after dinner to pray together for Brian's health and for Dave's parents, who were in a marital crisis. In my relationship with Dave, I learned how profound an impact spiritual friendship can have on one's emotional and spiritual development. Even though we were fierce competitors on the tennis court and at track meets, Dave and I sought only the best for

---

3. Ibid., 8.
4. Ibid., 20.

each other. Our deep connection with each other stimulated growth in our connection with God.

I thought of Dave and other spiritual friends when I studied the golden age of Celtic spirituality (fifth to seventh centuries A.D.).[5] Spiritual friendship was prominent among the famous saints who emerged during that period such as Kieran, Columcille of Iona, Enda of Aran, and Kevin of Glendalough. They were profoundly changed by their "soul friend" (*anamchara*) relationships. They were keenly aware that inner healing happens when we openly and honestly acknowledge to another person our concerns, griefs, joys, and spiritual struggles. They discovered that God is very close to those who speak as friends do, heart to heart. Often the seemingly insignificant events that we share with our soul friends can be vehicles for God to speak to us and through us.

Tragic Death of Uncle Dave

As I recounted in chapter 1, my mother's brother, Uncle Dave, was one of my childhood heroes. When I was seven, he married Emma Fabella, a very attractive and gracious woman from Salinas whose parents came from Mexico. They moved to Bay Farm Island, an extension of Alameda and soon had five beautiful children. I saw them quite often and became quite fond of Emma and my cousins. Uncle Dave and I continued to be very close. I asked him to be my sponsor (*padrino*) for my Confirmation in eighth grade.

Uncle Dave quickly developed a prestigious career at the Lawrence Radiation Laboratory in Livermore. He moved the family to a new home in Orinda, where he also had a shop in which he developed his inventions. Uncle Dave had an exceptionally attractive personality. He was fun, bright, creative, and loving. Lots of friends hung out with him regularly in his shop.

On July 4, 1965, I was about to serve Mass at our parish church when Brian came to the sacristy with the alarming news that Uncle Dave and his eight-year-old daughter, Gina, had been in a car accident and

---

5. Edward C. Sellner, *Wisdom of the Celtic Saints* (Notre Dame, IN: Ave Maria Press, 1998), 8–9.

were in the hospital. My mother and grandmother were outside the church in the car waiting to take me and Brian to the hospital. We were all extremely anxious but hopeful that they would be okay.

When we arrived at the hospital, we expected to be able to visit Uncle Dave and Gina in their hospital rooms. As we sat in the waiting room, Emma's sister, Dee, entered from the Intensive Care unit weeping and hugged Ma saying, "I'm so sorry, I'm so sorry." We didn't immediately know what she meant. She looked at our silent faces and said, "Dave is gone. The doctors couldn't save him. Gina suffered serious injuries, but she will be all right."

We were absolutely stunned and devastated. I was so overwhelmed with shock and grief that, to this day, I don't remember what happened during the next several minutes. Dee tried to comfort my mom and grandmother while Brian and I remained very disoriented. We very much wanted to visit Gina, but the hospital personnel would not allow us because of her serious injuries. Eventually, we left the hospital and drove back to Alameda. I remember my mom was overcome with grief. Ma tried to remain composed in order to comfort my mom.

Never had our family experienced so much grief and sadness. The next few days my mom and grandmother were constantly on the phone spreading the heartbreaking news and inviting people to the funeral services for Uncle Dave.

The vigil service and Rosary occurred a few days later, followed by the funeral Mass the next morning at Santa Maria Parish in Orinda. The vigil and Rosary were led by a kind young priest named Father Michael Tobin. He led the Rosary in a new way called the "Scriptural Rosary." Before each Our Father and Hail Mary he read a short phrase from the Bible related to the mystery we were reciting. We all found the service uplifting and consoling. Afterwards, many friends and family members went to Dave and Emma's home for fellowship. I remember Emma sitting silently on the living room sofa. Her second son, Karl, was sitting on the arm of the sofa and stroking her face. It was such a poignant scene witnessing five-year-old Karl trying to console his grieving mother.

Some minutes later, Emma gave me an envelope on which was written, "A letter that was never delivered." I opened the letter and discovered that it had been written to me by Uncle Dave the previous year. I knew I was going to burst into tears, so I quickly exited the house and got into our family car to read the letter. Uncle Dave had written it shortly after attempting to take the family to visit me at the seminary. They had gotten lost and decided to return home. In the letter, he apologized for disappointing me, and referred to how disappointed he had often been as a youth when his uncles backed out of trips they had scheduled with him. I wept as I had never wept before. A few minutes later one of Uncle Dave's best friends, Harold Silva, opened the door and said, "Come on, Kevin, your Uncle Dave would not want you crying like this." He then told me that he had never loved another man like he had loved my uncle. I was extremely touched by his compassion for me and by his love for Uncle Dave.

The next day we celebrated Uncle Dave's funeral Mass. What I most remember were about fifty Holy Names sisters in the congregation, all in full habit. They loved my Aunt Jeanne and demonstrated great solidarity with her and our family.

Thanks be to God, Gina survived the accident and was able to return home a few weeks later. For the next year, Emma tried to care for her five children, all under the age of nine. It proved to be more than she could handle. She was approaching a mental breakdown and decided to enter a psychiatric hospital. The children were sent to live with other family members for a couple of years. When Emma was released from the hospital, she sold the house in Orinda and moved her family to Salinas, where her parents and siblings lived. Despite the enormous challenges faced by Emma, she was able to provide a secure, loving family life for her children. My mom, Ma, Aunt Jeanne, and I would visit them periodically. I have fond memories of hanging out with the children and taking them to the beach when I was on vacations from the seminary.

Occasionally Emma would speak about her time in the hospital. She said that the person who most helped her recover was the hospital chaplain, a Jesuit priest named Father Tom Burns. He would converse with her often and helped her develop a deep prayer life. Her conviction was that prayer and spiritual direction promoted her healing more than all the psychiatrists. I filed that report in my mind as I thought about what kind of priest I wanted to be. Going through the family tragedy made me much more sensitive to those going through their own heartbreaks.

Relationships with Women

Beginning in my junior year (1965–1966), the seminary began to open up to the outside world. Prior to that time, apart from a weekly walk into town, seminarians left the seminary only for the major vacation periods. Our families came once a month for Visiting Sunday, during which we enjoyed a picnic lunch on the grounds and a long visit.

The seminary president-rector, Father Al Giaquinto, felt that seminarians were too isolated from the world that we were being prepared to serve. So, in 1965 his administration organized a pastoral placement program through which seminarians were sent to parishes to serve in a variety of ministries.

Classmates Tom Jackson, Bob Cleek, and I were assigned to a high school religious education program at St. Joseph of Cupertino Parish in Cupertino. Since students had no cars, we relied on transportation supplied by parishioners. It so happened that our first parish engagement was a Sunday retreat day for the teens that occurred on the annual seminary Open House Sunday. All seminarians were to be on deck to provide guided tours of the seminary for the several hundred visitors who would attend. Because of our parish commitment, Tom, Bob, and I were dispensed from the obligation.

We waited on the front steps of the seminary for the as-yet-unknown parishioners who were to pick us up. A stylish late-model convertible, top down, drove up with three young women inside. They asked if we were the seminarians who needed a ride. We couldn't believe our good fortune! We introduced ourselves, briefly showed them a few sights, and then returned to the car. The girl who owned the vehicle asked me if I would like to take the wheel. Without hesitation I jumped into the driver's seat and headed down the long seminary driveway passing dozens of classmates who gawked at us with jaws dropped. The sight of three seminarians driving out with three young women in an open-top convertible was mind-boggling in those days.

On the retreat we met lots of kids our age. The public school teens, especially the girls, seemed fascinated by the presence of seminarians. We had such a good time being the center of their attention that we stayed beyond the seminary curfew. The same three girls who picked us up drove us back to campus and offered to return the following months to provide us with transportation. We were more than happy to accept, gave them a warm send-off, and then realized that the door to the seminary was locked. We found an unlocked window, climbed through, and escaped being caught.

The next morning when I entered the classroom for the first class of the day, I was stunned by what was written on the blackboard: "The three Casanovas!" "Kevvy, the dynamic lover," and similar phrases designed to achieve maximum embarrassment from my (envious) classmates. Our adventure the previous day had clearly been noticed. I was mortified and quickly erased as much of the incriminating material as possible before the priest-professor arrived. Despite my fear that the faculty would suspect the three of us of unseemly behavior with the girls or discover we had broken curfew, no repercussions ensued except a slight rise in status among our peers and the beginning of delightful friendships with the three girls.

As I wrote this section of the book, I sent the above paragraphs to Bob Cleek to ensure that my memories were accurate. He wrote back reminding me of a detail I had forgotten:

> I do recall you managed to lure two of the girls up to St. Joe›s and had a visit with them on the front lawn one time. That was pretty daring of you. I remember one was a very cute blonde.

That "very cute blonde" (Kathy Price) was one of the only non-Catholic teens in the parish program. One of the most significant long-term outcomes of my involvement in that parish teen program was a close friendship with her. I used to visit Kathy at her home in San Jose during vacations where she introduced me to the world of modern classical music, in particular, Carl Orff's *Carmina Burana*. She also was responsible for my escaping from the seminary (in her MG sports car) during my first year in college (1967) to see the landmark film of our generation, *The Graduate*, starring Dustin Hoffman and Anne Bancroft. That was the nearest I ever came to having a classic "date night" as a seminarian.

A New Meditation Practice: Lectio Divina ▸

A transformative experience during senior year was my initiation into the practice of meditation. Until that time, our primary training in meditation was a morning group meditation during which a priest would read from a spiritual book and periodically pause for us to reflect on the passage. The evening Rosary also served as a meditative practice for many of us. At the beginning of my senior year, Father Giaquinto announced a new practice: the half hour before dinner would become a period of silent, personal meditation during which we could pray as we wished.

The problem for many of us was that we didn't know how to practice personal meditation, apart from the Rosary. In order to gain some instruction, I bought a book called *Meditations for Seminarians* that contained a scripture passage for every day of the year along with a short commentary and application. My practice was to sit in the chapel for half an hour, read the brief scripture passage with frequent pauses during which I would close my eyes, ponder the texts, and speak to the Lord.

Using this method, I would find myself periodically drifting off – sometimes to a spontaneous flow of thoughts, sometimes to nod, and at other times to a silent place. While in that silent place, I didn't know what was happening. I knew I wasn't asleep, but I wasn't thinking about anything in particular. It was uniquely peaceful. I would emerge from the periods of meditation refreshed and extraordinarily quiet inside. The silence would often remain with me after meditation and would positively affect my interaction with fellow students during the meal that followed. A deeper joy grew within me throughout the year, and I soon realized that the half-hour of daily meditation on the Word of God had a lot to do with a growing awareness of God's presence.

Without knowing what I was doing, I was practicing an ancient Christian method of meditation called *Lectio Divina* ("Divine Reading"). I didn't know that the Catholic tradition calls the prayerful experience of interior silence "contemplation"—a way of becoming aware of the interior presence of God, who is always present.[6] What follows are classic instructions for practicing *Lectio Divina*:

---

6. The term *mysticism* is often used interchangeably with *contemplation*—mystical prayer often serving as a synonym for contemplative prayer. The word *mystical*

To begin, invoke the guidance of the Holy Spirit. Choose a passage from Sacred Scripture. Proceed with faith that the Lord will guide you in the four-step process:

Lectio (Reading): Read a few lines or paragraphs slowly, trying to understand the meaning of the text.

Meditatio (Meditation): Think about the text and its meaning for you and your circumstances. Linger on any words or phrases that touch you.

Oratio (Prayer): Speak to the Lord spontaneously in words of contrition, petition, gratitude, or praise.

If you practice the first three steps in a simple, serene manner, you will find that sometimes you are led to the fourth stage of Lectio Divina,

Contemplatio (Contemplation): You feel drawn to rest in silence, and so you cease working with the mind. When thoughts appear, return serenely to the text.

Throughout the session random thoughts will come and go. Don't fight them, but don't entertain them either. When you become aware of aimless thoughts, calmly return to the text. The process may repeat itself many times in the course of a session.

My daily practice of meditation brought me much peace and joy. The fact that my overall high school experience was happy, despite the inevitable adolescent struggles, I assumed that I would have a smooth path ahead of me in my journey to the priesthood. I never suspected how much turbulence would enter my life in college.

---

comes from the Greek *mystikos* meaning "hidden." Until the sixth century, the adjective *mystikos* applied to the hidden Christian meaning of the Old Testament, to the hidden presence of Christ in the Eucharist and, eventually, to interior "infused" supernatural prayer and higher states of consciousness.

3

Unsettled College Years and an Awakening

I entered the college seminary in 1967 just after the "summer of love" in the San Francisco Bay Area. It felt as though the Bay Area and much of the United States had entered into a cultural revolution overnight. For the young adult generation, "drugs, free-love and rock-and-roll" seemed to reign, or as the Twelve-Step program might describe it, "self-will run riot."

Turbulence after the "Summer of Love"

The seminary was not immune from such destabilizing influences. Traditional Catholicism became widely dismissed as irrelevant—in particular, its practices of solemn liturgy, popular devotions, and silent meditation. The focus was on social transformation and work on behalf of the disadvantaged—an essential part of Catholic teaching—but it became disconnected from its spiritual foundations. My generation was quickly forgetting Dorothy Day's timeless insight that the only power that can lead to liberation of the oppressed and the oppressors is Divine love.[1]

---

1. Dorothy Day is best known as the co-founder of the Catholic Worker movement and a newspaper by the same name. Since 1933, both have been passionately devoted to serving the poor and fighting for a radically Christian society. Her poignant autobiography is *The Long Loneliness: The Autobiography of Dorothy Day* (1952; repr., San Francisco: Harper & Row, 1981).

Many of us seminarians found ourselves caught up in the spirit of the new age. What caused the dramatic change from a Christ-centered, virtue-centered spirituality to a more secular self-seeking way of life in the seminary? It was not only the secularizing influences. The seminary administration, with good intentions, naively believed that if the emphasis were on personal initiative and motivation, we seminarians would develop disciplines that would sustain us as future priests when we no longer would be living in an institution guided by a common rule of life. Spiritual exercises were dropped from the daily schedule, except daily Mass. We were expected to meditate, pray, and do spiritual reading on our own without much guidance. We were not taught how to meditate, nor was a wise, personal rule of life proposed. The previous year, a half hour was set aside in the seminary schedule for personal meditation. An environment was created that supported personal spiritual practice, and many of us meditated daily with great profit. As I began my freshman year of college, the daily program set aside no time for meditation, and I did not take the initiative to meditate.

Institutional structures don't necessarily lead to healthy personal habits; but spiritual practices based on the experience of spiritual masters are enormously helpful in one's spiritual development and psychological integration.

I began to adopt the prevailing attitude that real Christianity was activism for social justice. Although my intention was to live the gospel more radically, I gave up most traditional spiritual practices, believing that work with the poor was true spirituality. During my sophomore year I worked at least twenty hours a week in a project for disadvantaged Latino children in the inner city of San Jose—in addition to carrying a full load of classes. A brother seminarian, John Dean, and I organized after-school arts and crafts programs for middle school pre-teens. On the weekends we would take them in a couple of old cars to recreational and cultural locales—to the beach, the Aquarium, and the Planetarium in San Francisco, and to swim at the seminary. The work was good, and I relished connecting with the Latino community, but I became exhausted and acutely missed my former periods of meditation. In those days of social revolution, however, it wasn't cool to spend time in the chapel meditating.

After seven months of working night and day, I burned out. During Holy Week I participated in the Easter celebrations and felt nothing—just emptiness and even hopelessness. I was trying to live a "radical" Christian life, yet I felt no peace or consolation, just exhaustion.

A Spiritual Awakening

A close friend at the seminary, Dennis Stradford, invited me to join him for a three-day retreat beginning the day after Easter at the New Clairvaux Trappist monastery in Vina, California, located on an old ranch of the Stanford family about three hours north of Sacramento. I accepted the offer simply to get some rest. We arrived on a sunny Easter Monday morning. The guest master showed us to our quarters in an old farmhouse. After unpacking, Dennis showed me a book that a monk friend, Father Dunstan, had given him called *Gravity and Grace* by Simone Weil. The book comprises selected passages arranged thematically from her personal notebooks. Simone Weil was a gifted philosopher and spiritual genius who died young during the Second World War.[2] She was born into a Parisian secular Jewish family in 1909. She completed a brilliant course of study in philosophy and later plumbed the depths of Christianity, Hinduism, Taoism, the Greek philosophers, St. John of the Cross, and Shakespeare, among many other traditions and authors. Eventually the Gospels became her daily spiritual food.

Taking the book from Dennis, I opened to the table of contents and found a chapter titled, "To Accept the Void." I resonated with the chapter heading, so I opened to the chapter and read a line that changed my life:

> Grace fills empty spaces but it can only enter where there is a void to receive it, and it is grace itself which makes this void.[3]

Instantaneously I was filled with light from the core of my being to the top of my head. It was not only an intellectual and emotional experience. It was physical as well. I sensed energy rushing upward within me. I exclaimed to Dennis, "Listen to this! Grace enters where there is a void

---

2. Simone Weil, *Gravity and Grace* (London: Routledge & Kegan Paul, 1952), x.
3. Ibid., 10.

to receive it, and it is grace itself that makes this void!" Dennis looked at me with a blank stare. I was overwhelmed by a joy and excitement that I had never known before. Suddenly, in an instant of divine inspiration, I understood what had been happening to me the previous seven months. I was being purified of superficial beliefs about Christianity and illusions about myself. After trying for seven months to live a radical Christian life by my own efforts alone, and trying to prove my worth by excessive work, I had bottomed out. I found myself completely empty. The Holy Spirit then filled that emptiness. It was sheer grace.[4] I had done nothing to deserve this enlightenment. I didn't even ask for it. At that moment I realized that God had been pursuing me, just as he pursues all of us. Finally, I was humbled to the point where God could fill me. A passage in John's Gospel that had always mystified me shed light on the experience:

> The wind blows where it wills, and you can hear the sound it makes, but you do not know where it comes from or where it goes; so it is with everyone who is born of the Spirit. (John 3:8)

Throughout the three-day retreat, I devoured *Gravity and Grace*, finding illumination on every page. I also immensely savored the monastic liturgies and the chanting of the psalms. The prayer services were full of Easter themes with which I completely resonated. When the monks chanted "Christ is risen," I would respond within myself, "Yes, Christ is risen! And he is risen in me." When I took meditation walks through the monastic orchards and encountered a monk picking plums, I would stop and joyfully share the fruits of my awakening. The monks, who were certainly more spiritually advanced than I, indulged my youthful enthusiasm and seemed genuinely moved by my testimonies.

On the final day of the retreat, Dennis and I prepared to drive home after dinner. As we loaded the car, about seven monks arrived to bid us a

---

4. This is the first explicit reference to one of the main themes of this book referred to in my introduction: "Divine Providence"—which refers to divine interventions in the course of our spiritual growth. These interventions are manifestations of "grace," the gratuitous gift that God makes to us of his own life, infused by the Holy Spirit into our soul to heal it and to sanctify it (*Catechism of the Catholic Church* [Vatican City: Libreria Editrice Vaticana, 1994; various publishers and printings] §§1999–2000).

fond farewell. We had mutually inspired each other during those three blessed Easter days, and I could hardly contain my joy. In fact, I could not contain it. As Dennis and I began driving down Highway 5 toward Sacramento, I could not speak during the first hour. As the sun set, I simply stared out the window with a huge smile on my face, enveloped by deep silence and a palpable sense of Christ's presence.

I returned to the seminary a changed man. Throughout the next two months I found myself in a heightened state of awareness and a constant sense of communion with God. Although it sounds like an exaggeration, there wasn't a single day when I didn't feel the joy of Christ in me—the fruit of going through a death and resurrection experience. Sharing the experience with friends deepened my joy. In particular, I savored sharing with a dynamic young Sulpician priest, Father Jerry Coleman, and with my spiritual brother, Dennis.

The day after the retreat I encountered Father Coleman at the seminary pool. With over-the-top enthusiasm I recounted what happened to me at the monastery. I exclaimed, "Now I understand the whole death-resurrection foundation of Christianity! The seed has to die in the earth in order for new life to sprout! We have to be emptied out of what is not God in order to be filled with God! Grace only enters where there is a void to receive it!"

Looking back on that encounter, I admire Father Coleman's forbearance as this nineteen-year-old seminarian presumed to explain the foundations of Christian spirituality to an eminent theologian. He likely was amused by my uninhibited fervor, but he did nothing to discourage it. On the contrary, he expressed interest and asked me questions in order to more deeply appreciate my new state of awareness. Throughout the rest of the spring quarter, when Father Coleman was scheduled to celebrate the daily community Mass, I would often go to his room beforehand and offer him suggestions for his homily. Most priests would probably think, "Who does this kid think he is?" But Father Coleman was most indulgent. He knew that I was going through a spiritual awakening, and he good-naturedly listened to my passionate outpourings.

Dennis participated in my conversion from the first moment. He too had recently undergone a spiritual awakening while a student at San Jose State University. When he decided to pursue priestly formation after graduation, he was sent to the college seminary to pick up philosophy classes before entering the graduate seminary in Menlo Park. He became the big brother I never had and an *anamchara*.[5] After the retreat, he would come to my room at night and we would pray Night Prayer (Compline) together. We would also gather with a couple of seminarian brothers to share our spiritual experiences while drinking Galliano on the rocks with a twist of lime in a small, abandoned chapel (alcohol was not allowed on campus). The spiritual brotherhood, along with my daily meditation and Mass, helped sustain my new heightened state of consciousness.

Years later when I wrote a doctoral dissertation analyzing higher states of consciousness in the Vedic-Hindu and Christian traditions, I discovered that St. Teresa of Avila describes a "fifth state of consciousness" beyond waking, dreaming, sleeping, and contemplation. She describes it in her book *The Interior Castle* in terms that are somewhat like what I experienced after my retreat at Vina.[6] The fundamental characteristic of the fifth state is conformity of the human will with the Divine will, and an enduring sense of the Divine Presence accompanied by abiding peace and joy. Some Catholic theologians call the fifth state, "Conforming Union."[7] Ordinarily it emerges after years of ascetical training[8] and deep meditation. However, it sometimes happens that a person may be propelled into the fifth state temporarily by means of profound suffering and emptiness or through a powerful conversion experience. I believe that is what happened to me.

An Auspicious Journey to Mexico ▸

Two days after the retreat, Father James Poggi, nine seminarians, and I traveled to Mexicali, Mexico, for four days as part of a course called "The Mexican-American Experience." It was taught by Father Poggi, who was

---

5. "Soul Friend" in the Irish language.

6. St. Teresa of Avila, *The Interior Castle*, in *The Collected Works of St. Teresa of Avila*, trans. Otilio Rodriguez and Kieran Kavanaugh, 3 vols. (Washington: Insitute of Carmelite Studies, 1976–1985), "The Fifth Dwelling Places," chap. 2, section 12–chap. 3, section 5. All further references to *The Interior Castle* will be found in the text, abbreviated *IC* plus the locating numbers.

7. John G. Arintero, *The Mystical Evolution in the Development and Vitality of the Church*, trans. Jordan Aumann, 2 vols. (St. Louis: Herder, 1951), 2:162.

8. Ascetical training involves spiritual disciplines that help purify mind and body.

my spiritual director. I took the course because I sensed a call to work as a priest with Spanish-speaking people. I needed more training in the language and culture.

One day during our excursions around Mexicali I voiced my desire to study Spanish in Mexico. Another student, David Mugridge, informed us that he was going to study in Mexico City the following year through a Junior Year Abroad program. He offered to arrange for me to live with a Mexican family. His offer enticed me, and I decided to pursue it.

Upon returning to the seminary, I shared my plans with Steve Rickard, my tennis partner, who was always ready for new adventures. He expressed keen interest in joining me for the Mexican experience and we began to make plans. This was to be the first of many adventures I would share with Steve over the next several years.

I apprised Father Giaquinto of my plans to take a leave of absence from the seminary. He supported my decision but offered a word of caution. He said, "Several seminarians have taken a leave of absence in recent years to participate in programs in Mexico, but none has returned to the seminary." I was puzzled by his comment, but I didn't ask this wise priest for his counsel regarding how to protect and nurture my vocation outside of the seminary. That was a mistake.

Exposure to Transcendental Meditation in a Factory ▸

After completing my sophomore year at St. Joseph's College, I returned to my family in Alameda and began working at the American Can Company in Oakland. I needed to earn sufficient funds to pay for my Junior Year Abroad program in Mexico City. The morning I entered the factory to begin my job as a janitor, the heightened state of awareness that I had experienced after the Trappist monastery retreat vanished just as suddenly as it had appeared. It was a huge disappointment and surprise. I expected the "high" of my spiritual awakening to last forever. If I had read St. Ignatius of Loyola's *Spiritual Exercises*, I would have known that periods of intense consolation are gifts—graces that sometimes accompany spiritual awakenings—and are given to encourage us to continue on with our spiritual journey. These consolations invariably fade over time until we have reached sufficient purification of body, mind, and spirit to sustain such heightened states of consciousness without the ego becoming attached to the consolations. This will become clearer when we examine the higher states of spiritual development in later chapters.

After a couple weeks, I graduated from janitor to assembly-line worker, where I met two co-workers who would disappear during the afternoon break and return refreshed and relaxed, whereas the rest of us workers were usually stressed out by that time of the day. I asked the two guys what they were doing during their break, and they told me that they practiced Transcendental Meditation—or TM—a mental technique taught by the famous Indian teacher, Maharishi Mahesh Yogi. I told them I was a Catholic seminarian and they asked me what type of meditation I practiced. I was embarrassed to tell them that I didn't meditate. (I had discontinued practicing *Lectio Divina* when I returned home for the summer.)

I was intrigued by their description of TM as a simple technique for gaining mental clarity and physical relaxation. I was struck by their claim that TM was not a religious practice although it came from an ancient spiritual tradition from India. I decided that I would take the TM course because I was frazzled and needed some inner peace. However, my work schedule was so tight that I was unable to free up the time to take the four-day course. TM instruction would have to wait until I returned from Mexico.

After working all summer, I still needed another $500 to cover my studies in Mexico (about $3,500 in today's money). A fellow seminarian told me about Rex Lindsay, a wealthy Catholic Silicon Valley executive who supported programs for the poor and for disadvantaged Latino youth in the valley. I contacted Rex who invited me to his ranch near Mount Hamilton to check me out. After an hour of chit chat, he asked me "How much do you need?" I responded, "I have worked all summer, but I still need about $500." Rex then said, "Are you sure that's all you need?" I said, "I think so." He responded, "I'll give you $600." That was typical of Rex Lindsay–generous beyond the call of duty.

Father Dunstan, a Modern-Day Desert Father ▸

Before I left for Mexico in September of 1969 to begin my Junior Year Abroad, I met Father Dunstan Morrissey, a Benedictine monk whom my friend Dennis befriended a couple of years earlier. Father Dunstan gave Dennis the book by Simone Weil, *Gravity and Grace*, that impacted me so powerfully at the Trappist monastery. Because Father Dunstan would later play a pivotal role in my spiritual journey, I am going to present a brief overview of his early life in order to provide a context for his witness and teachings.

I have never met anyone quite like Father Dunstan. He reminded me of the great Desert Fathers of the fourth century—full of wisdom but completely unpretentious, a Christlike man of enormous integrity and uncompromisingly committed to knowing and living the truth. When we first met, Father Dunstan was forty-six years old and had been a monk for about twenty years.[9] He lived to the age of eighty-seven. He was raised a Protestant and studied at Notre Dame University in Indiana, where he was baptized a Catholic. After his baptism he told the university chaplain that he felt called not only to be a Catholic but to be a monk as well. The priest suggested that he wait a couple of years. So, Dunstan applied to work at the State Department and was accepted for the foreign service. He then served as a vice consul in Alexandria, Egypt.

After two years in the Foreign Service, Dunstan still felt a strong desire to become a monk and eventually ended up at St. Bede Abbey, about sixty miles down the Illinois River from Chicago. When he first entered, he told the abbot that his interest was really solitude. The abbot said, "That's very dangerous, unless you've been trained in community." Dunstan accepted the abbot's word and underwent the traditional monastic training according to the Rule of St. Benedict. In 1953 he was ordained a priest and served as dean of the academy connected to the monastery. All during that time he had a deep longing for solitude.

---

9. Fr. Dunstan's story is found in a small booklet edited by Susan Moon titled *To Hear Thoroughly: Father Dunstan Morrissey Talks about His Life* (Berkeley: Open Books, 1998).

After fifteen years of living in the monastic community, one day the abbot said to him, "If you still look for solitude, the Camaldolese (an Italian order of semi-hermits, a branch of the Benedictines) have arrived in California and if you'd like to go, you can go now." So, in 1960 Father Dunstan left for Big Sur, California, and spent a year going through a second novitiate with the new community. At the end of the year, the prior wanted to make him novice master, but Father Dunstan felt the call to live in solitude. He left the Camaldolese and asked his abbot at St. Bede's if he could live in solitude under the direction of Father Jacques Winandy, a retired French abbot living on the island of Martinique. Dunstan joined Father Winandy's small colony of hermits in 1963 and lived under his spiritual direction for four years.

What drew Father Dunstan to become a monk and live in solitude? In the short book that speaks of his life, *To Hear Thoroughly*, he reflected on the meaning of his monastic vocation:

> The early church fathers felt that solitude provided the chance for purification. The Roman Empire was falling apart, and great masses of people came from Rome to live in the deserts of Egypt. They'd live there for a year or two, and then they would suddenly remember that some relative really needed them back in Rome, so they would go to the abba [a spiritual father] and ask to leave. The abba would say—this is repeated in several anecdotes—"Go to your cell. When you're hungry, eat. When you're sleepy, go to sleep, have a rest. But don't leave your cell. Your cell will teach you everything."
>
> In some way one is dwelling with all beings while in solitude. That's why I have the sense that the vocation is beyond the opposites because I do feel great solidarity with everything in the world. But one has to be careful not to get carried away by that idea.
>
> When one remains in solitude for a long time, horizons just give way to other horizons, constantly. That's a kind of built-in dynamic. And so your response is a willingness to follow that movement.[10]

In 1967, Father Winandy directed Father Dunstan to return to the world and live his monastic vocation there. Father Dunstan commented, "I never asked Jacques Winandy why I'd been given this direction. I wanted to carry through on the idea of obedience without tinkering with

10. Ibid., 34.

it."[11] Father Dunstan believed that the Holy Spirit had spoken to him through his spiritual father, so he left Father Winandy's colony of hermits. He made his way to California and waited for a sign from Above with regard to next steps.

In the meantime, Father Dunstan needed to find a way to support himself and decided to become a potter. He studied with Marguerite Wildenhain, a distinguished potter who lived in Guerneville, California. Upon completion of his training, Marguerite told him, "Don't dare present a pot to the public until you've made five thousand pots and thrown them away." Father Dunstan's response was,

> Again, it was a matter of obedience. I thought, "How am I going to make five thousand pots if I have no place to live?" Then it came to me: "I've got to get a night job that will allow me to pay for my board and room, and I'll work on pottery during the day."

Someone in Marguerite's class told Father Dunstan about a job opening for a janitor at the University of California in Santa Cruz. He got the job and rented a cabin in the Santa Cruz Mountains. It was at that time that my friend Dennis invited me to meet Father Dunstan.

When we entered Father Dunstan's cabin, he greeted us warmly, offered us refreshments, and then asked me who I was. I explained that I was a seminarian taking a year's leave from the seminary to learn Spanish at a university in Mexico. I then told him that I had just begun working as a janitor at a can company. Here's how the rest of the dialogue proceeded:

Father D: "Very good, very good."
Kevin: "What do you mean 'very good'? I hate the job."
Father D: "You know, the Zen masters say that the most important activity of the day is washing the dishes."
Kevin: "What do you mean?"
Father D: "We priests and seminarians need to know our place."

At that point, I knew that I was in the company of a rather extraordinary teacher who had wisdom far beyond what I could fathom. But rather than being put off, I was intrigued. When we left the cabin, I knew that

---

11. *Ibid.*, 16.

I would return. In a later chapter I will relate more of my encounters with Father Dunstan.

Shortly after my meeting with Father Dunstan, I took leave of my family and seminary and set off for my Junior Year Abroad program in Mexico City. Little did I know that studying in Mexico would propel me into the biggest vocational crisis of my life.

4

Vocational Crisis in Mexico

Arrival in Mexico ▶

IN THE FALL OF 1969, STEVE RICKARD AND I FLEW TO MEXICO City as "seminarians on leave" to begin a Junior Year Abroad program at the University of the Americas.[1] We were picked up at the airport by our host families and were immediately confronted with the fact that our college Spanish classes in California had not prepared us to speak Spanish. During the car ride to my host home, I used the twenty or so phrases I had memorized but fell silent when the family began to respond to me in their customary rapid-fire Mexican Spanish. Fortunately, two of the teenage children spoke English, so they saved me temporarily from remaining *incomunicado*.

The family household comprised the parents, five children, and three full-time servants. The servants were *indigenas* from Oaxaca: a cook, a housekeeper, and a young man who took care of maintenance, the cars, and the garden. They lived in the basement and were never allowed to sit at table with the family. I was stunned by the chasm between the upper and lower classes of Mexican society. At that time the population of Mexico City was about twelve million, most of whom were working class and poor. But there were many affluent neighborhoods (*colonias*) in the city including San Angel, where my host family lived in a

---

1. At that time the university was in Mexico City. Today it is in Puebla, Mexico.

large, elegant, modernistic house designed by the father of the family, who was a renowned architect.

The family was non-practicing Catholic, but since I was a seminarian, they took me to Mass at the local church the first Sunday. The liturgy was celebrated in a very traditional manner without the priest adding a personal touch. There was no noticeable sense of community or hospitality, although, had I paid attention, I probably would have become aware of the devotion and reverence of people around me. The Second Vatican Council had ended only four years earlier. I had become accustomed to a very modern American way of celebrating the liturgy with a strong emphasis on promoting community interaction and contemporary music. The liturgy at the parish church in San Angel really turned me off. In a fit of late-adolescent self-righteousness, I decided that if they didn't celebrate Mass the way I wanted, I wasn't going to attend.

As I reflect on that ill-considered decision, I am amazed that I had forgotten so quickly the implications of the extraordinary, grace-filled spiritual awakening that I had undergone only five months earlier at the Trappist monastery. Even though I had been touched deeply by God and by the Church's liturgy at that time, I was still under the influence of the prevailing 1960s ideology that valued novelty and self-expression over traditional doctrine and practices. More insidious was the prevailing philosophy of "willfulness" in place of seeking the Divine will. Thus began a six-month hiatus in my Mass attendance and personal prayer, which proved quite damaging to my connection with God and to wise decision-making.

The family and servants of my host family treated me graciously, but, within a couple of weeks, the older teenage children were sent off to boarding school and I was left without translators and peers with whom to speak. I felt quite lonely because the parents were often away on trips, and I was not yet able to converse comfortably with the two remaining children and servants. I began my studies at the university where I knew no one except Steve Rickard and our classmate, Dave Mugridge, who had arrived before us. After having studied in a small college seminary the previous two years, I felt lost in the new international university environment.

Fortunately, Dave began to invite me and Steve to the midafternoon meal at the home of Miguel and Susana Mayorga, who were his host family. They had twelve children, the three oldest being around my age. I relished the opportunity to hang out with such a large, loving, and very Catholic family. The parents treated me and Steve like sons and were happy for us to join the fourteen of them and Dave for family meals.

Father Donald Hessler and el Nuevo Guadalupanismo

Miguel and Susana were quite active in an international organization of Catholic families called the "Christian Family Movement" (*Movimiento Familiar Cristiano*, or MFC). Their chaplain in Mexico City, Father Donald Hessler, was a legendary priest of the Maryknoll missionary order. In the midst of my adolescent religious rebellion, Father Hessler proved to be a thread that kept me somewhat connected to the Church and my vocation.

I met Father Hessler at the Mayorga home and asked him about his background. He said that he credited his priestly ordination to the influence of Dorothy Day, the founder of the Catholic Worker movement. Father Hessler was born in Ann Arbor, Michigan, in 1912 and developed a strong connection with Christ and the Church during his adolescence. After high school he joined the seminary of the Maryknoll Foreign Mission Society because he felt a strong call to share the gospel and serve the poor in the Third World.

One summer during his seminary studies he traveled to New York City to work with the homeless who sought help at the Catholic Worker House of Hospitality. He was captivated by Dorothy Day and the Catholic Worker ministry. At the end of the summer, he told Dorothy that he wanted to take a leave from the seminary and establish a Catholic Worker House in Detroit. He assumed that Dorothy would be pleased that an idealistic young man would commit himself full-time to promoting the movement that she founded. To his great surprise, Dorothy responded severely, "You will do no such thing! The world needs good priests and missionaries. Return to the seminary and pray. Your prayers will do more good than your presence in Detroit. I will attend your ordination."[2]

2. My translation from a privately published booklet of interviews compiled by

Commenting on that exchange, Father Hessler said "From anyone else I would not have accepted the directive, but her firmness convinced me." Throughout the rest of his life, he would periodically say, "A woman ordered me to be a man and a priest."

After his ordination, he was sent to serve as a missionary in Kweilin Kuan Tsi in the south of China. A few months later Japan attacked Singapore, Hong Kong, and Pearl Harbor, all on the same day (December 7, 1941). Soon Father Hessler and other foreign missionaries were sent to a Japanese concentration camp where he remained for four years until the end of the war. He could have been released earlier from the camp through diplomatic channels, but he chose to remain in order to minister to the other prisoners until they were freed.

After seven years in China, Father Hessler returned to the United States and was sent to serve in Mexico, where he remained for fifty years. When I met him in 1969, he was focused on connecting middle- and upper-class MFC families with poor families in remote villages where little ministry was carried out by the Catholic Church. During our first conversation he asked me, "What are you doing for the poor in Mexico?" With embarrassment I answered, "Nothing." He said, "There is a small medical missionary team headed by two medical students, including Eduardo Mayorga, the oldest son of the Mayorga family. They travel monthly for a weekend to an isolated village of Otomi Indians in the Valley of Mezquital to provide medical services. The village has no priest, so they invite one of us priests from the capital to offer Mass on the same weekend. Why don't you join the team?"

I was too embarrassed to refuse, so within a couple of weeks I accompanied two medical students on a two-hour drive to the village where my responsibility was to go door-to-door announcing that doctors were in town and that Mass would be celebrated on Sunday. My role was challenging because my Spanish was still rudimentary and many of the residents spoke Otomi, not Spanish. Most homes did not have running water or electricity, but the people were generous and hospitable with what they had.

Working alongside Father Hessler, I quickly gained a sense of the theology that inspired his pastoral practice and that would impact my

---

Pietro Ameglio: Donald Hessler, *La Fuerza de la No-Violencia* (Col. Ampliación Los Reyes, Los Reyes La Paz, Edo. De Mexico, 1994), 12.

future ministry. He called the center of his theology, "*El Nuevo Guadalupanismo*" which refers to the encounter between Our Lady of Guadalupe and the indigenous Juan Diego that occurred in December of 1531. The Catholic Church believes in the historicity of the encounter, but even if one were to interpret it only as a foundational legend of Latin American Christianity, Father Hessler's interpretation would not change.

The story begins with recently baptized Juan Diego walking from his village to the conquered Aztec capital (now Mexico City) in order to attend Mass. On his way, he walked over the hill of Tepeyac, where a beautiful celestial woman appeared to him and spoke in his native language, Nahuatl. She told him she was the Blessed Virgin Mary, Mother of the true God, and made known to him her desire that a shrine be built on Tepeyac from where she could pour forth her love, compassion, and protection. "For I am your merciful Mother," she said, "to you and to all mankind who love me and trust in me and invoke my help. Therefore, go to the dwelling of the Bishop in Mexico City and say that the Virgin Mary sent you to make known to him her great desire."

Juan Diego delivered the message to Bishop Zumarraga, who said that he could not accept it without some proof that it came from the Virgin Mary. Eventually, the Blessed Virgin did send a sign—Castilian roses that would not be found on that dry hill in winter. Juan Diego wrapped them in his garment, a *tilma*, and delivered them to the bishop. To everyone's enormous surprise, the image of the Virgin Mary appearing as a pregnant indigenous woman was impressed upon the inside of the *tilma*. (In the twentieth century, scientists and artists have studied the *tilma* with the best scientific instruments and have been unable to explain how the image was created.) For almost five hundred years, the miraculous *tilma* has been enshrined above the high altar at the Basilica of Our Lady of Guadalupe, which is the spiritual center of Mexican Catholicism.

From the Guadalupe story, Father Hessler developed his philosophy of ministry:

> The Virgin Mary did not usurp the voice of the poor. This is *guadalupanismo*: Mary did not speak once with the bishop. She insisted that Juan speak. At first Juan failed in his mission, saying that he was not the right person and even defended the bishop for paying no attention by defining himself as *gente menuda, cola, escalerilla, hoja seca, mecate*

["an insignificant person, a tail, a little staircase, a dried leaf, a coarse rope"]. He was very graphic and had a tremendous inferiority complex. Then Mary became even more serious and silenced him saying: "Look, I firmly command you to return to the bishop and he has to listen." A woman ordering a man to be a man. I have needed this several times. This is the role of the Virgin, and of those who advocate on behalf of the poor. Finally, Juan returns to the bishop who then kneels down and accepts. Who evangelized whom?[3]

The obvious answer is "Juan Diego evangelized Bishop Zumarraga." Father Hessler connected the story with Jesus's first public preaching in the synagogue at Nazareth: "The Lord has anointed me to bring good news to the poor" (Luke 4:18). Father Hessler rephrased the message:

> I am anointed to deliver all the Good News to the poor, so that they can evangelize the Church and the Church, more humble and poorer, can evangelize the world.

Father Hessler lamented that often the voice of the poor has been taken away instead of affirmed.

> The Virgin Mary took away the poor man's inferiority complex by taking away his humiliation and making him humble. Juan Diego returned dignified, not bowed. The Virgin made him humble, and she gave him the virtue without which humility is worth nothing: audacity. There is no humility without boldness. This is the [preferential] option for the poor: that they have voice and vote in the Church, that the Church listens to them even on our knees. But they will not have a prophetic voice if there are no advocates: men, women, the wealthy.

Father Hessler's vision is not uncommon among a certain group of priests and other pastoral workers in Latin America who are often identified with the "Theology of Liberation." What distinguished Father Hessler's pastoral approach was his absolute commitment to nonviolent change and to adoration of the Blessed Sacrament. Whenever I would visit him in the various churches where he served, he would often be found deep in prayer before the Blessed Sacrament. He did not adhere to an ideology. His motivation for giving his life in service to the poor (and to the wealthy) was his love for Christ and for all who are dear to

---

3. Ibid., 8.

Christ. His vision attracted and challenged me. He planted a seed in me that would bear fruit several years down the road—a commitment to put the message of Our Lady of Guadalupe in practice by giving special attention to the poor and other disadvantaged of society.

An Undeclared Romance

I continued to join the Mayorgas for social gatherings, where I would often play the piano. A guest at one of the gatherings told me about his sister who was a pianist. He invited me to his home to meet his family and to hear his sister play.

When I arrived at his home, he introduced me to his sister, Antonia, who was a lovely young woman and quite talented. She had recently graduated from high school and was working in the field of art restoration. She and her family received me warmly and then invited me to play the piano. After playing I asked Antonia to play. Her music and her way of being captivated me.

A few weeks later I broke my ankle playing tennis with Steve and was hobbling around on crutches. In that disabled condition I attended a party at which Antonia was present. As everyone danced, I stayed on the sidelines feeling sorry for myself, at which point she sat down next to me and tried to cheer me up. I was touched by her thoughtfulness and concern.

As Thanksgiving approached, Dave, Steve and I decided to introduce this distinctly American holiday to our Mexican friends. We invited about thirty people to the traditional turkey dinner. We spent all day preparing the meal at the Mayorga home. When we gathered everyone for the meal, by happenstance Antonia and I were seated next to each other. We began an animated conversation even though my Spanish was still quite limited. I was amazed at how my linguistic abilities suddenly improved dramatically! Within about fifteen minutes I was overcome by a feeling that I had not experienced since middle school. I felt that I was falling in love. For an hour and a half, I didn't notice anyone else at the table. My attention was irresistibly fixed on Antonia. She seemed quite taken with me as well which only fueled my excitement.

After the dinner I told Steve that I had something big to share with him. We went to a bar, and I breathlessly shared with him what had happened to me during the dinner with Antonia. Steve understood very well because he had recently fallen in love with a beautiful girl whom he met while working on youth retreats in California. In fact, he had pretty much decided to pursue a relationship with her. He encouraged me to follow my heart.

Antonia and I began to spend time together at family gatherings and parties. An obvious challenge for me was how to justify entering into a romantic relationship while being a seminarian-on-leave. Nonetheless, I didn't want to admit to myself this evident truth. Being with Antonia brought me much happiness, but I wasn't considering the effect of our friendship on her.

A New Host Family ▸

After the Christmas vacation, I moved into the home of Armando and Liduvina Limon and their three teenage sons. They treated me like a son and brother. I enjoyed my life with them. The father was an atheist, but he respected and supported my plans to become a priest. Since the family did not worship, I found it easy to continue absenting myself from Sunday Mass. Strangely, I did not yet take seriously the contradiction between maintaining a desire to become a Catholic priest and failing to participate in the central act of Catholic worship.

I began hanging out with the oldest son, who was a year younger than I. He was a rock musician and had been introduced to marijuana in that subculture. One evening he took me to a park and invited me to smoke a joint. I told him I had never taken drugs and was not interested. He kept on insisting and tried to motivate me by saying that he had some of the best marijuana in Mexico—"Acapulco Gold." Finally, I accepted and smoked a joint. I felt nothing. He gave me another joint and still I felt nothing. Then he gave me a third joint and suddenly the effects of the drug overpowered me. I was high as a kite. Then Armando suggested we travel to downtown Mexico City to *Sala Chopin*, a high-class piano store.

Arriving at *Sala Chopin*, my eyes immediately caught sight of a Steinway grand piano. I sat down and began playing some classical music. The manager approached me, irritated that this young *gringo* was playing a very expensive piano without permission. Without blinking I invented a story: "I am the son of a wealthy American who asked me to locate a fine piano that he could purchase." The manager's eyes lit up. He believed my tall tale and led me to the most expensive nine-foot Steinway Concert Grand located in a small enclosed circular courtyard with a terrace above where listeners could gather. I proceeded to play one of the most loved Latin American pieces, *La Malagueña*. I played the piece with great passion which helped cover up the mistakes generated by my intoxicated condition. After the grand finale, I heard thunderous applause. The terrace above me had filled up with a highly enthusiastic crowd of Latin music devotees. I told the manager that I loved the piano. He was thrilled thinking that the "wealthy father" of this young *gringo* pianist would purchase the piano. He proceeded to give me piano brochures and tickets to an upcoming concert. Armando was amazed by the drama I had created.

That was the last time I smoked marijuana in Mexico. The next morning, still reeling from the effects of the drug, I said "no more!" I realized how deadened was my conscience the night before, telling one lie after another and utterly deceiving the store manager. At least I provided him and his customers with a free, intoxicating concert!

However, I did smoke a few more times when I returned to the United States. When I compared the use of recreational drugs with the effects of prayer and meditation, I realized how drugs dulled my consciousness and fostered self-absorption. Prayer and meditation had the opposite effects: greater clarity of mind, awareness of the needs of others, and connection with the "Higher Power."

Vocational Crisis ➤

After a couple of months of going out with Antonia, one weekend we attended a party and were dancing when she began to express her misgivings about our relationship. She had a lot of respect for the Church and the priesthood, and she felt ill-at-ease with our tacit romance. After the party I plunged into the depths of depression. For several days I thought and thought about how to respond. Significantly, I do not recall asking for divine guidance. The lack of regular worship and prayer had impaired my ability to distinguish my willfulness from God's will. If I had been tuned in to the Holy Spirit, I would have concluded that I was living a double life, and that it was insensitive and wrong for me to expect Antonia to remain in an undeclared quasi-romantic relationship with a young man who was unable to make a commitment.

After agonizing for several days, on St. Valentine's Day (*dia de la Amistad* in Mexico), I went to Antonia's house with flowers, chocolates, and a card in which I acknowledged how my vocational turmoil was confusing her. I told her how much she meant to me and that I wanted to try and work out a way to continue our friendship. She hesitantly accepted my hope, but in the ensuing two months, we were not able to get beyond the mutual uneasiness.

Finally, the tension was more than I could bear. During Holy Week while on a vacation in Veracruz with the Limon family, I remember walking in front of a Catholic Church on Good Friday from which I heard liturgical music. My heart ached to enter the church, but my pride kept me out. The next day I became violently ill with a stomach infection. The combination of a longing to reconnect with God and the Church, my severe sickness, and my confusion regarding Antonia led me to make the abrupt decision to return to the seminary as soon as possible. I felt that I could not resolve my vocational issues and internal turmoil while remaining in Mexico.

Upon return to Mexico City, I phoned the rector of the seminary who graciously allowed me to reenter immediately since the third quarter was just beginning. I announced my sudden decision to my Mexican friends. Everyone was shocked, especially the Limon family and Antonia. Within four days I was on a plane to California.

5

Simone Weil, Meditation, and Jung

THE EMOTIONAL TURMOIL THAT CHARACTERIZED MY LAST couple of months in Mexico subsided somewhat once I returned to the college seminary. Surprisingly, the first real breakthrough occurred not in the seminary but rather during the summer vacation of 1970, when I worked as a forklift driver at Plastronics, one of the early Silicon Valley high tech companies whose CEO was Rex Lindsay. I lived at the San Jose State University Catholic campus ministry residence with Dennis Stradford and two other seminarians. Working the swing shift afforded me ample time in the morning for personal pursuits.

Simone Weil ▸

Feeling acutely the need for spiritual renewal, I revived my former practice of daily spiritual reading. Each morning after breakfast, I would ride my bike to serene William Street Park, where I would sit under a tree on a blanket for a couple of hours and read inspiring books. In particular, I read the works of Simone Weil, whose book *Gravity and Grace* catalyzed my spiritual awakening at the Trappist monastery.

As I noted in chapter 3, Simone Weil was a brilliant philosopher and spiritual genius from a secular Parisian Jewish family; she died young during the Second World War.[1] Because

---

1. Gustave Thibon "Introduction," in Simone Weil, *Gravity and Grace* (London: Routledge & Kegan Paul, 1952), x.

of Nazi laws governing France at that time, she needed refuge in a home that would not attract the attention of the Nazis. A Catholic intellectual, Gustave Thibon, learned of Weil's dilemma and invited her to live with his family. He became her close friend and biographer. Concerning that period in Weil's life Thibon writes,

> She was just then beginning to open with all her soul to Christianity, a limpid mysticism emanated from her; in no other human being have I come across such familiarity with religious mysteries; never have I felt the word *supernatural* to be more charged with reality than when in contact with her.
>
> Such mysticism had nothing in common with those religious speculations divorced from any personal commitment which are all too frequently the only testimony of intellectuals who apply themselves to the things of God. She actually experienced in its heart-breaking reality the distance between "knowing" and "knowing with all one's soul," and the one object of her life was to abolish that distance.[2]

In relation to my recent struggles, I found encouragement in Thibon's reflection on the role of suffering in Weil's life:

> [Simone Weil] firmly believed that creation of real genius required a high level of spirituality and that it was impossible to attain to perfect expression without having passed through severe inner purgation.[3]

Having recently passed through a period of extreme willfulness and forgetfulness of God, I was painfully conscious of my need for purgation. Through Simone Weil, I began to see how the anguish and void I experienced in Mexico could be vehicles for purification.

> To accept a void in ourselves is supernatural. Where is the energy to be found for an act which has nothing to counter-balance it? The energy has to come from elsewhere. Yet first there must be a tearing out, something desperate has to take place, the void must be created. Void: the dark night.[4]

My withdrawal from worship and personal prayer had been a serious mistake, and it led me into emptiness. It was clearly not God's will that I abandoned spiritual practices, but I do believe the resulting void

---

2. Ibid., viii–ix.
3. Ibid., x–xi.
4. Weil, *Gravity and Grace*, 10.

was a divine gift. Sometimes suffering is what wakes us up to the fact that we are traveling in the wrong direction. The emptiness can create a space in us for future blessings.

Likewise, the pain that emerged in my relationship with Antonia was a sign that my desire for her companionship had become self-centered and was sabotaging true love. As St. Thomas Aquinas said, "Love is willing the good of the other." I was not willing her good but rather my happiness. Thus, as Weil wrote, "there must be a tearing out, something desperate has to take place, the void must be created. Void: the dark night." And then what happens?

> To detach our desire from all good things and to wait. Experience proves that this waiting is satisfied. It is then we touch the absolute good.
> .... The good which we can neither picture nor define is a void for us. But this void is fuller than all fullness.
>
> If we get as far as this we shall come through all right, for God fills the void.[5]

Transcendental Meditation

The previous summer, two co-workers at the American Can Company had told me about their practice of Transcendental Meditation (TM). I felt a strong desire to learn the method because of the stress and anxiety I was undergoing before traveling to Mexico. Upon my return from Mexico I felt even greater longing for the settled mind and release of stress that the TM literature promised.

Just before beginning my work at Plastronics, I decided to attend a TM introductory lecture at the local TM center. However, I had reservations since the method taught by Maharishi Mahesh Yogi comes from a Asian, non-Christian tradition. Can a Christian practice such a method without compromising his or her Christian commitment?

I asked a priest from the seminary, Father Gene Konkel, to accompany me to the introductory lecture to help me answer the question. The lecturer was Jerry Jarvis, one of Maharishi's close associates. He began

---

5. Ibid., 13.

the lecture by referring to neurophysiological studies summarized by a researcher, Dr. Keith Wallace, who compared the three ordinary states of consciousness (waking, dreaming, and sleeping) to a fourth state of consciousness. According to Jarvis, what human beings consider normal waking consciousness is in fact a very limited experience of consciousness that is confined to the more surface levels of the mind. Transcendental Meditation, which allows mental and physical activity to settle down, gives rise to a fourth state, a settled or ground state of consciousness. This fourth state of consciousness is referred to as transcendental consciousness or pure consciousness, a state in which there are no thoughts, no sensory experiences, and yet full conscious awareness. It is said to be the experience of consciousness itself.[6]

He continued by describing the procedure for experiencing transcendental consciousness as turning the attention inward toward the subtler levels of a thought until the mind transcends the experience of the subtlest state of the thought and arrives at the source of the thought. In Transcendental Meditation one uses a specific thought, a "mantra," and then experiences that thought at successive prior stages of its development. While in principle any thought could be so experienced, the TM technique finds as one of its principles of procedure that a thought associated with sound value is most universally appropriate for this purpose. There is a particular set of sounds, or mantras, handed down in Maharishi's tradition that seem to have the special property of settling mental activity and leading one's attention to a state of interior quiet.

Jarvis went on to explain that anyone of any background who can think a thought can practice Transcendental Meditation and that TM is not a religion. No particular belief is required to practice the method. When people ask Maharishi about what they should believe and how they should behave, he answers "Follow your own religious tradition."

After the lecture I asked Father Konkel what he thought. He answered, "What they call "meditation" the Catholic tradition calls "contemplation." I didn't know much about "contemplation," but I mentally filed Father Konkel's observation for future investigation. Father

---

6. Robert Keith Wallace, *The Maharishi Technology of the Unified Field: The Neurophysiology of Enlightenment* (Fairfield, IA: MIU Neuroscience Press, 1986), 9.

Konkel and I didn't see any harm in the TM practice, so I decided to take the four-day course of instruction.

When I learned the method, there was something about it that felt familiar. The mental and physical dynamics were similar to what I had experienced by practicing *Lectio Divina* as a senior in high school: a settled mind and physical relaxation. The main difference had to do with the religious dimension. Practicing *Lectio Divina*, my intention was to engage in an interior dialogue with Christ by reflecting on the Word of God and speaking to him from my heart. Often during and after the practice I would sense closeness with God and an enhanced desire to follow the scriptural teachings upon which I had been meditating.

When I practiced TM, my purpose was to relax, settle my mind, and gain more energy for my daily activity. For me, the TM technique was mental hygiene. The only impact it had on my personal relationship with God was that it helped quiet my mind in preparation for prayer and worship.

Over the coming years I would come to see further implications of TM and the tradition from which it comes. Eventually, I would undertake a serious academic study comparing Maharishi's understanding of spiritual development with the Christian understanding; but as I began the TM practice in the summer of 1970 my motivation was simply to gain peace of mind and release of stress.

Senior Year: Return to a Spiritual Routine ➤

Beginning my senior year at St. Joseph's College brought a welcome return to a healthy rhythm of life and to regular spiritual practices. Almost daily, I took long walks in the hills and orchards above the college (which are now part of Rancho San Antonio County Park in Cupertino). For the first time since my spiritual awakening at the Trappist monastery two years earlier, I began to meditate on the Gospels. I have read hundreds of spiritual texts from the Christian and non-Christian traditions, but no text touches my heart more than the Gospels.

On my meditative walks, I began with the heart of Jesus's ethical and social teachings—the Sermon on the Mount, chapters 5–7 of Matthew's Gospel. During the previous few years, I had been under the influence of one of the classic enemies to the spiritual life: the enslaving power of attachments. I had been attached to people's esteem, which I tried to win through excessive involvement in social-justice ministries. I had been attached to "being in love" without considering how my attachment was affecting Antonia. I was attached to being popular among my peers. As I continued to feed these attachments, anxiety and exhaustion increased. I didn't realize that feeding unhealthy desires only strengthens them and creates dependency.

Jesus breaks through all those illusions:

> No one can serve two masters. He will either hate one and love the other or be devoted to one and despise the other. You cannot serve God and mammon [the craving for possessions]. (Matthew 6:24)

> Therefore, I tell you, do not worry about your life.... But seek first the kingdom of God and his righteousness, and all these things will be given you besides. Do not worry about tomorrow; tomorrow will take care of itself. Sufficient for a day is its own evil. (Matthew 6:25–34)[7]

This timeless reading reconnected me with the enlightenment that I had received at the age of fourteen when I resolved the doubts regarding my future. I believed that Divine Providence is a reality. As St. Paul writes in Romans 8:28, "We know that all things work together for good for those who love God, who are called according to his purpose."

Reading the Gospels provided me with the inspiration I needed for a new commitment to the spiritual journey. The above passage, and others like it, renewed my trust in the providential ordering of events. At the same time, I knew that trust in Divine Providence did not dispense me from doing my part. I read somewhere: "Pray as if everything depended on God, and work as if everything depended upon you." Analyzing the turbulence of the past couple of years made me realize that there were many unresolved issues within me and that I had to deal more intentionally with my psyche.

The Psychology of Carl Jung ▸

My spiritual director at the seminary, Father James Poggi, was a serious student of the great twentieth-century pioneer in analytical psychology,

---

[7]. Unless otherwise noted, all biblical citations are from the RNAB (Revised New American Bible).

Carl Jung. In fact, during my senior year, Father Poggi was undergoing weekly analysis with a Jungian analyst. Using Jung's insights, he had been helping me process my psychological and emotional issues. For my senior research paper, I decided to undertake an in-depth study of Jung's investigations into the structure and dynamics of the psyche.

Jung understands the psyche as the totality of all the psychic processes, both conscious and unconscious. His years of studying the structure and dynamics of the psyche revealed four prominent contents: the Persona, the Shadow, the Anima/Animus, and the Self. His clinical practice led him to conclude that, in order for full human growth and development to occur, we must make contact with the deep, inner layers of our person. In order to encounter ourselves, the ego must encounter the ever-recurring typical form-elements of the psyche that he called "archetypes."

As part of my study, I began to record my dreams each morning on a tape recorder. Jung found that paying attention to our dreams can help reveal what is happening within our psyche, especially our unconscious psychic processes. These revelations often appear under symbolic form. Within a short period of time, I found that I could remember the details of multiple dreams each morning. Most of my dreams seemed nonsensical, but some revealed issues that I had either repressed or to which I paid insufficient attention such as unresolved tensions, unrealized potential, fears, romantic longing, sexual desire, and occasional messages that seemed to come from the Lord.

An example of something I learned about myself from dream analysis had to do with my "shadow." Jung describes the shadow in his autobiography, *Memories, Dreams, Reflections*:

> The shadow is the inferior part of the personality; the sum of all personal and collective psychic elements which, because of their incompatibility with the chosen conscious attitude, are denied expression in life and therefore coalesce into a relatively autonomous "splinter personality" with contrary tendencies in the unconscious. The shadow behaves compensatorily to consciousness; hence its effects can be positive as well as negative.[8]

---

8. Carl G. Jung, *Memories, Dreams, Reflections* (1963; repr., New York: Vintage Books, 1965), 398–99.

The conscious image that I had of myself at that stage of life was that of a relatively liberal, free-thinking, and hang-loose young man. However, a series of dreams revealed something else about my personality. On many occasions I dreamed of a priest on the faculty whom I considered to be rigid and authoritarian—just the opposite of what I imagined myself to be. Yet fellow students who observed me operate in positions of responsibility and leadership accused me of being bossy and dogmatic at times, especially in stress situations when I would react emotionally without thinking. So, despite my conscious image of being "liberal, free-thinking, and hang-loose," my unconscious was telling me to be aware of the other side. The priest whom I perceived as rigid and authoritarian who appeared recurrently in my dreams was really a symbol of my "shadow side." When I admitted that such tendencies were part of my repressed personality, I began to deal with them instead of projecting them onto others.

Jung postulates the shadow as a storehouse of energy; therefore, he encourages us to make friends with our shadow. Befriending the shadow often propels us into action. For example, awareness of repressed anger and redirecting it appropriately can propel us into constructive action in response to that which triggers our anger.

Herman Hesse's Narcissus and Goldmund ▸

My Jungian studies led me to read Herman Hesse—a popular novelist of the mid-twentieth century who was strongly influenced by Jung. One can gain insight into Hesse by reading his autobiographical novel *Steppenwolf*, which presents "a lonely, reclusive intellectual who struggles to reconcile the wild primeval wolf and the rational man within himself without surrendering to the bourgeois values he despises. His life changes dramatically when he meets a woman who is his opposite, the carefree and elusive Hermine."[9]

The theme of a struggle between two components of a man's psyche, is also found in another novel by Hesse, *Narcissus and Goldmund*—a book that impacted me during my senior year and for some time there-

---

9. Herman Hesse, *Steppenwolf* (New York: Henry Holt, 1929), Back cover.

after. Narcissus and Goldmund are two friends sometime in the Middle Ages who meet while pursuing the possibility of monastic life. Both are seeking to live a meaningful life. The intelligent, virtuous, serious-minded Narcissus finds what he is looking for in monastic ideals and practices, while the warmhearted, passionate, and handsome golden-haired Goldmund gradually becomes disillusioned with the monastic environment.

> . . . he wanted to go on a trip and try wandering once more. It was not good to live in a cloister for so long, with men only. It might be good for monks, but not for him. One could speak intelligently with men, and they understood an artist's work, but all the rest—chatting, tenderness, games, love, pleasure without thought—did not flourish among men, for that one needs women, wandering, freedom, and ever new impressions. Everything around him was a little gray and serious here, a little heavy and manly, and he had become contaminated; it had crept into his blood.

Goldmund then leaves the monastery and travels far and wide seeking happiness. His goal was simply to be free, to wander, and to experience whatever life presented. Being a charming, sensitive, and handsome young man, he attracted women wherever he went and entered into one romantic encounter after another. Finally, at the end of the novel he returns to the monastery many years later, where he meets Narcissus, who has become the abbot, and they share deeply their years of divergent experiences.

Narcissus and Goldmund represent two male archetypes: the *senex* (the "wise elder") and the *puer eternus* (the "eternal youth"). The *senex* represents the stable, virtuous, spiritual man, while the *puer eternus* represents the adventurous, sensual man who wants to remain always a youth psychologically. The novel attracted and disturbed me. I found myself identifying with both men. To some degree I was living the life of Narcissus the monk, but I also felt an attraction to Goldmund's spirit of adventure and romance.

I continued to live with a divided psyche, as symbolized by the two types of literature I was reading on my meditation walks: the Gospels and Hesse's novel. The Gospels motivated me to live a life of virtue and closeness to God. Hesse's novel encouraged me to seek natural happiness without the boundaries and guidance commended by religious tradition. Reflecting years later, I concluded that Hesse's philosophy represented to some degree the "shadow" side of Jungian psychology—the tendency to reduce the human search for meaning to self-actualization based on guidance from the unconscious and its archetypes. Conversely, the Christian search for meaning finds guidance not only from intuition and instinctual forces but from Jesus, the saints, and the spiritual masters, all of whom comprise the driving force within the history of Christianity. However, this realization came some years later. As I was coming of age, Goldmund continued to entice me and create conflicts with my chosen path.

6

Encounter with Christian Mysticism: Meister Eckhart

Near the end of my senior year, I had a conflict with a friend that threw me off balance. I felt the need to get away for a weekend to process what had occurred. I traveled to a monastery on a mountain above the Big Sur coast called New Camaldoli Hermitage—a community of Camaldolese Monks who form a branch of Benedictine monasticism. On the way out of my room at the seminary, I searched my bookshelf for a good spiritual text, and I noticed an unread book that a friend had highly recommended by the fourteenth-century mystic and scholastic named Meister Eckhart about whom I knew nothing. For the next two days, I walked the mountains around the monastery reading Eckhart, who helped me recover my perspective. He also served as my first significant entrée into the world of Catholic mystics.

This was my unplanned introduction to Meister Eckhart, a German Dominican and world-famous mystic. The Dominican religious order was founded by St. Dominic of Guzmán in the early 1200s in southern France. Like his contemporary, St. Francis of Assisi, St. Dominic was committed to living a simple life as a wandering beggar, preaching through word and example the teachings of Jesus. Unlike Francis, Dominic emphasized the importance of study. The Dominicans were the first religious order to abandon manual labor and to put intellectual work in the forefront.

Forty years after the founding of the Dominicans, Eckhart (1260–1328) was probably born at Tambach near Gotha. As a young man he joined the Dominicans and studied in their monastery in Cologne. His teachers saw in him great intellectual ability, and they sent him to study at the University of Paris, which was then the center of the Western intellectual world.[1]

Paris was also a center of controversy, partly due to what could be called a new "enlightenment," fed from Greek, Arabic, and Hebrew sources. This new knowledge was increasingly influencing the arts, sciences, and theology in the universities. This new enlightenment was manifested in the academic philosophy that came to be known as Scholasticism, especially as it was promoted by Thomas Aquinas (d. 1274). One of Thomas's major contributions was the integration of Aristotelian philosophy into Christian theology.

Eckhart completed his studies at Paris in 1302, earning the title of "Meister" (Master), and from then on he was known as Meister Eckhart. Soon he rose to positions of prominence in the Dominican order.

Eckhart's "Talks of Instruction" ▶

During my weekend at the New Camaldoli Hermitage I read Meister Eckhart's "Talks of Instruction," which contain questions his students addressed to him as they sat together in evening table conversation. One of the first teachings that hit me in my distressed state was how to deal with frustrations and disappointments in life. Eckhart begins by describing people who feel that they must get away from where they are to get to a place where they can find peace or live a more spiritual life. His answer is the following:

> The truth is that you yourself are at fault in all this and no one else. It is pure self-will. Whether you realize it or not, there can be no restlessness unless it come from self-will.... This is what I mean: people fly

---

1. "Introduction," in Edmund Colledge and Bernard McGinn, *Meister Eckhart: The Essential Sermons, Commentaries, Treatises, and Defense*, Classics of Western Spirituality (New York: Paulist Press, 1981), 6.

from this to seek that—these places, these people, these manners, those purposes, that activity—but they should not blame ways or things for thwarting them. When you are thwarted, it is your own attitude that is our of order.[2]

In another talk Eckhart teaches in the same vein:

Those who do well, do well wherever they are, and in whatever company, and those who do badly, do badly wherever they are and in whatever company. But if a man does well, God is really in him, and with him everywhere, on the streets and among people, just as much as in church, or in a desert place, or a cell. If he really has God, and only God, then nothing disturbs him.[3]

This teaching of Eckhart hit me between the eyes. Instead of blaming my circumstances for my suffering, Eckhart was telling me that my attitude was what needed to change. So, what was I to do? I continued reading:

Begin, therefore, first with self and forget yourself! If you do not first get away from self, then whatever else you get away from you will still find obstacles and restlessness. People look in vain for peace, who seek it in the world outside, in places, people, ways, activities, or in world-flight, poverty and humiliation, whatever the avenue or degree; for there is no peace this way. They are looking in the wrong direction, and the longer they look the less they find what they are looking for. They go along like someone who has missed his road; the farther they go the more they are astray. What, then, is to be done?

Let everyone begin by denying self and in so doing he will have denied all else. Indeed, if a man gave up a kingdom or even the whole world and still was selfish, he would have given up nothing. If, however, he denies himself, then whatever he keeps, be it wealth, honor, or anything else, he is free from it all.[4]

---

2. Raymond B. Blakney, *Meister Eckhart: A Central Source and Inspiration of Dominant Currents in Philosophy and Theology since Aquinas* (New York: Harper & Row, 1941), 5.

3. Ibid., 7.

4. Ibid., 5.

This was not the teaching of my generation. In the 60s and 70s the cry was: "Assert yourself!" Eckhart was telling me, "Forget yourself!" He writes, "To the extent that you eliminate self from your activities, God comes into them—but no more and no less."[5]

So, if forgetting self is the way to true peace, how was I to move in this direction? Eckhart answers:

> This is the basis on which human nature and spirit are entirely good, and from which our human actions receive their worth: a mind completely devoted to God. Direct your study to this end, that God shall be great in you, so that in all your comings and goings your zeal and fervor are toward him. . . . Seek God and you shall find him and all good with him.[6]

Eckhart's Experience of God

"A mind completely devoted to God." This is the key that Eckhart discovered and communicated to his disciples, that if we really have God, nothing disturbs us. He explains why in audacious language:

> Because he has *only* God and thinks only God and everything is nothing but God to him. He discloses God in every act, in every place. The whole business of his person adds up to God. His actions are due only to him who is the author of them and not to himself since he is merely the agent. If we mean God and only God, then it is [God] who does what we do and nothing can disturb him—neither company nor place. Thus, neither can any person disturb him, for he thinks of nothing, is looking for nothing and relishes nothing but God, who is one with him by perfect devotion.[7]

In this passage Eckhart teaches that, if we want to find peace in life, no matter what the circumstances, we must take care how we think of God. We are not to think of God only during times of prayer, meditation, and worship, rather we are to hold on to God throughout the day in all our

---

5. Ibid., 6.
6. Ibid., 7.
7. Ibid., 8.

experiences. Eckhart writes, "Take him with you among the crowds and turmoil of the alien world." How are we to do this? Eckhart answers, "It depends on the heart and an inner, intellectual return to God and not only steady contemplation by a given method."[8]

Eckhart's answer echoes Jesus's first teaching in his public ministry: "Repent, for the Kingdom of Heaven is at hand" (Matthew 4:17).[9] Repent means "change your mind," or "go beyond your mind." Thus, if I am upset with a friend who stood me up, or angry with someone who cut me off in traffic, or lusting after someone who attracts me, "repent" at that moment would mean, "redirect the thought or feeling to God immediately." Change the direction of my mind from the preoccupation at hand to the presence of God within me. This is how I first interpreted what Eckhart means by an "intellectual return to God."

A deeper interpretation is given by Eckhart:

> The more [a person] regards everything as divine—more divine than it is of itself—the more God will be pleased with him. To be sure, this requires effort and love, a careful cultivation of the spiritual life, and a watchful, honest, active oversight of all one's mental attitudes toward things and people. It is not to be learned by world-flight, running away from things, turning solitary and going apart from the world. Rather, one must learn an inner solitude, wherever or with whomsoever he may be. He must learn to penetrate things and find God there, to get a strong impression of God firmly fixed in his mind.[10]

When Eckhart says to regard everything as divine, he understands that everything is upheld in existence by God, the sourceless source of all existing beings. God is existence itself. No being, no thing could exist unless God gives it existence and, in this sense, God is the deepest reality of any being.[11] Eckhart teaches that we must learn to get beyond the

---

8. Ibid., 9.

9. Pope Benedict XVI explains that the "heavens" is an alternative expression for the word *God*, which the Jews largely avoided out of reverence for the mystery of God. Thus, "Kingdom of heaven" speaks of God, who is as much in this world as he is beyond it. A better translation would be to speak of God's being Lord, of his Lordship (Pope Benedict XVI, *Jesus of Nazareth* [New York: Doubleday, 2007], 1:55–56).

10. Meister Eckhart, *Talks of Instruction*, 9.

11. Eckhart invoked the distinction between the "absolute existence" (*esse absolutum*) of God and the "formally inherent existence" of creatures, which is to say that God

surface value of things and "learn to penetrate things [and circumstances] and find God there."

A related counsel is that we must avoid all negative attitudes and behavior. Eckhart says, "one must learn an inner solitude, wherever or with whomsoever he may be." This means that we don't allow ourselves to be overshadowed by others or by our own emotions. We remain "sober," witnessing our thoughts and reactions to people and circumstances. This requires constant vigilance.

Vigilance or watchfulness is a spiritual practice recommended by Eckhart. He writes,

> One should be, as our Lord said, "Like people always on the watch, expecting their Lord." Expectant people are watchful, always looking for him they expect always to find him in whatever comes along; however strange it may be, they always think he might be in it. This is what awareness of the Lord is to be like and it requires diligence that taxes a man's senses and powers to the utmost, if he is to achieve it and to take God evenly in all things—if he is to find God as much in one thing as in another.[12]

Jesus declares that the person who practices repentance does so for the sake of experiencing the kingdom of heaven (God's lordship over us). Repentance requires mental discipline. Eckhart teaches in the same vein: "The man to whom God is ever present, and who controls and uses his mind to the highest degree—that man alone knows what peace is and he has the Kingdom of Heaven within him."[13]

The Unity of God and Human Beings ▶

The more I read Eckhart during my weekend at the New Camaldoli Hermitage, the more I realized that his experience of God and his theology of God were far beyond me. I felt strongly attracted to his teachings

---

is the existence of all things in an absolute sense, but not as formally inhering in them (Bernard McGinn, "Introduction," in *Meister Eckhart: The Essential Sermons*, 33). Thus, a human being has existence that is created, and such existence is dependent on divine existence.

12. Meister Eckhart, *Talks of Instruction*, 10–11.
13. Ibid., 11.

and to the possibility of a deeper, contemplative experience of God—an experience I tasted during the period of my spiritual awakening at the Trappist monastery two years earlier—but I knew that further study would be required before I could more fully appreciate his "mystical theology."

Years later I undertook a sustained examination of Eckhart during a three-week retreat at the New Camaldoli Hermitage, especially of his teachings about "union with God." His key teaching supporting all others is the unity of God and human beings, a belief that flows right from the New Testament. Jesus teaches that God is "my Father and your Father" in John 20:17. At the end of the Last Supper discourse, Jesus prays, "Father . . . , I have given them the glory you gave me, so that they may be one, as we are one, *I in them and you in me*, that they may be brought to perfection as one" (John 17:22–23). Eckhart, however, expressed the unity between God and humans in language that struck some people as extravagant. He used the analogy of marital relations. God is a procreator, a begetter, and thus the Father. The soul is the virgin wife, in whom the Son is begotten, and this is the secret of God's eternal delight and ours as well. God is the tireless lover of the soul, and he eternally begets his Son in the receptive soul.

Eckhart's teaching is a supreme example of "apophatic theology." *Apophatikos* in Greek means "negative." The word "negative" refers to the process of negation by which we must gradually renounce all attributes of God in order to attain to the experience of God. God's nature is always beyond what we can think and understand, and so, only through entering into the contemplative process can we move beyond created reality, all images, all thought and so move into the darkness of the Godhead. The great scholar of mysticism Louis Dupré explains, "In doing so the human mind surpasses its own created being and, in the ecstatic ascent, loses itself in the divine super-essence. It thereby becomes deified."[14] "Ecstatic" refers to going beyond oneself. This continual movement beyond what we know, feel, and think directs the mind to its union with God.

---

14. Louis Dupré and James A. Wiseman, O.S.B., *Light from Light: An Anthology of Christian Mysticism*, 2nd ed. (New York: Paulist Press, 2001), 80.

I began to wonder how the Christian understanding of contemplation related to my experience of interior silence through Transcendental Meditation and to the teachings of the primordial Indian tradition from which it springs, Vedanta. The summer following my graduation from college provided me with an exceptional opportunity to begin a decades-long study of the relationship between Christian spirituality and Asian spirituality. This exploration became the grist for a doctoral dissertation that I completed twenty years later.

7

Encounter with an Eastern Tradition

THROUGHOUT MY SENIOR YEAR, I PRACTICED Transcendental Meditation (TM) twice daily for twenty minutes. I noted in chapter 5 that I undertook the practice because I was looking for more peace of mind and release of stress. Along with daily Mass and meditative walks in the hills reading the Gospels, the Eastern meditation practice proved quite helpful in enabling me to recover from the emotional and spiritual turbulence of my junior year in Mexico.

By the end of my college career, I had settled down considerably. I had temporarily resolved the confusion regarding my vocational path by concluding that I did want to be a priest even though the desire for marriage still attracted me and the Goldmund archetype continued to intrigue me. When I expressed my doubts to the seminary rector about whether I should continue on to St. Patrick's Seminary in Menlo Park, he saw no impediment since one of the purposes of a seminary is to help a candidate work out vocational issues.

After graduating with a degree in psychology, I returned to live with my family in Alameda for the summer and began working as a janitor at the Kaiser Center in Oakland. One of my summer reading books was Maharishi Mahesh Yogi's commentary on the *Bhagavad Gita*.[1] I was intrigued by Maharishi's claim

---

1. Maharishi Mahesh Yogi, *Maharishi Mahesh Yogi on the Bhagavad-gita: A New Translation and Commentary with Sanskrit Text*, chapters 1 to 6 (Baltimore, MD: Penguin Books, 1969; reprint, 1973; cited hereafter as *BG*).

that his method of meditation is a way to gain "Enlightenment," which he also calls "Self-realization." I began to find connections between his teaching and Jung's description of "individuation" and the notable psychologist Abraham Maslow's notion of "self-actualization." The question arose within me, How does all this relate to Christian theology and spirituality?

Near the end of June, I received a flier from the Berkeley TM center inviting meditators to attend an August TM teacher-training course to be led by Maharishi at Humboldt State University in Arcata, California. I had no interest in becoming a TM teacher, but, upon reading the flier, I immediately felt a strong desire to attend the course. It was an impractical option because I needed to work the entire summer in order to save enough money to cover my expenses for the upcoming academic year. Nevertheless, I decided to follow my gut.

I told my parents that I planned to quit my job a month early so that I could participate in Maharishi's course. They sensibly reminded me that I needed sufficient funds to pay my seminary expenses, and they did not understand my intense interest in Eastern meditation. Yet they recognized my compelling desire, and they supported my decision even though they did not understand it. That was an endearing attitude that my parents have demonstrated throughout my entire life and for which I am immensely grateful.

Encountering Maharishi Mahesh Yogi ▸

At the beginning of August 1971, I drove my 1953 Buick Special (I was an old car enthusiast) to Humboldt State University, where I spent four stimulating weeks with Maharishi and about two thousand meditators from all over the country, most of whom were idealistic young adults. We resided in the university student housing and attended three daily lectures by Maharishi in the university gymnasium. Maharishi sat on a stage, cross-legged on a sofa, spoke without notes, and entertained questions from the floor.

This was the first time I encountered Maharishi. Although I had read some of his writings, I knew very little about his background. I was fascinated by what I learned about him.

When Maharishi speaks about himself, he assigns all credit for who he is and what he teaches to his master. Consequently, his story begins with the story of Swami Brahmananda Saraswati (1868–1953), whom Maharishi calls "Guru Dev" (Divine Teacher).

In his early twenties, Maharishi was studying physics at Allahabad University. Besides studying, he also was seeking a spiritual guide. Upon meeting Guru Dev, he knew that he had found his master:

> As a thirsty man arrives at a well, so I arrived at the feet of my Master. The quest of a perfect Master was there. The first sight of his personality was enough to make me surrender at his feet. He was the most highly revered sage in India and was held as the embodiment of Divine Consciousness.[2]

From 1941 until Guru Dev's death in 1953, Maharishi lived as his devoted disciple, attempting to attune himself perfectly with Guru Dev's thoughts and feelings. He started by doing simple chores in order to be around the master, to "breathe his air." One day he had the opportunity to draft a letter for Guru Dev. The master liked what he had done, and the young disciple soon became Guru Dev's private secretary. It is said that Maharishi was the favorite disciple, and those who knew Maharishi at that time say that he spared nothing in Guru Dev's service.[3]

After Guru Dev's death in 1953, Maharishi retired to the caves of the "Valley of the Saints" in Uttar Kashi. He lived there in peaceful solitude for two years until an idea occurred to him to visit the temple of Rameshvaram in south India. Although he had no intentions of leaving solitude, the idea persisted. When Maharishi consulted an older holy man in the valley, the elder suggested that he go.

Soon Maharishi traveled across India to the southernmost tip, where he spent several weeks visiting temples and shrines around Rameshvaram. Back in the world, he was struck by the gap between the inspiring words of the Vedic literature and the miserable daily life of the Indian people.

---

2. Maharishi Mahesh Yogi, *Thirty Years around the World: Dawn of the Age of Enlightenment, Volume One 1957–1964* (Vlodrop, The Netherlands: MVU Press, 1986), 184.

3. Jack Forem, *Transcendental Meditation: Maharishi Mahesh Yogi and the Science of Creative Intelligence* (New York: E. P. Dutton, 1974), 208.

... I was so naturally and deeply moved between the two realities: life being lived on a completely wretched level and life described [in the Vedic scriptures].... This was the natural feeling that was deep in my mind, that something should be done so that people don't suffer, because there is no reason to suffer.[4]

One day when he was in the southern city of Trivandrum, a man approached him and asked, "Do you speak?" Maharishi answered that he did not lecture. But the man persisted and set up a series of seven talks for Maharishi in the public library.

Maharishi spoke for seven evenings to crowds that doubled each day. His message was simple and novel:

> The suffering and misery so common to human existence are unnecessary. Life in its essential nature is bliss, and every person can experience unbounded bliss consciousness and integrate it into daily life through the effortless technique of Transcendental Meditation.[5]

The people were surprised to hear the spiritual path described as simple and natural. For centuries in India, spiritual growth had been presented as requiring renunciation, detachment, and withdrawal from the world.[6] Meditation was understood to be difficult and requiring rigorous concentration and control of the mind. Maharishi had learned the contrary from Guru Dev. The crowds were anxious to practice the "effortless" and "natural" method of meditation about which Maharishi spoke. He had never instructed the masses in meditation before, but he could not refuse the people's request; and so, Maharishi began to teach Transcendental Meditation. That was the beginning of his worldwide movement.

Maharishi's Religious and Philosophical Tradition ▸

Maharishi's daily lectures at Humboldt State provided my first in-depth exposure to the spirituality of the Far East. In order to provide the

---

4. Maharishi, *Thirty Years around the World*, 190. The following account of Maharishi's decision to begin teaching Transcendental Meditation is found on pp. 190–200.
5. Ibid., 193 (editor's summary).
6. Maharishi Mahesh Yogi, *On the Bhagavad-Gita*, 15.

context for his teachings, I will present a brief overview of Maharishi's tradition.

Maharishi belongs to the "Vedic" tradition, the original source of Indian philosophy and religion, especially Hinduism.[7] The Vedic tradition is based on the "Vedas," the ancient sacred scriptures of India. The word *veda* means "knowledge." Vedic literature also includes other works that developed during the course of the tradition, such as the *Upanishads*. Upanishadic wisdom is preserved in the "Vedanta"—the "end of the Vedas," the final stage of the Vedas. It is the sixth and most elevated of six systems of Indian philosophy.[8] Although Hindus refer to Vedanta in the singular, several Vedanta systems that developed after the first millennium A.D. interpret the Upanishads in widely divergent fashion.[9]

The most widely known of classical Vedanta systems is called Advaita ("nondualism"). Advaita is usually closely associated with the philosopher Shankara, a reformer of the Vedic tradition whose traditional dating is 509–477 B.C., although some modern scholars place him in the eighth or ninth century A.D.[10] Maharishi claims that the meditation practice taught by Shankara and himself can lead a person to experience higher states of consciousness and, thereby, realize in oneself the truths taught by the Vedas and Vedanta.

Maharishi teaches that meditation leads a person to transcend thought and to experience the "Higher Self" (also described as the "source of thought" and "pure consciousness")—a fourth state of consciousness beyond waking, dreaming, and sleeping. He also calls the fourth state "Transcendental Consciousness." Repeated experience of Transcendental Consciousness purifies the mind to the point that the attachments and disordered habits that inhibit a person from being grounded in the Higher Self are gradually released from the mind and the nervous system. Once the purification process is complete, one enters the fifth state,

---

7. See Solange Lemaître, *Hinduism*, trans. John Francis Brown (New York: Hawthorn, 1959), 9.

8. Ibid., 44–57.

9. K. H. Potter, "Vedanta," *The Perennial Dictionary of World Religions*, ed. Keith Crim et al. (San Francisco: Harper & Row, 1989), 786.

10. Maharishi explains the discrepancy by opining that some modern scholars "have perhaps confused an illustrious successor with Shankara himself, because all his successors are known as Shankaracharyas; the name has become a title" (*BG*, 256 n. 5).

"Cosmic Consciousness," also called "enlightenment." Continued growth in higher states of consciousness is accomplished through devotion to God resulting in "God consciousness" (the sixth state), and finally to union with God, "Unity Consciousness" (the seventh state).

As I listened to Maharishi and took copious notes, I realized that the knowledge he was presenting was of a much higher order than the analytic and humanistic psychology I had been studying in college. I detected similarities with Jung's notion of the Self, although Jung did not posit a transcendent source to the dynamics of the psyche.

My attempts to relate Christian philosophy and theology to Maharishi's teachings proved more difficult. Both traditions speak of God, Being, creation, the soul, and higher states of spiritual development, but to what degree were they speaking about similar or different realities? I had heard that one of the great Catholic spiritual masters, St. Teresa of Avila (1515–1582) also describes seven stages of the spiritual journey in her book *The Interior Castle*, but I had no idea whether her "seven dwelling places" correspond in any way with Maharishi's system.

Because my own theological education was limited, I needed more knowledge of my own tradition before I could develop an informed dialogue with the Vedic tradition and respond to important questions, such as the following:

- What is the difference in the two traditions' understanding of creation, the human soul, and God?
- How does the Christian understanding of union with God compare with that of Vedanta?

I looked forward to pursuing these questions when I would begin graduate studies in theology the following month. In the meantime, my experiences at the Humboldt course continued to fascinate me. Part of the fascination was simply living with two thousand idealistic young spiritual seekers from a variety of religious and philosophical traditions. Early in the course, stimulating and challenging discussions increased dramatically once it became known that I was a candidate for the Catholic priesthood. I revealed my identity during one of Maharishi's lectures when I approached the floor microphone and asked him a question.

> Maharishi, I am a Catholic seminarian studying for the priesthood. I have been practicing TM for about a year and have found it supportive

to my Christian spiritual practices. I would like to invite other Christians to take advantage of TM. Would you consider offering TM instruction in church environments?

Maharishi responded:

We respect all religious traditions, and all are welcome to learn TM. But it would be better to leave Christianity in the church and TM in the TM Center.

Immediately after the lecture, a number of meditators approached me and asked me questions such as:

- What kind of meditation does the Catholic Church teach?
- Isn't the Catholic Church against Eastern meditation?
- What is unique about Jesus Christ? Wasn't he one of many masters who have reached "Christ-Consciousness?"
- Aren't all religions simply different paths to the same goal?

I was unsure how to answer some of the questions but was intrigued by all of them. Many of the meditators who questioned me were Christians who no longer practiced their faith and had unresolved issues about Christ and Christianity. Others were non-Christians who were curious about Christianity. The interactions challenged me to deepen my knowledge and experience of both the Christian and Vedic traditions.

Spiritual Practices during the Course ▸

Prior to arriving at the teacher-training course, my experience of Eastern meditation had been limited to two twenty-minute meditation sessions daily. During those sessions, I mentally repeated a mantra according to the TM method and usually found myself entering into a deep state of rest. My mind would become settled. Occasionally, I would briefly enter a state of complete silence. When I resumed normal activity after meditation, I periodically noticed that the settled state of mind and physical relaxation would last for a period of time. The experience of interior quiet during and after meditation was similar to what I had experienced during my senior year in high school when I practiced *Lectio Divina* for half an hour each day before dinner.

During the course at Humboldt State, the participants engaged in an advanced meditation practice called "rounding." A "round" consists of ten minutes of yoga postures (*asanas*), five minutes of a simple breathing exercise called *pranayama*, and twenty to thirty minutes of meditation. We practiced two rounds in the morning and two in the later afternoon in the privacy of our student housing. After my morning rounds, I would usually engage in *Lectio*, using the New Testament, especially John's Gospel, commonly considered the most mystical of the four Gospels.

The *Lectio* practice involved quiet reflection on the texts interspersed with periods of silence. Whereas TM led me to interior quiet, *Lectio* led me to a quiet devotional dialogue with God. I listened to the Word of God, and I spoke to him from my heart. The dialogue would periodically fade away and I would enter into contemplation, complete stillness. The scripture passages that especially resonated with my *Lectio* experience are from Jesus's Last Supper discourse in John's Gospel (chapters 13–17):

> Whoever loves me will keep my word, and my Father will love him, and we will come to him and make our dwelling with him. (John 14:23)

> I am the true vine, and my Father is the vinegrower. He takes away every branch in me that does not bear fruit, and everyone that does he prunes so that it bears more fruit. You are already pruned because of the word that I spoke to you. Remain in me, as I remain in you. (John 15:1–4)

At times I would attempt to relate my *Lectio* experiences to what Maharishi was teaching. Maharishi taught that one could experience the Higher Self through meditation. Jesus taught that those who are faithful to him and to his words would experience his presence in themselves. I began to reflect on a fundamental question that would occupy my attention for years: What is the relationship between the Higher Self experienced when one transcends thought during TM and the presence of God experienced during contemplation?

My daily practices gradually led me to a preliminary conclusion about the relationship between Far Eastern and Christian spiritual practices. The primary purpose of Far Eastern meditation is to cultivate silence leading to purification of the mind and nervous system and realization of the Higher Self. The primary purpose of Christian *Lectio* is to cultivate a personal relationship with Christ, who reveals himself through his words and his Holy Spirit. Receiving and obeying his words leads to "abiding in him." "Abide in me as I abide in you" (John 15:4 RSV).

Aftereffects of the Course ▸

After four weeks of rounding, listening to Maharishi's daily lectures, and engaging in challenging conversations with other meditators, I felt the urgent need to speak with someone who possessed deep knowledge of the Eastern and Christian traditions to help me process and digest all that had occurred. I needed to speak with Father Dunstan.

By this time, two years after we had met in his Santa Cruz Mountains cabin, Father Dunstan had completed his training in pottery, had made five thousand pots and destroyed them all (as per the instructions of his teacher). Now he was teaching pottery at the Mendocino Art Center, which was on my route back to the Bay Area.

As soon as I drove away from Humboldt State University and headed south along the coastal highway, the first significant effect of the four-week course occurred: I felt enveloped in a profound silence and joy. The last time something like this happened to me was when I was propelled into my spiritual awakening at the Trappist monastery on Easter Monday, 1969. The difference between the two experiences was that the earlier spiritual awakening had happened suddenly and without any conscious preparation. At that time, I was in a state of extreme emptiness, having exhausted myself trying to live an authentic Christian life by excessive service to disadvantaged people. It was by the sheer grace of God that I entered into a heightened state of awareness and a sense of communion with God that remained for a couple months.

The experience of interior silence and joy following the month at Humboldt State seemed to be a direct result of prolonged meditation each day. The interior silence and peace that I underwent during meditation carried over into my waking state of consciousness. I believe the cause of the spiritual awakening at the monastery was supernatural. The cause of the interior silence and joy flowing from a month of deep meditation was natural,

The distinction between "natural" and "supernatural" mysticism was explored by the great twentieth-century Catholic philosopher Jacques Maritain. He explains "natural mysticism" in the following way: "The natural desire to see the Cause of being derives from the natural desire of knowing being.... Every great metaphysic is indeed pierced by mystical aspiration."[11] Supernatural mysticism is our natural capacity to know being elevated by the grace of God, who enables us to experience the Divine Presence. God transcends the center of the soul because God created the soul.

Processing with Father Dunstan ▸

When I arrived at Mendocino, I shared with Father Dunstan my experiences of the course. I asked his opinion about Transcendental Meditation. He responded that he had attended a lecture by Maharishi in Canada in the early 1960s and concluded that Maharishi was "legit." Father Dunstan knew much about Eastern philosophy and meditation. He had been practicing Zen meditation and studying Buddhism and Hinduism for some years. He considered Zen and TM to be methods of mental hygiene that are helpful for dismantling unhealthy desires and attachments. He did not consider them to be prayer. He found Zen to be helpful for settling and clearing the mind.

His perspective confirmed my initial conclusions with regard to the relationship between Eastern meditation and my Christian faith. At the same time, he tempered my extravagant enthusiasm regarding my meditation practices by adding a note of realism: "Remember, it's the long haul that counts."

---

11. Jacques Maritain, "The Natural Mystical Experience and the Void," in *Ransoming the Time*, trans. Harry Lorin Binsse (New York: Charles Scribner's Sons, 1941), 260–61. The article was based on a talk Maritain gave to the Fourth Congress of Religious Psychology in 1938. For a summary, see Henry Bars, "Maritain's Contributions to an Understanding of Mystical Experience," in *Jacques Maritain: The Man and His Achievement*, ed. Joseph W. Evans (New York: Sheed & Ward, 1963), 119–20.

In Maritain's 1931 Appendix to *The Degrees of Knowledge*, trans. Bernard Wall and Margot R. Adamson (London: G. Bles, 1937), he describes an intuitive, experimental, and indirect knowledge of the soul's existence through its own acts—the nucleus of his own view of natural mysticism defended in his 1938 talk referred to above.

8

Graduate Seminary and a Life-Changing Decision

Arrival at St. Patrick's Seminary ➤

THE INTERIOR SILENCE AND JOY THAT CHARACTERIZED MY state of mind after the TM teacher-training course stayed with me as I began graduate studies in theology at St. Patrick Seminary in the fall of 1971.[1] Built in 1898, heavily damaged by the 1906 earthquake, and rebuilt in 1908, St. Patrick's Seminary is a splendid Romanesque-style brick building constructed on eighty-five acres of land studded with ancient oaks.[2] It is not unlike some of the great nineteenth-century French monasteries. It serves as an oasis of quiet and a nature preserve in the midst of a San Francisco Bay urban environment.

I arrived at St. Patrick's with a great thirst for knowledge. The course at Humboldt State University had opened my mind to an entirely new body of knowledge and questions about the nature and destiny of the human person. Fortunately, at St. Patrick's I was to study with a brilliant, dynamic professor who would be able to address many of these questions from a Catholic perspective.

---

1. Now called St. Patrick Seminary and University.
2. In 1995 the seminary sold forty-three acres of land for housing development. The seminary retains forty-two acres.

From 1967 to 1970, the St. Patrick Seminary community had gone through the cultural upheaval common on most American campuses at that time. Happily, St. Patrick's regained equilibrium by the time my class arrived and provided a fertile climate for ongoing spiritual growth as well as academic investigation. The daily Masses were prepared with care, and students generally participated with enthusiasm. The rector, Father Mel Farrell, was a wise, serene leader who helped create a stable, positive environment. Students were open to fresh ideas, and many were interested in my exploration of Eastern spirituality. Soon after my arrival, I invited a teacher of Transcendental Meditation to give a lecture introducing the TM technique. Several students signed up for the four-day course of instruction.

My circle of spiritual friends grew. Dennis Stradford was a third-year student, and we continued to share a deep spiritual brotherhood and a common interest in Simone Weil and Father Dunstan. Another older student entered my life as well, whom I will call Leo. Leo was seven years older than I and had been a Dominican brother for a few years. He left the order, became a popular high school teacher, but again felt a call to the priesthood. He joined a local diocese, which sent him to St. Patrick's to complete his theological studies. While there, he became restless. He concluded that his call was to be a priest among the poor in Calcutta (Kolkata),[3] India—a call that had its origins in his childhood.

As a child, Leo had traveled to Calcutta with his father, who was a member of the Foreign Service. One day they were eating lunch at a restaurant when several hungry people approached the window next to their table and stared at them wide-eyed. Leo was overcome with compassion and sorrow, and he burst into tears. His father told him, "Leo, you must make a decision. Either you decide to do something to help such suffering people, or you must learn to accept their reality as it is." At that moment, Leo knew that his vocation in life had something to do with service to the poor.

During his time as a student at St. Patrick's, Leo's childhood conviction reappeared with great force, and he contacted the archbishop of Calcutta, who agreed to accept him as a candidate for ordination. The

---

3. In 2001 the government of West Bengal decided to officially change its capital city's name to Kolkata to reflect its original Bengali pronunciation

archbishop told him to continue studying at St. Patrick's for another year and then they would decide how to proceed with ordination.

Leo and I became the best of friends and spiritual brothers. For me he was a great inspiration, and we understood each other deeply. Although I did not intend to serve in the Third World, my experiences among the indigenous people in Mexican villages had sensitized me to the plight of underprivileged people. I fully supported Leo's plans. Little did I realize that he would soon have a dramatic impact on my life.

The seminary professor who helped me deal with philosophical and theological questions was Father Peter Chirico, a priest of the Society of San Sulpice (the Sulpicians). He had profound knowledge of both traditional and modern theology—especially the thought of two heavyweights of the mid-twentieth century, Bernard Lonergan and Karl Rahner. Father Chirico taught the first-year fundamental course, "Faith, Revelation, and Dogma."

Dogma ›

I shared the common reaction of my generation toward "dogma"—that the very notion was sterile and legalistic. Father Chirico soon opened our minds to a deeper understanding. For the universal Church to have declared "dogmatic" a formulation of faith, it must have had a great impact on people in the past and be based on Sacred Scripture and the consensus of great saints and theologians. He urged us to investigate what each dogma reveals about the human person, about God, and about our relationship with God.

The dogma that most occupied our attention in Father Chirico's class was "Jesus Christ is true God and true man." "Son of Man" was Jesus's most characteristic way of referring to himself. The title had two fundamental meanings for Jews. First, it meant the ideal, archetypal human being. Second, in the Book of Daniel the title "Son of Man" is given to the one in whom and through whom the salvation of God's people would come to be realized (Daniel 7:13–14). The following are notes I took during one of Father Chirico's classes:

> Through his life, death, and resurrection, Jesus declared that the goal of human life is infinity itself, union with God. To be true to our

human nature—as expressed in and by the Son of Man, we can never become complacent and self-righteous, believing that we have "finally arrived." The function of Christian liturgy which celebrates the "mystery of Christ" is to call us to the truth, and to empower us to grow beyond where we are toward full humanity. Traditional Christian spiritual practices such as the sacraments, prayer, meditation, and asceticism, are meant to help people reach union with God. In that state, the divine and human come together in an integral unity. In this state human love is perfectly realized.

Faith ▸

Father Chirico demonstrated that Catholicism does not believe in blind faith, but in faith and reason. Faith is reasonable. Scientists operate on the basis of a natural faith in the intelligibility of the universe. If they did not *believe* that they could understand the workings of nature, they would not continue investigating. A natural faith leads them on. Again, I quote my class notes from Father Chirico:

> Christian faith involves a psychological and emotional openness to the meaning of life as revealed in Jesus Christ. Because of one's faith in Jesus Christ, the Christian sees infinite possibilities for his or her growth and development. The possibilities don't end at death. Although Christians don't rely on scientific proof for their faith, we can extrapolate from our own experience to understand the ultimate teachings of Christianity.
>
> We can compare knowledge to the circumference of a circle with the circle's area representing the mystery of life. As the circumference enlarges (knowledge), the area (mystery) grows proportionately. New circumstances always elicit new developments in a person. Bernard Lonergan describes the process in this way: One tries to *understand* the new experience. Then one makes a *judgment* about it which enables one to *decide* about the new possibilities which arise from judging the experience. Having decided, one must *articulate* or *implement* the decision which, in turn, brings the person to *reflect* on the results of the implementation. Then the whole process begins anew: experience, understand, judge, decide, act.

There seems to be no end to this process, which leads us to believe that our goal is infinite. This leads to an extrapolatory understanding of God. Since we have not yet realized the goal, we cannot define it. But we can see the process of our development and we can project understandings based on this process. We can interpret "moving toward unity with God" as the infinite prolongation of these processes. We have *faith* in an infinite, sourceless source (God) behind it all. This is one way to describe the reasonableness of faith.

Jesus and the Avatars

A common theme in my discussions with meditators on the TM teacher-training course had to do with the person and nature of Jesus Christ. They posed questions such as, What is unique about Jesus Christ? Wasn't he one of many masters who have reached "Christ-Consciousness"? Wasn't he an incarnation of God like Krishna and the other Avatars of Hinduism? (*Avatar* in Sanskrit means "incarnation.")

As the course with Father Chirico continued, I developed my initial responses to these questions. God eternally expresses and communicates himself. God's Word, God's self-communication is the Second Person of the Blessed Trinity, the Son of God who is eternally begotten of the Father. The Father is the source and origin of the Godhead. The eternally begotten Son of the Father became a human being, born of the Blessed Virgin Mary. That human being, Jesus of Nazareth, is truly human in all things but sin, and is truly God, making him unique among all beings.

The Hindu tradition describes avatars as gods who appear as human beings but do not actually become human.[4] They do not suffer and die. The Eternal Word of God (the Son), *became* human, incarnating as Jesus of Nazareth. He emptied himself of his divine prerogatives to enter fully into human existence, experiencing what all human beings experience, including suffering and death. Jesus was not simply a human being who became enlightened and entered God-consciousness. He was God from

---

4. N. J. Hein, "Avatar, Avatara," *The Perennial Dictionary of World Religions*, ed. Keith Crim (San Francisco: Harper & Row, 1989), 82.

the moment of his conception, "conceived by the Holy Spirit" without the mediation of a man.[5] He is called "the Christ" because Christians believe that he is the Messiah, the anointed of God. *Christos* in Greek means the "anointed one."

Other questions from my meditator friends still filled my mind, in particular: Aren't all religions simply different paths to the same goal? This question and many more would command my attention in a very different environment the following year.

Decision to Leave the Seminary ▸

I was filled with creative energy and joy throughout the fall quarter. Not only did I enthusiastically engage in academics and community life, but I also participated in stimulating extracurricular service projects: a monthly Catholic radio show, periodical weekend retreats for married couples, leadership of a parish choir, and advanced seminars offered by the local TM center.

However, my attitude soured in the winter quarter. The core theology course for first year students was no longer taught by Father Chirico, but by a professor who did not inspire me. I found his classes boring and I felt disheartened. At the same time, my vocation struggles, which had subsided for a year, came back with a vengeance. Some of the married couples with whom I socialized were challenging me to rethink celibacy both by their words (they didn't believe in the celibacy requirement for priestly ordination) and by their actions (their happy marriages attracted me). Significant friendships with women with whom I could share deeply had become an important part of my affective life. Put together, these influences were creating in me more desire for marriage than for priesthood. I desperately needed help in my discernment process. I could not make a vocational decision relying solely on feelings. I needed deeper knowledge and wisdom.

---

5. The angel Gabriel was sent by God to Mary of Nazareth with the following message: "The Holy Spirit will come upon you, and the power of the Most High will overshadow you; therefore, the child to be born will be called holy ... the Son of God." (Luke 1:35)

Help arrived in the spring quarter through a course taught by Father Chirico called "Vocation and the Sacraments." The course focused on the generic Christian vocation, marriage, celibacy, priesthood, and religious life. The course proved to be exactly what I needed.

In the above sections on "Dogma" and "Faith," I recounted how Father Chirico described the generic Christian vocation in developmental and evolutionary terms. Faith in Christ's resurrection leads to the conclusion that human beings are made for the infinite. There will never be an end to our development as persons because our destiny—as articulated by Jesus Christ—is union with the Father. However, a great tension exists between that teaching and our corporeal finiteness. The more we learn and the more potential we actualize, the more we are made aware of how limited we are in our present state of existence.

In the course, Father Chirico focused on specific vocations through which Christians grow in their generic Christian vocation. He emphasized that we become persons through relating with creation, other people, and the Triune God (Father, Son, and Holy Spirit). We cannot love all people without first loving a particular person; and we cannot relate with all sectors of life without first concentrating on one aspect of life. Thus, each must live out a specific limited Christian vocation in order to develop into the full generic Christian vocation.

Father Chirico's vision of the priesthood flowed directly from his understanding of the generic Christian vocation:

> The priest is to be the minister in the church who witnesses to Jesus Christ in His universal unifying activity. The priest is to be the "ultimate unifier" of the Christian community, the one who helps others see infinite possibilities for their growth and development because of their faith in Christ. He must have experience and knowledge of how to catalyze such growth. This requires internalization of the processes that Jesus and the Christian tradition provide for the spiritual journey.
>
> As the "ultimate unifier" the priest must have the capacity to relate deeply with men and women and the capacity to relate to a wide variety of human situations. The celibacy of the priest is an expression of a transcendent vocation, a sign that no matter how beautiful and good a particular relationship may be in this world [e.g., marriage], it is not the ultimate. The celibate must have an abiding spirit of hope in the

completion implied in accepting the Risen Christ. One believes that one will be fulfilled in all aspects of life, even in the area renounced.[6]

Father Chirico's vision of the priesthood was inspiring and highly idealistic. Years later I would come to critique Father Chirico's theology for paying inadequate attention to the reality of sin and the Cross. I believe that Father Chirico was trying to find a Christian response to the prevailing human potential movement of 1970s humanistic psychology. His class provided me with valuable tools for thinking concretely about what would be required for making a priestly commitment. The more he described the role of a priest, the less prepared I felt to make such a life commitment. Instead, I felt more attracted to the vocation of marriage. In a final reflection paper for the course, I wrote the following:

> To FULLY realize the generic Christian vocation, one must become a person who relates totally with the material universe, other persons, Christ, and God. Clearly then, no one has ever fully realized the Christian vocation except Jesus Christ. How do we *move toward* realizing "total relatability?"
>
> . . . . For many years I have seriously considered the priesthood as the way I would live out my Christian vocation. The more I understand the requirements for priestly ministry, however, the more I see that I cannot develop the necessary capacities within the seminary context, nor can I grow as the person I am within the structure of the Roman Catholic priesthood.
>
> . . . . No one can give that which one does not have. The same holds true for "giving up." I cannot grow to love all people if I have not really grown through a love relationship with one person first. I have never concentrated on one person to the point where we became *real lovers*. I want and need that kind of relationship—which will probably mean marriage."[7]

I concluded the reflection paper optimistically regarding my future:

> . . . . We all live by a natural faith which means being open to new experiences. I do not know what is going to happen to me when I leave the

---

6. Father Peter Chirico (from my class notes).
7. Kevin P. Joyce, "A Reflection Paper on the Christian Vocation" (St. Patrick's Seminary, May 19, 1972), 5–7.

seminary—where I am going to go, what I am going to do, whom I am going to love. But the natural faith in the future by which we all live is given an absolute quality because of my consciousness of Jesus Christ in my life. I have an absolute future, a future which may involve much suffering. It cannot include ultimate failure, however. "Which of you would hand his son a stone when he asks for a loaf of bread . . . ? (Matthew 7:9). How much more will our heavenly Father give us—his children—bread when asked. With faith in infinite possibilities for growth and development, verified and made possible by the Resurrection of Jesus Christ, I enter the mystery-filled future with hope.[8]

8. Ibid., 9.

9

Breaking the News

Having made a firm decision to leave the seminary, I proceeded to tell the people around me. My intention was to speak first with my parents. It happened, however, that my bishop, Floyd L. Begin of the Oakland Diocese, paid a visit to the seminary the same day I finalized my decision. He announced that he wished to speak privately with each student of his diocese.

When I entered the seminary parlor for the chat, I decided that I was not going to tell him about my decision. It was too fresh and momentous, and I wasn't ready to face any potential disapproval. Bishop Begin greeted me genially and asked me how I was doing in the seminary. I told him that I enjoyed the community life and classes very much. Then, without further small talk, he proceeded directly to the issue I was not ready to address:

"Well, Kevin, how do you feel about the priesthood?"

I was tempted to say something trite and evasive like, "Oh, I think the priesthood is a great vocation! I'm taking a terrific course on it right now. . . . " But my conscience got the better of me and I told him the truth. He responded graciously and warmly,

> Kevin, you have given nine years of your life to consider a priestly vocation. You have given your best and you have made a conscientious decision. I thank you for your generous spirit and perseverance. May the Lord bless you abundantly as you begin a new path.

I can only marvel at Bishop Begin's largeness of heart and kindness. He had hoped for nine years that I would one day serve as one of his priests. The diocese had spent tens of thousands of dollars on my education. Yet Bishop Begin's concern at that moment was entirely focused on my well-being. He was a fine example of what a priest is supposed to be: a loving, spiritual father.

Within a day or so I went home to tell my parents and brother. Unfortunately, I had not kept them in the loop with regard to my vocational struggles. When I shared my decision with them, they were stunned. My dad said, "I am shocked." My mom burst into tears. Brian remained silent. I had never indicated to them that I was thinking of leaving the seminary. I deeply regret that I had not shared my process with them along the way.

Nor had I shared my process with anyone else. This was a major error I repeatedly committed throughout the previous three years. Even though I had a spiritual director at the seminary, I did not open up my fantasy life to him. My fantasies had a lot to do with the Goldmund archetype (see chapter 5), which had become a shadow personality within me. Externally I lived like a responsible young seminarian. Inside I longed for adventure and romance. There's nothing unusual about a young adult feeling such attractions. But if I had been consciously following Bernard Lonergan's discernment process that I presented in the last chapter (experience, understand, judge, decide, act), I would have been analyzing my experiences and feelings with someone wiser than I so that I could better *understand* their meaning, *judge* them to be helpful or harmful, make prudent *decisions*, and *act* on them wisely.

St. Ignatius of Loyola (1491–1556) is the great expert with regard to discernment of spirits—how to determine whether one is being led by the good spirit or the evil spirit. One of the Rules of Discernment from his classic book, *The Spiritual Exercises*, asserts that the evil spirit acts as a false lover in wishing to remain secret and not be revealed. If one has evil or foolish intentions and reveals them to a spiritual director, one is unlikely to carry them out.[1]

---

1. St. Ignatius of Loyola, "Thirteenth Rule," in *The Spiritual Exercises* (various editions; e.g., Classics of Western Spirituality; New York: Paulist Press, 1991).

The most grievous error I had been committing was a sin of omission. I had not been praying about my fantasies and decisions. During the three months following my spiritual awakening at the Trappist monastery in 1969, I regularly prayed about my thoughts, feelings, and decisions, asking God for light and wisdom. Despite inevitable challenges, my decisions usually led me to positive outcomes.

Yet, during my senior year in college and my year at St. Patrick's Seminary, I was practicing TM each day and occasional *Lectio Divina*, but I did not engage in conscious dialogue with the Lord regarding my decisions. I followed my feelings. My process reflected the spirit of the 1960s and '70s: "do your own thing, follow your bliss, be free of external authority," which is assessed by the Twelve-Step programs as "self-will run riot." My generation should have been reflecting on the insight of the prophet Jeremiah: "More tortuous than all else is the human heart, beyond remedy; who can understand it?" (Jeremiah 17:9).

After announcing my decision to my parents, I went to my grandmother's home a few blocks away. We sat in her outdoor gazebo and I told her my story. Her response was remarkable, yet it didn't surprise me: "Kevin, I have never prayed that you would become a priest. I have always prayed that you would follow the guidance of the Holy Spirit and I shall continue praying for that." The way Ma responded to my announcement reflected her deep trust in Divine Providence. She believed that if it was God's will that I should become a priest, the will of God would eventually prevail.

Gradually I shared my decision with priests and fellow seminarians. Most tried to support me in my decision, although I knew that Father Chirico and Father Konkel felt I was making a big mistake.

Challenged by Father Don McDonnell, Cesar Chavez's Mentor ▶

One priest who challenged my decision is one of the most remarkable priests I have ever known: Father Donald McDonnell. Father McDonnell is well known by those familiar with the story of Cesar Chavez and the United Farm Workers. Cesar always gave Father McDonnell the credit for training him in social justice and the principles of nonviolence. Chavez also credited Father McDonnell for launching him on his decades-long struggle for just and safe working conditions for farmworkers throughout the United States.

The two men became close friends in the early 1950s, when Father McDonnell came to the impoverished east San Jose barrio of *Sal Si Puedes* ("Get Out If You Can") to establish a ministry among the Hispanic population. Cesar and his wife were among the Father McDonnell's first parishioners of what would later become Our Lady of Guadalupe Parish in San Jose. Cesar drove him to farmworker camps to celebrate Mass and accompanied him to local prisons.

Father McDonnell was one of a handful of priests known as the Spanish Mission Band of the Archdiocese of San Francisco, who traveled throughout Northern California, aiding farmworkers and other Spanish-speaking Catholics. His work impressed a young seminarian, Roger Mahony, during a summer assignment with Father McDonnell:

> "During that summer, my heart and soul were converted to the work of service to our migrant brothers and sisters, and since then, my life and ministry have been focused on them," said Mahony, now the retired cardinal archbishop of Los Angeles.[2]

In 1961, Father McDonnell responded to a Vatican appeal for priests to serve in Latin America and was sent to Cuernavaca, Mexico, to teach the Spanish language, culture, and history to priests, brothers, sisters, and lay volunteers preparing to work in Latin America. Three years later, he went to Tokyo to learn Japanese, and in 1964 he traveled to Brazil to minister to Japanese immigrants. He also learned Mandarin to serve the Chinese in Our Lady of Guadalupe Parish in San Francisco, where he was pastor from 1970 until his retirement in 1989.

Father McDonnell was also a strong pro-life advocate and once spent thirty days in jail for blocking a Planned Parenthood entrance. He was among the first people arrested at an Operation Rescue demonstration in the San Francisco area. During his time in jail, he had most of his fellow prisoners praying the Rosary with him daily.

---

2. Monica Clark, "Priest Who Inspired Cesar Chavez Dies at Age 88," *National Catholic Reporter*, March 2, 2012 (online edition).

I met Father McDonnell at the seminary swimming pool shortly after my decision to leave the seminary. He asked me what I was doing with my life, and I shared with him my decision to leave the seminary. In a most friendly manner he began to tell me about the joy of serving as a priest. He said to me, "There is a beautiful, wide road out there waiting for you if you choose to take it." I responded, "I thought the Lord said that it is the narrow road that leads to life." Laughing, he replied, "Well, we've been making some improvements on it!"

That was my introduction to Father McDonnell. Little did I realize at the time what an impact he would have on my life in the future.

Breaking the News in Mexico ▸

I made my decision to leave the seminary midway through the spring quarter. After sharing the news with family and friends, I decided to spend the spring break in Mexico with Dennis Stradford and Tom Barni (my friend from middle school). We took a forty-eight-hour bus ride from Tijuana to Mexico City. On the trip down I fantasized about proposing marriage to Antonia. As per my usual *modus operandi*, I didn't share my intentions with Dennis or Tom, afraid that they might judge my thoughts as unrealistic or premature.

In Mexico we proceeded to visit the friends I had made during my Junior Year Abroad. Most of them were not entirely surprised by my decision to leave the seminary since they had witnessed my vocational confusion during my time with them.

When we arrived at Antonia's house, I informed her and her family about my decision (without mentioning anything about marriage). Her father said, "Kevin, we have watched you the past few years, and you seemed like a toreador in the bull ring. I am very happy that you have finally made a decision and are at peace with it. My family and I are taking a short vacation at a beach house in Acapulco, and we would like to invite you and your friends to join us." I was thrilled with the invitation, and I looked forward to some long conversations with Antonia in such a romantic atmosphere.

Once in Acapulco, I decided that I would raise the topic of a possible future together with Antonia while walking on the beach at sunset. I had become temporarily an incurable romantic. As we walked along the beach, enjoying the exquisite Acapulco coastline at Puerto Marquez, I was about to speak but suddenly I froze. I said nothing. We returned to the house, both feeling uneasy. The next evening, we again walked the beach at sunset, and I had the same reaction. I wondered what was the matter with me? I had just gone through a long, painful process to leave the seminary. I was now available for a serious relationship with the woman who had captured my heart three years earlier, and I couldn't speak. I was furious with myself.

On the third and final day of our stay in Acapulco, I decided that my hesitation the previous two evenings was simply a case of cold feet. I was determined that we were going to have "the talk" that evening. Again, we walked down the beach and I was trying to rouse my courage when suddenly I began speaking without any forethought. The words just tumbled out of me. Reality finally caught up with me: "Antonia, I am twenty-two years old and I have been in the seminary for nine years. I don't know myself and I don't know the world. I am not ready to make any permanent commitment."

Antonia was stunned. At that moment not only did the reality of my life become clear to me, so too did the reality of Antonia's life. She knew of the deep affection I had for her. She had just learned a few days earlier that I was leaving the seminary. I had asked her to walk the beach with me three evenings in a row. What was she supposed to think? I realized for the second time in the history of our friendship just how selfish I had been in the relationship. My main concern had been my happiness, not hers. I felt deep sorrow over how I had led her on, and I couldn't do anything to put things right.

A couple of hours later, Dennis, Tom and I boarded a bus for Tijuana. Seven years would pass before the wound would heal in a most remarkable way.

10

Seeking a New Direction in Spain

AFTER THE DEBACLE IN ACAPULCO, I RETURNED TO ST. Patrick's Seminary to complete the 1972 spring quarter and to celebrate my twenty-third birthday. I had no plans for the future nor any money. No particular career attracted me at the moment, and I knew I wasn't ready for marriage or any other long-term commitment. I still l had high spiritual ideals and the desire for new adventures.

Since the TM teacher-training course at Humboldt State had been so stimulating and transformative, I decided to apply to the second and final phase of the teacher-training that was to begin in the fall of 1972. The course was to be held in La Antilla, Spain, and would last for six months under the leadership of Maharishi. I learned that La Antilla was a resort town in the south of Spain on the Atlantic coast near the border with Portugal, so I intended that the six months of training would double as a six-month Andalusian vacation. Upon completion of the course in March 1973, I planned on traveling in Europe for three months. My strategy was to witness the birth of spring from the south in Greece to the north in England.

In order to carry out my plan I needed to earn about $2,000 ($10,000 in today's money). Once summer arrived, I worked three jobs simultaneously: as a catering service waiter/bartender, a clerk at a liquor store, and organist at Sacred Heart Church in

San Jose. I worked hard and made a lot of money quickly. But by the end of the summer I was still short of my goal, so I parted with my beloved 1953 Buick Special for $300 to make up the difference. That was a sad day for this lover of classic cars.

An Emotional Departure ▸

On the day of my departure for Spain, my parents, brother, grandmother, and some good friends came to Oakland Airport to bid me farewell at 7:00 A.M. It was a very emotional moment. For almost a year I was leaving everyone I knew and loved. I was entering an unknown future with no clear goals.

After the warm farewells, I walked down the tarmac toward the plane. I looked straight ahead toward the horizon and beheld the most amazing full moon I had ever seen. I interpreted it as a sign that something awesome was awaiting me.

The flight was chartered by the TM organization's Students' International Meditation Society (SIMS). All the passengers were heading for the same course. We arrived in Seville thirteen hours later and were taken by bus to the coastal town of La Antilla, where SIMS had leased all the apartments, small beach-side villas, and one large hotel. Seven hundred course participants from around the world, mostly young adults, descended on La Antilla that day. It was virtual chaos as the course staff attempted to arrange housing. I was determined to be assigned to one of the beach villas. Because I was one of the few arrivals who spoke Spanish, I made myself useful to the SIMS staff as they tried to communicate with the Spanish facilities staffs. My services were rewarded with a villa right on the beach.

The modest three-bedroom villa was designed as a summer vacation residence. It had no glass windows, only wooden shutters, and no heating system. That didn't bother me and my two roommates in the Indian summer of mid-September. I had periodically fantasized about the possibility of living a simple, rustic life without creature comforts. That's what I got. My bedroom had no furniture except for a mattress on the red tile floor. My window looked out onto the beach and the Atlantic Ocean about a hundred yards beyond. I felt like I was in paradise. Here is a description of La Antilla written by the celebrated playwright Bill Gibson who later would visit our course:

> Apart from a cluster of new high-rise apartments with a few stores in their bottoms, La Antilla was a strip of two hundred or so villas set down along the ocean for a mile, all white-plastered and roofed in red tile, low and modest, and deserted for the winter; with no more than three autos in sight, the streets were overblown with sand, and the white town dozed in the sun as quiet as meditation itself. The only sound was the huff of the breaking sea for miles in either direction along a beach as unspoiled as when the Phoenicians walked it.[1]

The next day all the course participants met in a hotel ballroom. I was delighted to encounter someone I knew: a young Canadian meditator, Mary Ann Radley. She and a group of girlfriends had befriended me during the Humboldt State course, intrigued by the presence of a Catholic seminarian. We discovered that our villas were only a few doors down from each other. We made plans to walk to dinner together that evening.

Arriving at the serving table in the hotel dining room we were confronted with one of the best vegetarian spreads I had ever seen. All the meals throughout the course were to be vegetarian, following Maharishi's custom.

The kitchen staff went beyond the call of duty to ensure that we had delicious, wholesome meals. They were unable to find whole-grain flour, so they tracked down the closest flour mill and arranged with the owner to sell them unrefined flour each week. They made from scratch all the food, including delectable baked goods. Mary Ann and I spent a good part of the evening catching up and agreed to meet again the next day for the morning lecture.

Mary Ann was a bright, refined, attractive woman. Soon many young men in the course were seeking her attention. She and I were not romantically interested in each other, but we did become good friends. She told me about the would-be Casanovas, and I offered to be her "protector." So, most days we walked to the lecture hall together and sat next to each other. Within a short time, the frustrated suitors figured she had a California boyfriend and gave up their pursuit.

1. William Gibson, *A Season in Heaven* (New York: Atheneum, 1974), 17.

The East–West Dialogue Resumes

The daily routine included two or three "rounds" (yoga positions, breathing exercise, meditation) in the morning and in the afternoon. Lectures were held after lunch and dinner. The great disappointment at first was that Maharishi was going to be delayed for a month. In the meantime, surrogates presided over the gatherings and played audiotapes of Maharishi's lectures. Despite his absence, a great deal of intellectual ferment was catalyzed, and I periodically found myself in the middle of it.

Word spread that an ex-seminarian was on the course. I had thought that since my seminary days were over, I would no longer be sought out as the local "expert" on Christianity and Catholicism. I discovered that an ex-seminarian was just as intriguing to the meditator community as the real deal. I began to be peppered with questions similar to those addressed to me at the Humboldt course: How do Catholics meditate? Do you think the pope is an enlightened master like Maharishi? What does the Church teach about reincarnation?

Paradoxically, my mind was fully engaged with theological and spiritual issues, but I was not worshiping. I had not even discovered where the local Catholic church was. I was intensely interested in the questions that were being posed to me, in particular, What is unique about Christianity? The prevailing belief among many meditators was that "all religions are just different ways to reach the same goal." I did not accept that theory, but I was struggling to explain the uniqueness of Christianity.

After a few weeks wrestling with this question, one afternoon during meditation an insight hit me with such force that I had to stop meditating and record the insight in my journal—November 24, 1972:

> The Last Judgment scene of Matthew's Gospel (25:35–36, 40) provides the key to the uniqueness of Christianity: Jesus said, "For I was hungry and you gave me food, I was thirsty and you gave me drink, a stranger and you welcomed me.... And the king will say to them in reply, 'Amen I say to you, whatever you did for one of these least brothers of mine, you did for me.'" The Christian message is incarnated not only in who Jesus *is*, but also in what Jesus *did*, what St. Francis *did*, and what Mother Teresa and Dorothy Day are *doing*. The compassionate outreach to suffering people by great Christians flows from

their connection with Jesus, and from their conviction that suffering people manifest the presence of Jesus. In a sense, they *are* Jesus.

The revelation occurred on a Thursday afternoon. That evening before dinner, I checked my mailbox and found a letter from my grandmother who informed me that her neighbor's granddaughter, Sally Bolce, was in my course in La Antilla. Sally's grandmother had sent her a similar letter the same day. I left a note in Sally's mailbox suggesting that we meet at the mailbox the following evening before dinner.

On schedule, we met Friday evening and Sally effusively greeted me with, "Oh Kevin, I have wanted to meet you for so long! About six months ago I had a reversion to Catholicism after having left the church many years ago. Since then, I have attended Mass every day and my life has changed. My grandmother told me about you, and I was so looking forward to meeting another meditator who is a strong Catholic!"

In the presence of this enthusiastic, newly reverted Catholic, I felt mortified that I hadn't been to Mass throughout our time in La Antilla, so I said to her sheepishly, "I haven't found the church here in town. Where is it and what time is Mass tomorrow?" She told me the hour of the Saturday evening Mass and we agreed to meet there.

The following evening, we met for Mass at the simple, whitewashed church on the beach with its front doors open to the sea. When the moment arrived for the Gospel reading, the padre proclaimed, *Lectura del Santo Evangelio segun san Mateo* ("a reading from the Holy Gospel according to Saint Matthew"):

> Jesus said, "When the Son of Man comes in his glory, and all the angels with him, he will sit upon his glorious throne, and all the nations will be assembled before him. And he will separate them one from another, as a shepherd separates the sheep from the goats. He will place the sheep on his right and the goats on his left. Then the king will say to those on his right, 'Come, you who are blessed by my Father. Inherit the kingdom prepared for you from the foundation of the world. For I was hungry and you gave me food, I was thirsty and you gave me drink . . .'"

I was stunned. I knew deep in my heart that it was no coincidence that the Last Judgment Gospel reading that had come to me in meditation two days earlier as containing a key to the uniqueness of Christianity was proclaimed at the Mass. I received two strong messages from the occurrence. First, the Lord was validating the message that had come to me the previous day. Second, I was being told "get serious about practicing your faith!"

Getting Serious about the Faith Again ▸

Joining Sally Bolce for the Saturday evening Mass during which the Last Judgment Gospel was proclaimed so moved me that I decided I would join Sally daily for Mass. The following Monday we both showed up for the 5:30 P.M. Mass, along with a few wives of the local fishermen who lived at the far end of La Antilla. After Mass Sally introduced me to the padre, a jovial, middle-aged Spanish priest who spoke no English. He invited us into his modest house for some sherry and snacks, and he expressed curiosity about the meditation movement that had just invaded his sleepy town. He showed particular interest when I told him that I had been a seminarian for nine years and was seriously engaged in comparing the Christian and Far Eastern traditions.

Mary Ann learned that I had begun to attend Mass each day. She expressed interest in joining me even though she was not a baptized Christian, did not belong to any faith tradition, nor did she understand Spanish. She did have some interest in Catholicism because of her love for the poetry of Gerard Manley Hopkins, the renowned nineteenth-century Jesuit poet. I told her she was more than welcome, so the daily congregation of meditators grew from two to three. Mary Ann entered right into the rituals and gestures just like a cradle Catholic, even though she didn't understand much of what was happening at first. She reminded me of Dorothy Day who, while still a socialist and an agnostic, had begun to enter a Catholic church at 6:00 A.M. for a quiet morning Mass after a night of dancing and carousing with her socialist friends. Here is a relevant quotation from her moving autobiography, *The Long Loneliness*:

> I went to an early morning Mass at St. Joseph's Church on Sixth Avenue and knelt in the back of the church, not knowing what was going on at the altar, but warmed and comforted by the lights and silence, the kneeling people, and the atmosphere of worship. People have so

great a need to reverence, to worship, to adore; it is a psychological necessity of human nature that must be taken into account.[2]

Within a few days, one of the meditators who shared the cottage with Mary Ann, a young, lapsed Catholic from New York, asked Mary Ann if he could join us for Mass. I don't remember his name, but Mary Ann called him "Darling Boy." He was several years younger than she.

A Unique Christmas

Now the daily congregation of meditators had grown to four, and the padre continued to invite us to his little house each day for sherry and appetizers after Mass. By this time, we had entered the Advent season, and the padre was thinking about the coming Christmas celebrations. One day during our little social hour, he said to me,

> Christmas is coming and I suspect that a large group of English-speaking meditators will attend the Christmas Masses. Already a few dozen are coming on Sunday mornings. I feel bad that I can't preach in their language, so I am wondering if you could deliver the homily for the Christmas Midnight Mass and the noon Mass on Christmas morning? Since you were a seminarian for nine years, I don't think you will preach heresy!

His invitation appealed to me. I began to think about designing a bilingual liturgy with music and biblical readings in English and Spanish. For my homily, I decided to use a story that I had recently heard about Mother Teresa of Calcutta, who was asked why she devoted so much time to caring for the dying. Her answer touched me deeply: "So that they can die in the sight of a loving face." She emphasized that one message of Christmas, the feast of God taking on human flesh, is the absolute value of every human being.

On Christmas Eve the course participants and guests joined in a festive evening of carols, a Nativity play, and other Christmas traditions

---

2. Dorothy Day, *The Long Loneliness: The Autobiography of Dorothy Day* (New York: Harper & Row, 1981), 84–85.

in the hotel ballroom. By this time, Maharishi had been in La Antilla for several weeks. He presided over the celebration seated cross-legged on the stage's sofa. At least seven hundred people were packed into the ballroom, and they applauded appreciatively after each presentation. I had been requested to conclude the evening by singing a couple of Gregorian chants. I sang the ancient "Ave Maria" and the "Kyrie Eleison" from the "Mass of the Angels."

There was no applause after my chanting. The entire assembly remained in complete silence with their eyes closed. Their reaction showed me the power of Gregorian chant. It had its beginnings in the early centuries of Christian monasticism. It is "soul music," music that comes from deep contemplative and devotional experience. People of any tradition who appreciate meditative silence are drawn into a state of quiet recollection by the chants.

I decided to take advantage of the moment for a bit of promotion:

> Tonight, at midnight and tomorrow at noon, there will be bilingual Christmas Masses at the local Catholic church, which is located on the beach three blocks from the hotel. Anyone of any tradition is warmly welcome to attend.

The padre and I expected a good turn-out, but we did not expect the overflowing crowd that showed up at midnight. The atmosphere was exceptionally joyful. Everyone sang the bilingual carols, and my homily seemed to touch hearts. The only grousing came from some of the local Spaniards who couldn't get inside their own church.

The next day, more Spanish parishioners and many meditators showed up for the noon Mass. After Mass, the padre and I were greeting people in front of the church. The mood was light-hearted and upbeat. Then an older American who was visiting his son on the course approached me and asked, "Do you believe that Jesus Christ literally rose from the dead?" I was quite surprised by such a serious-minded question on a joyous Christmas morning. I answered, "Certainly." He responded, "Can I speak with you sometime?" We exchanged addresses and agreed to meet later.

Bill Gibson Enters My Life ➤

I didn't realize that the man who asked to speak with me was the renowned playwright, William Gibson, who had written *The Miracle*

Worker, which recounts the story of Helen Keller and Annie Sullivan. The play served as the foundation of the popular film by the same name starring Anne Bancroft, who won the Oscar for Best Actress.

We waited until after the New Year for our talk. The last week of the year is always a "week of silence" for Maharishi and for those around him. He instructed the seven hundred meditators to enter into complete silence and to meditate most of each day. The weather that week was spectacular—not a cloud in the sky and no vehicles to break the silence. Most of us picked up food in the dining room and brought it to our residences so that we could remain for long periods of time without interruption in our "caves."

To break the silence on January 1, 1973, Maharishi emerged from his silence thinner and radiant. He slowly sipped a cup of water as he quietly began delivering a lecture. After the lecture I met Bill Gibson at his villa late in the evening. We shared good Spanish red wine, French bread, and sardines. He initiated the conversation by telling me how he was moved by the Gregorian chants I had sung and the Christmas Mass. He needed to speak with me about it. He was fifty-eight years old and an agnostic. Later he would write a book about his La Antilla experiences, *A Season in Heaven*, in which he relates what happened to him during that Christmas noon Mass:

> I sat among the black garments of fishermen's widows, not knowing why I was there; I hadn't been a believer since my fourteenth year, nor heard mass since my mother's requiem a dozen years ago. I felt at home. Unexpectedly, the young meditator was again up front. . . . He took the pulpit to give his homily in English.
>
> Speaking to what Christmas meant, he told of a nun in Calcutta who had abandoned her nunnery to care for those dying in the streets, and quoted Christ's tale of the King who said to the blessed, "Come, inherit the kingdom, for I was hungry and ye gave me meat, I was thirsty and ye gave me drink. I was a stranger and ye took me in. . . . Inasmuch as ye have done it unto one of the least of these my brethren, ye have done it unto me."
>
> I sat there with my eyes wet, not caring why, but suffused with some blessing that I felt nowhere else; I loved those rhythms as much as Maharishi his Vedas, and I had never left off reading in that mystifying book, which in its veriest nonsense somehow embodies our deepest wisdom, and on occasion with an hour to kill in a city I had wandered into some church and sat for a while, also knelt, surrender-

ing to my childhood and mother again, for kneeling takes us down to that size, and always with this same awakening of my heart, unique to church, like some sweet plum in me that most of the time I was denying; and I thought, why? If my brain kept me from eating, and I chose to go hungry with my brain, we had thought out a poor bargain with life.[3]

Bill told me that he had decided to change his plans and not return home with his wife after the Christmas holiday. His older son, Tom, who was a course participant, wanted him to stay to attend a new series of lectures that Maharishi had video-taped called "The Science of Creative Intelligence (SCI)," which was a packaging of ancient Vedic wisdom in scientific terms. Bill was mildly interested in the lectures and desirous of spending an extra month with his son; but the crucial factor in his decision to stay was what happened to him in that white-washed church on Christmas day.

The primary topic of our first late-night conversation was the historicity of the resurrection. Bill was haunted by the person of Jesus Christ. For decades he had rejected the supernatural elements of the Gospels, but he had always taken the New Testament with him when traveling. As noted in the quotation above, he had "never left off reading in that mystifying book, which in its veriest nonsense somehow embodies our deepest wisdom."

We both were energized and challenged by the dialogue and agreed to meet again the following night. I invited Mary Ann to join us for the second dialogue on religion and meditation. Despite having no formal background in things theological, Mary Ann entered the intellectual fray with gusto and with insight. She also injected her quick wit quite regularly. During the conversation, we were poking fun at the common belief among meditators that too much exercise works against the good effects of long meditations. I protested that vigorous exercise gives me a high. Bill commented on our conversation in his book:

[Kevin] recalls a meet in which he was the favorite, running the 880 in two laps, so embarrassed to be the last in a field of fifteen that he sprinted the entire second lap—"which nobody does"—and came in

3. Gibson, *Season in Heaven*, 54–55.

first. It "wrecked" his lungs; for days he couldn't breathe without coughing.

"Everyone here would call it a terrible stress," he says, "but I lived for a month on that win; it's one of the memorable experiences of my life."

"Oh Kevin," says Mary Ann, "it'll be a pity when the rest of us are in cosmic consciousness and you're just 880 yards short."[4]

During our conversation, I told Bill about the quartet of meditators that was attending Mass each day. Bill asked if he could join us, which he did for the remainder of his time in La Antilla. His eyes would often mist during the Mass. He told us that he still didn't understand the whole "Christian thing," but he had decided to "leave his brain at the door of the church" for a while and just accept whatever happened.

Bill picked up his brain again on the way out of church, and we continued to engage in heady theological conversations most evenings over wine and sardines. At the same time, we were attending Maharishi's new video course on SCI along with about two hundred other meditators. It was facilitated by John Black, a young TM teacher about five years older than I who had been Maharishi's personal assistant for a time. We participants were always on our best behavior when Maharishi was present. But with John in charge, we turned rowdy, partly because of the long hours of silent meditation we were practicing each day. We needed an outlet. But the primary cause of our dissatisfaction was the new scientific vocabulary. We were all fond of Maharishi's spiritual and philosophical language. The new terminology was difficult for many to accept. Poor John Black was the recipient of much critical questioning and muttering during the Q & A that followed the videos. He was a good sport and handled us unruly rabble without getting flustered. He was a good example that long-term meditation promotes serenity.

Near the conclusion of the SCI course, Bill invited Mary Ann and me to join him on a tour of legendary Andalusian cities: Seville, Cordova, and Granada. It was against the rules for meditators to leave the course before its conclusion, but Bill was greatly admired by the course hierarchy. By dropping his name, I was able to convince John Black to liberate Mary Ann and me for a week.

---

4. Gibson, *Season in Heaven*, 118–19.

It was a marvelous tour, and at its conclusion, Mary Ann and I bade a fond farewell to Bill as he took a cab to the airport for his trip back to the Berkshires in Massachusetts. It was the end of an extraordinarily stimulating period for the three of us.

The End of the Course ▸

Lest the reader think that all was bliss and light, the second three-month period of the course for me was a letdown. In January, several hundred of us course participants moved from La Antilla to a nearby coastal town called Punta Umbria to make room for new arrivals. I was assigned to a modernistic hotel, cold and sterile. I sorely missed my little villa on the beach. The local Catholic church was some distance away; consequently, our quartet of daily Mass participants discontinued the practice. The late-night powwows with Bill and Mary Ann provided a relief from a daily routine that had lost some of its charm.

I continued to engage in frequent philosophical and theological conversations with meditators, but I was becoming a bit put off by the prevailing obsession with "enlightenment" and the mood-making that often accompanied it. Although I was still enthusiastic about the meditation practice, my primary interest was Christ and his teachings. The revelation that came to me in La Antilla about the centrality of active love for those who suffer, and the example of Mother Teresa showed me that the goal of Christian spirituality does not end with enlightenment. Rather, the purpose is transformation into loving human beings and intimacy with God. As I reflected on the two greatest commandments—love of God and love of neighbor as oneself—I was convinced that, without a conscious, intentional love of God, the spiritual journey remains imbalanced and incomplete.

Maharishi did speak about love of God and unity with God, but he quite deliberately did not promote his religion. For him, meditation clears the way for "devotion to reach the feet of God" (his words), but he did not teach us how to practice devotion. He expected us to find God-centered spiritual practices in our own faith traditions.

The problem was that most meditators were not actively engaged in a faith tradition and were using the practice of meditation as their only spiritual practice. I knew from my own experience and from reading the lives of saints that, without conscious contact with God through prayer, worship, and participation in a faith community, our spiritual journey is incomplete. We can become self-absorbed as we seek "Self-realization."

Ironically, I was falling into the same defect of "mood-making" that I was criticizing. As the teacher-training course neared its completion, Maharishi gave us final instructions as we prepared to return home and to begin teaching meditation. He emphasized our noble roles as "knowers of reality" as we brought "enlightenment to the world." He wanted us to serve always as dignified representatives of the exalted knowledge that we would be communicating to the society around us—dressing formally in public, and not appearing in public when we were "unstressing." (Unstressing is a term Maharishi used to describe disagreeable attitudes and moods that may accompany the purification process.)

There was nothing pretentious or artificial about Maharishi. But he was instructing a group of twenty- and thirty-year-old young adults to act as if we were spiritual masters. Many of us were novices on the spiritual path, and we compensated by trying to imitate the gestures and words of Maharishi. We tried to act as if we were in a higher state of consciousness.

I was not immune from this tendency. My speech and behavior began to take on somewhat of an artificial and pretentious air. This defect would adversely affect my relationship with old friends who were about to join me on an odyssey through Europe.

11

A European Odyssey

MIDWAY THROUGH THE TEACHER-TRAINING COURSE, I INVITED four friends to join me on a three-month trip through Europe that was to begin once the course ended in March 1973. Mary Ann Radley readily accepted the invitation as did her old friend, Bob Galletuck. Dennis had decided not to pursue priestly ordination and would be leaving the seminary program in March, so I invited him to take a break and join the European tour. I also invited a close friend, Mary Anne Tomacci (whom I will call "M.A."), who sang in the choir I had directed in San Jose. She was well educated in European languages, art, and architecture. I knew that she would very much appreciate the itinerary.

Once the course ended, Dennis, M.A., and Bob joined Mary Ann and me in La Antilla. Our plan was to spend a week or so in Andalucía, then off to Madrid and Barcelona. From there we would make a quick trip to Rome on our way to the Adriatic coast of Italy to take a boat to Athens. This was to fulfill my dream of witnessing the birth of spring from the south to the north of Europe.

Tension with Old Friends ➤

When we started traveling, I entered into a mild culture shock, having spent the better part of the previous six months with my eyes closed in meditation. The culture shock, together with my new self-awareness as a teacher of meditation led to subtle conflict with my old friends. The spiritual affectation I had taken on was off-putting to M.A. and Dennis. They didn't express their discomfort with me, but I felt it—just as they felt the distance that my pretension created between us.

Although M.A. and Dennis knew some Spanish, I was the only one who spoke the language fluently, so the role of travel organizer and translator largely fell to me. We did have good times enjoying the marvelous history and architecture of Andalucía, but by the time we reached Granada, I was feeling tired and frustrated leading and translating for a group of five. I respectfully asked Mary Ann and Bob if they would mind traveling on their own, explaining that coordinating the group of five was proving too demanding for me. They graciously accepted my proposal. Dennis, M.A. and I proceeded on to Madrid, Barcelona, the French Riviera, and Italy.

By the time we reached Italy I found myself in a full-blown depression. The strained communication—largely due to my spiritual pride, affected behavior, and spiritual turmoil— was more than I could process on my own. Even though I left the teacher-training course with a strong Christian identity, the Eastern teachings and vision had strongly influenced me, and I was unable to reconcile satisfactorily the two philosophies of life and spiritualties.

Back in the seminary, I would have easily discussed the issues with Dennis, my spiritual brother. But the traveling had created a subtle distance between us and I wasn't able to open up with him or M.A. about my depression and internal turmoil. The fact that Dennis was barely coming out of a vocation crisis also inhibited me from seeking his counsel. The one friend who kept coming to mind as someone with whom I could share my struggles was Leo. But that option seemed impossible since I didn't know where he was. The most recent communication I had had with him was several months earlier when he informed me that he was preparing to travel to Calcutta and prepare for ordination.

Meanwhile, the three of us reached Florence for some inspiring time drinking in Michelangelo's masterpieces. I knew little about art history, and I didn't know that Michelangelo had sculpted four *Pietàs*—the third of which was in the Duomo (Cathedral) of Florence.[1] When we entered the Duomo and walked to the sanctuary, I saw the *Pietà* that Michelangelo had sculpted in his old age. I was speechless. In fact, I couldn't take my eyes off that incomparable work of art for half an hour. It was more than

---

1. It was later moved to a small museum behind the Duomo.

a work of art. It was a work of love and devotion. It provides an intimate look at the relationship between the artist and Christ. The sculpture has four figures: the dead Christ in the arms of his mother, Nicodemus holding Christ's body from behind, and Mary Magdalene supporting the body (a later addition sculpted by a different artist). The figure of Nicodemus is an image of Michelangelo himself through which one can feel the intense love he had for Christ.

As I gazed at the *Pietà*, I wrote the following in my journal. My journal entry reveals my central preoccupation throughout the trip: how to bring together my Christian faith with Maharishi's Vedic teachings:

> The Eastern tradition sees little value in suffering. Suffering is regarded as the consequence of "bad *karma*." Vedanta teaches that the enlightened person does not suffer; the Self of an enlightened person would witness the pain of the body. Such a teaching ignores the fact that suffering is often born of love, such as the suffering that results from the death of a loved one.
>
> The Cross, the death of Jesus, has traditionally held a central place in our faith. Rightly so, for as Michelangelo clearly shows, here is a transforming object of devotion and love par excellence. Jesus was life and hope for those who loved him, and the *Pietà* incarnates grief and sorrow over the incomparable tragedy of his death. Not only that, but Jesus identifies with our suffering, having experienced its depths when he cried out "My God, my God, why have you abandoned me?"

The following day we reached Rome for an overnight in preparation for catching an early morning train to Bari on the Adriatic coast in order to board a ship to Athens. I was still deep in depression and thinking often of how much I would like to have a long talk with Leo.

The next morning we rose early and arrived at the Rome train station about 7:30 A.M. Hundreds of people were in multiple lines purchasing tickets. We took our place at the end of the line for the coastal city of Bari. Immediately in front of me was a man with a long black coat and a large duffle bag. He turned around. It was Leo!

A Providential Encounter ▸

I entitle this section "providential" because that moment of encounter with Leo was one of those rare moments in the history of my life when I knew without any doubt that God was right there. In that period of intense darkness and emptiness, God came to my rescue through the one person whom I had been longing to see throughout my depression. Grace was again filling the void.

Leo was as shocked as I. I said, "Leo! What are you doing here?!" He asked me the same question with amazement in his eyes. M.A. and Dennis were flabbergasted. They both knew Leo from his days at St. Patrick's. We all began rapidly explaining what we were doing in Rome, and to my great delight Leo told us that he was also on his way to Bari and Athens to take a train to Istanbul and then on to Afghanistan and India.

Our train was not to leave for a few hours, so Leo said, "This is your first time in Rome. Let's take a quick run to the Vatican and see the Sistine Chapel!" Dennis and M.A. weren't in the mood for racing to the Vatican, so they decided to find a quiet café for some cappuccino and breakfast.

Leo and I boarded a bus to the Vatican, and then ran to the Vatican Museums and through its halls to the Sistine Chapel. Needless to say, the sight was breathtaking. Again, Michelangelo spoke to my soul and created a longing within me for a long, leisurely sojourn in Rome.

That afternoon the four of us boarded a train for Bari and then a boat for the twenty-four-hour sail to Athens. Hour after hour, Leo and I caught up on what had occurred in our lives the past year. He had completed one more semester of theological studies at St. Patrick's, and then was told by the Archbishop of Calcutta to head for Calcutta, where he would be ordained a priest. I shared with Leo all that had happened to me at the TM teacher-training course and I opened up about my depression and spiritual turmoil.

Leo was a radical Christian willing to devote the rest of his life to serving the poor on the streets in Calcutta. He helped me reconnect more deeply with my Christian roots and gradually lifted me out of my depression.

When we reached Athens, Leo spent a few days with us touring. We then bade him farewell as he boarded a train to Istanbul. We knew that it was possible that we would not see each other again, at least not for several years.

After a few days enjoying the quiet and beauty of a Greek island, Dennis flew back to California. M.A. and I headed to Rome, where we planned to meet Doug, a seminarian friend from California. He had arranged for us to spend Holy Week in a convent near the Vatican.

When Doug met us at the Rome train station, he told us that he had a surprise for us the next morning. "Meet me at the Obelisk in St. Peter's Plaza at 10:00 A.M." He dropped us off at the convent, leaving us quite curious about the next morning's surprise.

M.A. and I arrived at the Obelisk at 10:00 A.M. There was Doug waiting for us. So was Leo.

Holy Week in Rome ›

"Leo, what are you doing here?!!" M.A. and I were again astonished by Leo appearing when we least expected it. He explained that when his train arrived in Istanbul, an unscrupulous immigration officer had taken his visa and would not return it unless he paid a bribe. Leo refused and so the officer confiscated the visa. Leo then phoned the archbishop of Calcutta and explained the dilemma. The archbishop told him to return to Rome and stay at the North American College, where the archbishop would arrange for another bishop to ordain him a deacon for the archdiocese of Calcutta, thereby making him an official member of the Calcutta clergy. This would make it easier for the archbishop to obtain immigration papers for Leo.

"What are you going to do now?" I asked Leo. "Stay in Rome for Holy Week and hope that within the next ten days the official ('tonsorial') papers will arrive from Calcutta." M.A. and I were planning on spending the same amount of time in Rome before traveling to visit my relatives in Switzerland, so we all were delighted that we would be able to spend ten days together in Rome.

Doug was able to obtain tickets for us to attend the Holy Week services at St. Peter's with Pope Paul VI. M.A. and I soon learned that Leo could be a bit outrageous at times. On Good Friday, the three of us had excellent seats toward the rear of the high altar at St. Peter's with a bird's-eye view of the pope. After the service, we walked toward the front row of seats where the cardinals sat, dressed in their deep red robes. Leo recognized one of them. "There's Cardinal Ciccognani, the former Vatican ambassador to the United States. He speaks English. Let's go say hello." M.A. and I were not thrilled with the idea of approaching a high-ranking Vatican official, but Leo charged ahead. M.A. had a cardinal-red umbrella with her. When we reached Cardinal Ciccognani, Leo took the umbrella, tapped him on the shoulder and said, "Look, it matches!" The cardinal looked at Leo with bewilderment while M.A. and I wanted to hide behind a pillar. After a few words, the cardinal made a hasty exit. From then on, we dubbed the umbrella, the "Cardinal-Banger."

For the Easter Sunday morning Mass on the steps of St. Peter's, we had tickets to a primo spot about fifty feet from the altar. When we arose that morning, however, the Roman sky was pouring torrents of rain. I was bummed out. We knew that if the rain didn't stop, the papal Mass would be moved indoors at the last minute and we would lose our precious seats. The three of us proceeded to walk to St. Peter's, bunched together under the Cardinal-Banger. Leo tried to cheer me up. "Have faith. The Lord will provide." I responded with, "Have faith!!? Look at the sky! This rain is going to last for hours." "Have faith," he repeated.

The Mass was to begin at 11:00 A.M. We arrived at our seats an hour early. The rain continued unabated. I remained in my disheartened mood. We were warned by officials that we might have to vacate the steps at a moment's notice. At about 10:45 the rain began to diminish. At 10:55 the rain stopped. At 11:00 the clouds broke slightly, and a ray of sunlight appeared just as the pope arrived at the altar. The story sounds like Catholic fantasy, but that is exactly what happened. Leo rubbed it in: "I told you to have faith!"

Encountering the Spirit of St. Francis ▸

After ten days enjoying the marvels of Rome and celebrating Leo's thirtieth birthday with abundant gelato, the tonsorial papers had not arrived. Leo decided that, instead of waiting in Rome, he would travel with me and M.A. for a few weeks, periodically checking in by phone with the North American College to see if the papers had arrived.

M.A. headed south to the town of Tricarico to visit relatives for a few days, while Leo and I set off for Assisi about two hours northeast of Rome. Assisi is the birthplace of St. Francis and the center of the Franciscan movement that changed the history not only of the Church, but of Western civilization. We planned to all meet in Assisi five days later.

St. Francis fascinated me and Leo, just as he probably fascinates everyone who comes to learn of his life story. In an early biography by Thomas of Celano, a disciple of Francis, we see that Francis began his life as an unlikely candidate for greatness, much less sainthood. Born in 1182 in Assisi, Francis was a worldly, somewhat wild young man. Thomas of Celano writes,

> From the earliest years of his life his parents reared him to arrogance in accordance with the vanity of the age. And by long imitating their worthless life and character he himself was made more vain and arrogant.[2]

As a teen and young adult Francis did what adults deplore in the youth of today: he wasted time and money, was preoccupied with expensive clothes, ran around with the wrong crowd, and chased after women. One of his biographers described him as a glutton and street brawler. But after the age of twenty-five we see a different Francis—a young man in love with God and willing to do anything to follow Christ and serve humanity. What caused him to change so dramatically?

It seems that Francis began to emerge from a superficial and thrill-seeking adolescence around the age of twenty when he became a soldier and went to war against a neighboring town. He was taken prisoner and held captive for about a year. After his release, Francis suffered a serious illness, during which he became dissatisfied with his worldly life. He underwent a major crisis and could no longer find the same joy in his former high life.

Spiritual crises often find some resolution through pilgrimages. Francis undertook a pilgrimage to the tomb of St. Peter in Rome, where he exchanged his clothes with that of a beggar and spent a day begging for alms. Because of his experience begging and his interaction with ostracized lepers back in Assisi, Francis knew that God was calling him to live a new way of life. He started spending much time in churches praying for light.

One day, when he was walking by the little church of San Damiano, located outside the walls of Assisi, he was moved by the Spirit to go

---

2. Thomas of Celano, *The Life of St. Francis*, in *Francis of Assisi: Early Documents*, ed. Regis J. Armstrong, OFM, J. A. Wayne Hellmann, OFM, and William J. Short, OFM, 3 vols. (Hyde Park, NY: New City Press, 1999), 1:182.

inside for a prayer. He knelt before the beautiful Italo-Byzantine crucifix and offered this prayer:

> All highest, glorious God,
> cast your light into the darkness of my heart.
> Give me right faith,
> firm hope,
> perfect charity
> and profound humility,
> with wisdom and perception,
> O Lord, so that I may do
> what is truly your holy will.

While praying, Francis heard Jesus speak to him from the crucifix, "Francis, don't you see that my house is being destroyed? Go, then, and rebuild it for me."[3]

This was a call to help rebuild the Catholic Church, which in many places was lax and corrupt. However, Francis first interpreted the message as a command to rebuild the ruined chapel of San Damiano. He immediately went home, took a horse-load of cloth out of his father's warehouse and sold it with the horse in order to purchase materials for restoring the church. Then he went to the priest who oversaw San Damiano, asked to stay with him, and he began to rebuild the church.

This was the beginning of a series of dramatic developments that led Francis to inaugurate a powerful reform movement of Church and society. By the time he died at the age of forty-four, he was the most revered spiritual man of his age. Over ten thousand men had joined his "Franciscan" movement by then, and women from around Europe were forming monastic communities under his inspiration and that of his beloved collaborator, St. Clare.

Breathing the Spiritual Air of Assisi ▸

On the train ride to Assisi, I was anxiously reading Arthur Frommer's *Europe on $15–$20 a Day* looking for an inexpensive *pensione*. Neither

---

3. Thomas of Celano, *The Legend of the Three Companions*, in Armstrong et al., *Francis of Assisi: Early Documents*, 2:76.

Leo nor I had much money to spend on a hotel. After watching me for a while, Leo said, "Why don't you just put the book away. The Lord will provide." I was not convinced, but memories of recent experiences of Divine Providence led me to close the book and hope for the best.

Upon arrival in Assisi, we saw a Franciscan friar in the train station. Leo said, "Tell him we are pilgrims and ask him if there's a place we can stay for free." I was the designated translator since I could speak Spanish with an Italian accent. The friar pointed us to the imposing Franciscan monastery next to the Basilica of San Francesco. When we knocked at the main door, the friar who opened told us that they could not take us in, but that there was a Franciscan seminary up the road that might have room.

We rang the bell of the seminary and, fortunately, the seminarian who opened was a Spaniard. I explained that we were pilgrims who wanted to make a retreat, and that Leo was a seminarian preparing to be ordained a priest in Calcutta. He went to fetch the superior of the house who also was a Spaniard. I repeated our story and he cordially invited us to stay.

The friars and seminarians could not have been more hospitable. Not only did they provide us with rooms without charge, but they invited us to take our meals with them. Leo and I had been eating sparingly in order to economize and were ravenously hungry at every meal. The seminarians were amused by our robust appetites and it almost became a joke among them to send us leftover platters of food.

The spiritual atmosphere of Assisi put Leo and me in a very devotional mood. One morning we attended Mass at the small crypt underneath the Basilica of San Francesco, where St. Francis is buried. Leo and I were the only people in attendance. The priest celebrated Mass reverently and softly. I felt immersed in a contemplative state. Suddenly, about fifty tourists came running down the steps into the chapel, flashing cameras and speaking loudly. I was outraged. Without a second thought, I turned toward the tourists and shouted at them in English: "Get out! Get out!" The tourists were shocked by my outcry. They left immediately, apparently frightened by the fanatical Americano.

After four days, M.A. rejoined us and we made plans to travel to Switzerland. I first wanted to stopover at the C. G. Jung Institute in

Zurich and then to visit my mother's cousins in the alps above Lucerne and her aunt in Geneva.

Synchronicity in Zurich ▸

We took a night train from Assisi to Zurich assuming that the train would not be crowded and we could sleep. Little did we know that the evening we chose for the trip was the same evening when large numbers of Italians who worked in Switzerland were returning to work after the Easter holidays. The train was so jam-packed that we couldn't find a seat. After an eight-hour trip we arrived in Zurich at 7:00 A.M., exhausted, but I was excited by the prospect of making a "pilgrimage" to the institute founded by Carl Jung, who continued to be one of my intellectual heroes.

We examined the large tourist map of Zurich on the train station wall but no C. G. Jung Institute was to be found. We asked the tourist center personnel where to find the institute, but they had not heard of it. I was amazed and deeply disheartened that no one at the station was aware of such a world-renowned institution. Leo tried to cheer me up by telling us that a friend in California had given him the address of the poet laureate of Switzerland and had encouraged Leo to visit him if he ever traveled to Zurich. I wasn't interested, but we had no better option, so we took a tram to the outskirts of the city to a lovely old neighborhood where the poet laureate lived. As we walked through the tree-lined streets I continued feeling deep disappointment. When we reached the poet's elegant nineteenth-century residence, I glanced at the large house next door and couldn't believe what I saw: the C. G. Jung Institute!

12

A Crisis Brews during the Odyssey

Synchronicity or Divine Providence? ▸

WE WERE ALL FLABBERGASTED WHEN WE SAW THE C. G. Jung Institute. What were the chances that, in the metropolitan area of Zurich of more than 1.5 million inhabitants, the destination that I most desired to find would be right next door to the only contact we had in the city? Jung was extremely interested in such extraordinary coincidences. He wrote extensively on what he termed "synchronicity"—meaningful coincidences that have no discernable causality.[1] At that moment, however, I knew in my heart of hearts that this was not simply a meaningful coincidence, but rather a manifestation of Divine Providence, as was my encounter with Leo in the crowded Rome train station the previous month.

Belief in Divine Providence affirms "the existence of a divine plan and purpose for creation that reflects God's loving care."[2] Such a belief pervades the Hebrew Scriptures—the conviction

---

1. C. G. Jung, "Synchronicity: An Acausal, Connecting Principle," in *The Collected Works of C.G. Jung*, ed. Herbert Read, Michael Fordham, and Gerhard Adler, 20 vols. (Princeton, NJ: Princeton University Press, 1966–), 8:417–519.

2. See Joan Slobig, "Providence," *The New Westminster Dictionary of Christian Spirituality*, ed. Philip Sheldrake (Louisville: Westminster John Knox Press, 2005), 512–13.

that, for those who seek the will of God and who obey his commands, blessings follow. A clear example of this teaching is found in Psalm 37:3–5

> Trust in the Lord and do good,
> > that you may dwell in the land and live secure.
> Find your delight in the Lord,
> > who will give you your heart's desire.
> Commit your way to the Lord;
> > trust in him and he will act.

Jesus teaches the reality of Divine Providence in the passage often called the "Lilies of the Field Gospel" from the Sermon on the Mount that I referred to in chapter 5:

> If God so clothes the grass of the field [with wildflowers], which grows today and is thrown into the oven tomorrow, will he not much more provide for you, O you of little faith? . . . Seek first the Kingdom of God and his righteousness, and all these things will be given you besides. (Matthew 6:30–33)

As I reflect on manifestations of Divine Providence, I am struck by the fact that they do not occur only when we are spiritually strong and righteous. They often occur when we are at the end of our rope, spiritually empty, and even when we are conscious of serious sin. It seems that our misery and suffering can provide openings for the grace of God to work. This was made abundantly clear to me during my spiritual awakening at the Trappist monastery in Vina five years earlier. At that time, I was completely empty spiritually. Then God spoke to me through Simone Weil:

> Grace fills empty spaces, but it can only enter where there is a void to receive it, and it is grace itself which makes this void.[3]

As will become apparent below, I interpret the remarkable "coincidence" of being led to the C. G. Jung Institute as God saying to me, "OK, I am going to help you fulfill your desire so that you can discover something beyond what Jung can offer you."

---

3. Simone Weil, *Gravity and Grace* (London: Routledge & Kegan Paul, 1952), 10.

Study at the C. G. Jung Institute

My two companions and I entered the lobby of the Institute and I asked if there were any seminars available. The receptionist informed me that one of Jung's prominent disciples, James Hillman,[4] would be offering seminars the next few days. I had read James Hillman during my Jungian studies in college, and I knew him to be one of the most eminent scholars in the Jungian world. I was thrilled with the idea of studying with him and so, without thinking of the obvious obstacles, I asked if a walk-in could participate. The receptionist responded affirmatively but then I faced the first obstacle. Leo and M.A. were not interested in attending the seminars, and they wanted to get on to Lucerne. Second, my meager budget could not afford to pay for a hotel in affluent Zurich.

At that very moment, a middle-aged American couple who overheard my conversation with the receptionist asked me, "Do you have a place to stay? If not, you are welcome to stay with us. We have rented a chalet in the country not far from here." Again, I felt the workings of Divine Providence. Leo and M.A. knew how much this opportunity mattered to me. They assured me that it was fine with them if I wanted to spend a few days at the Institute. They would simply proceed on with the original plan and travel to a seminary in Lucerne where Leo had a friend and await me there.

That evening the American couple prepared a lovely dinner, during which we talked excitedly about our common interest in Jung. We were all fascinated with Jung's ability to excavate multiple fields of knowledge to understand the psyche: medicine, psychology, anthropology, mythology, world religions, and even occult practices. We were unofficial members of a movement of Americans and Europeans who found Jung to be a sort of Western guru. After having studied with an Eastern guru for six months, I was interested in comparing Maharishi's understanding of the mind with Jung's teachings.

---

4. James Hillman was an American psychologist who studied at, and then guided studies for, the C. G. Jung Institute in Zurich. He founded a movement based on Jung's teachings on archetypal psychology and retired into private practice, writing and traveling to lecture, until his death at his home in Connecticut in 2011 (Wikipedia).

At the next day's lecture, James Hillman touched on Jung's notion of the "Self." For Jung, the Self is the innermost nucleus of the psyche and is distinct from the ego. The ego is only the subject of consciousness, while the Self is the subject of the person's totality; hence it also includes the unconscious psyche. This means that there is in each person an unknown something that has an overview, a vision, a scope, a knowledge, and comprehension about one's total life circumstances. That "Self" functions autonomously. It acts independently of one's conscious mind, wishes, and will—as if it had a mind of its own.[5] The Self is experienced by consciousness as if it were a central planning system that is not part of, but includes and affects, the conscious system. Jung found cross-cultural data that convinced him that his concept of the Self represents a typical human way of experiencing existence and, for that reason, he referred to the Self as an archetype.

> As described by Jung, archetypes are inborn or encapsuled symbols that suggest the most fundamental motifs and themes of human existence. The very same archetypes exist in people of all time and from all places. Since they are universally experienced, the archetypes form what Jung called the Collective Unconscious.[6]

Listening to Hillman's lecture led me to believe that, for Jung, there is nothing deeper or more fundamental in the human psyche than archetypes—basic, universal symbols and images. For Maharishi and his Vedic tradition, there is a source in the psyche from which all thoughts, symbols, and images emerge. He calls it "pure consciousness," and the "Self."

After the lecture, I approached Hillman and asked him if Jung posited a source of thought beyond archetypes—a foundation transcendental to thought itself. Hill replied that, for Jung, the archetype is the ultimate category beyond which nothing can be imagined in the psyche. I proceeded to dispute Jung's view by referring to Maharishi's teaching (the teaching of Vedanta) that there is a source of thought that is characterized by complete silence and unboundedness that can be experienced through deep meditation. Hillman reacted with some impatience

---

5. William Alex, *Dreams, the Unconscious and Analytical Therapy* (San Francisco: C. G. Jung Institute, 1971), 3–4.

6. J. E. Talley, "Archetypes," *Baker Encyclopedia of Psychology*, ed. David G. Benner (Grand Rapids: Baker Book House, 1987), 73.

at my insistence that Jung may have missed something in his theory of the psyche, and the conversation ended.

Although I very much enjoyed Hillman's lectures and my interaction with other seminar participants, my experiences at the institute convinced me that Maharishi had a more accurate understanding of the center of the psyche. Christian scholastic psychology also understands the psyche in ways similar to that of Vedanta, according to which the memory, intellect, and will are operations of the center of the soul, called the "spirit." I began to conclude that there was a negative side of Jungian psychology, namely, the tendency to reduce the human search for meaning to self-actualization based on guidance from the unconscious and its archetypes. The Christian search for meaning finds guidance not only from intuition and instinctual forces but from Jesus, the Gospels, the saints, and the spiritual masters, all of whom constitute the driving force in the history of Christianity.

I left the institute with continued admiration for Jung's extraordinary brilliance, but no longer as a "disciple."

Connecting with My Swiss Family in the Alps ▸

From Zurich I traveled to Lucerne, where I met up with Leo and M.A. We then took a train high into the alps of the Berner Oberland area to reach the alpine village of Brienz, where my maternal grandfather was born in 1887. Even though my grandfather died when I was four, I had a close relationship with him. I was the first grandchild of my generation, and he doted on me. I recall with relish that he regularly took me out on drives in Alameda along the San Francisco Bay in his 1940 Buick. One of my cherished dreams for the European odyssey was to meet my Swiss relatives for the first time.

As the train descended a high mountain pass toward a pristine Alpine lake, I caught my first glimpse of Brienz on its shore. I wept at the sight, having seen photographs of the village since my earliest years. The train pulled into the nineteenth-century train station, and I was filled with the emotion of arriving where my maternal family had lived for centuries. The village itself is ancient. The Romanesque church in Brienz was built in the twelfth century.

My mother's first cousin, Fritz Michel, met us as we got off the train and led us on foot to the family home, a quintessential Swiss chalet on a foothill with beautiful views of the lake in front and the alps behind. His wife, Vreni, greeted me with a huge embrace and the words, "*Mein kind*" ("my family"). Even though she was not a blood-relative, she treated me and my companions as if we were long-lost children. The four days we spent with them and their son, Hans-Ueli, filled my soul with delight as I connected with my Swiss roots.

Retreating to the Monastery of Taizé ▸

From Brienz, my friends and I traveled to Geneva to meet my grandfather's eighty-nine-year-old sister, Elizabeth, who received us with the same gracious affection as Fritz and Vreni had. From Geneva I had planned to go directly to Paris and then on to England and Ireland to meet my Irish relatives. But Leo convinced me that we should first spend some days at the ecumenical monastery of Taizé, located in the village of Taizé, Saône-et-Loire, Burgundy, in southeastern France. The monastic community is composed of more than one hundred brothers, from the Catholic and Protestant traditions. Taizé has become one of the world's most important sites of Christian pilgrimage, with a focus on youth from many religious traditions. Over one hunded thousand young people from around the world make pilgrimages to Taizé each year for prayer, Bible study, sharing, and communal work.

M. A. and I were both attracted to Leo's proposal to make a short retreat at the monastery of Taizé, but we were concerned that our Eurail passes were going to expire in five days, and we had already committed ourselves to meeting a friend from California in London just after the expiration date. Leo convinced us to make a quick three-day retreat at Taizé, which would allow us to reach England on time.

We arrived at the monastery without reservations, but the guestmaster received us with open arms. Throughout much of the year, the small village of Taizé that serves as the site of the monastery is overrun by hundreds and even thousands of teens and young adults who come from all over the world for spiritual retreats. They are housed in dormitories, but we were fortunate to be lodged in simple but comfortable cabins.

Prior to Leo's invitation, I had known nothing about Taizé. During our brief retreat, I became increasingly inspired by what I heard. The Taizé Community was founded in 1940 by Brother Roger Schütz, a Reformed Protestant who had strong Catholic sensibilities. His motivation for founding a monastic community came from pondering how to live a life faithful to the vision of the Gospels. He felt that the enormous crises of the twentieth century required a deeper and more radical following of Jesus than was usually available in conventional Christian parishes. The devastation of Europe during World War II led him to purchase a small house that would eventually become the home of the Taizé Community. Only miles south of the demarcation line that separated Vichy France and the occupied zone, Brother Roger's home became a sanctuary to countless war refugees seeking shelter. Gradually a few men joined Brother Roger's community, and on Easter Sunday 1949, seven brothers committed themselves to a life following Christ in simplicity, celibacy, and community.

In the 1960s young people began to visit the Taizé community, and soon the number of young pilgrims soared. The first international young adults meeting was organized in Taizé in 1966 with participants from 110 countries. The village church of Taizé, which had been used for the community's prayers, became too small to accommodate the pilgrims. A new church, the Church of Reconciliation, was built in the early 1960s with the help of German volunteers. In that church, we joined hundreds of young people and the monastic community three times a day for deeply moving prayer and worship.

In that joyful, enthusiastic community I felt that I had come home. After traveling for two months and undergoing intense interior struggles, I was exhausted and spiritually dry. Except for our time in Assisi, I had not dedicated any significant time to prayer throughout the two months of traveling. I found Taizé to be a sanctuary. I loved the community prayer, the liturgy, the Christian fellowship, the time for long meditative walks and contemplation. My heart ached to remain for a long retreat, but M.A. and I had committed ourselves to meeting our friend from California in London within a few days. Resisting the deepest longings of my heart, I agreed to leave Taizé after three days. It was the most wrenching decision of the entire European odyssey.

A Crisis Brews in Paris ▸

Leo accompanied us to the train station, and we said farewell with heavy hearts. M.A. and I had become very fond of Leo. We realized that we might not see him again for many years since we assumed that he would be serving as a priest in Calcutta. Saying goodbye to both Leo and Taizé, I felt like a plant being yanked out of the ground just when it was beginning to take root.

Our plan was to spend a night in Paris, take a ferry from Calais to Dover and on to London. On the train ride to Paris, where we would spend a night, both M.A. and I were filled with sorrow. I tried to overcome the sorrow by writing feverishly in my journal. M.A. wept silently. I tried to console myself by thinking of how excited I would be taking in the wonders of Paris for the first time and, especially, the renowned north rose window in Notre Dame Cathedral that had captivated me ever since I first read about it in *National Geographic.*

After finding lodging in Paris, we proceeded to Notre Dame Cathedral to attend an evening Mass. Upon entering the cathedral, I walked directly to view the north rose window. Years later, I would read a passage in Bishop Robert Barron's book *Catholicism*, which captures the power of that dazzling work of beauty. He relates what happened on the first day of his doctoral studies in Paris:

> I entered the cathedral . . . and then stood fixed and mesmerized for twenty minutes by the sheer beauty of that window. Every single day that I was in Paris until I returned home for Christmas, I went to that spot and stared. . . . Beauty occurs at the intersection of three elements: wholeness, harmony and radiance. . . .[7]

Bishop Barron's experience would eventually be mine. But on my first day in Paris, in my depressed state, I gazed at the rose window and felt nothing. I was so consumed by a mixture of emptiness, sadness, and fear that I could not appreciate one of the greatest works of art in the world.

---

7. Robert Barron, *Catholicism: A Journey to the Heart of the Faith* (New York: Image Books, 2011), 272–73.

Not only did I feel uprooted by leaving Taizé when I most needed the inspiration and spiritual regeneration that I began to taste there, but I also was beginning to sense a very disturbing type of fear. In the past when I had felt confused or disoriented, I usually found some modicum of consolation by thinking that there was something better waiting for me in the future. But once we arrived in Paris, I was attacked by the fear that I had no future. It seemed that all the plans I had pursued in the past had dissolved. My years of preparing for the priesthood had ended. My starry-eyed pursuit of marriage shattered in Acapulco. My dreams of enlightening people through teaching Transcendental Meditation seemed like a pipe dream. My European Odyssey was almost over. I was running out of money and had no profession or job prospects back in California.

Close to despair, I joined M.A. for Mass in a small chapel near the rear of the Cathedral. When the priest proclaimed the Gospel, I was able to capture enough French to understand:

> Jesus said to them, "I am the bread of life; whoever comes to me will never hunger, and whoever believes in me will never thirst. . . . And I will not reject anyone who comes to me, because I came down from heaven not to do my own will but the will of the one who sent me. And this is the will of the one who sent me, that I should not lose anything of what he gave me. (John 6:35–40)

As I listened to those words, I wept because I sensed they were addressed to me: "This is the will of the one who sent me, that I should not lose anything of what he gave me." It was another moment of Divine Providence for me. I had entered the Mass feeling so lost, and the Gospel of that Mass was about Jesus's desire to save the lost.

When M.A. and I left the cathedral and walked along the Seine, I couldn't stop weeping and she was weeping as well. We both found ourselves in a vulnerable and insecure state. I said to her, "Let's find a bench and read the Lilies of the Field Gospel" (my "go-to Gospel" in times of anxiety). I pulled out my little New Testament and read:

> Therefore I tell you, do not worry about your life. . . . Look at the birds in the sky; they do not sow or reap, they gather nothing into barns, yet your heavenly father feeds them. . . . Do not worry about tomorrow; tomorrow will take care of itself. Sufficient for a day is its own evil. (Matthew 6:25–26, 34)

We found the text consoling and agreed that we needed to let go of our fears, trust in the Lord, and enjoy a fine French dinner. We found a charming restaurant in the Left Bank area, ordered a bottle of Bordeaux, ate escargot for the first time, and briefly forgot our sorrows.

The next morning the void returned to me with a vengeance. The fear that I had no future was paralyzing me. The brief consolation I experienced during the Mass at Notre Dame seemed like a distant memory. Some verses from Psalm 77 captured my anguish:

> In the day of my distress I sought the Lord.
> My hands were raised at night without ceasing;
> My soul refused to be consoled.
> I remembered my God and I groaned.
>
> I pondered and my spirit fainted.
> You withheld sleep from my eyes.
> I was troubled, I could not speak.
> I thought of the days of long ago
> and remembered the years long past.
> At night I mused within my heart.
> I pondered and my spirit questioned.
>
> "Will the Lord reject us forever?
> Will he show us his favor no more?
> Has his love vanished forever?
> Has his promise come to an end?"[8]

---

8. Psalm 77:3–9 (The Grail translation; London: Collins, 1963).

13

Breakthrough

Upon arrival in London, my fears about the future were consuming me more than ever. I felt the fear in the pit of my stomach. M.A. and I walked around downtown London and noticed a billboard advertising a film that had just been released about St. Francis of Assisi: *Brother Sun, Sister Moon*, directed by Franco Zeffirelli. I desperately needed some distraction, so I suggested that we go see the film that afternoon and relive some of our Assisi memories. Entering the theater, I had no other expectations. Besides, some critics panned the film as being saccharine and somewhat inaccurate historically. I had no idea that this romanticized movie would tear me apart.

Breakdown and Breakthrough during Brother Sun, Sister Moon ➤

The film begins around the year 1206 by presenting young Francis Bernardone as the pampered son of Pietro and Pica Bernardone, wealthy cloth merchants in Assisi. The plot of the film coheres in parts with what I recounted earlier about Francis's life. In the film, Francis is seeking fame and worldly glory by becoming a knight and going off to fight in a war between Assisi and a neighboring city-state. He is captured and imprisoned. Once ransomed by his father, he returns home sick and disheartened. When he recovers, he feels the need for direction. He begins to visit churches and to pray seriously for the first time in his life. This leads to a revelation from Christ that he is to "rebuild the Church." He interprets the message as a command to rebuild the ruined church of San Damiano where he had been praying. He sells some of his father's fine cloth, buys bricks, and begins rebuilding the ancient chapel. When Pietro discovers what his son is doing, he becomes furious, thrashes Francis and drags him to Bishop Guido of Assisi to seek his support in the conflict and to demand that Francis make restitution.

The bishop attempts mediation, but Francis has other plans. He strips himself and presents the clothes to his father. Standing naked before the bishop, his father, and the bystanders, he says, "Listen to me, all of you, and understand. Until now I have called Pietro di Bernardone my father. But, because I have proposed to serve God, I return to him the money on account of which he was so upset, and also all the clothing which is his, wanting to say from now on: *'Our Father who are in heaven,'* and not 'My father, Pietro di Bernardone.'"[1] Then, he walks off naked toward the horizon with his arms outstretched, as if he were embracing the sky.

At this point in the film, I began to weep uncontrollably, not knowing why. As the film progresses, Francis proceeds to devote his life to Christ and the Gospel. My tears continued to flow, especially whenever images of Jesus appeared on the screen.

Young men begin to follow Francis, attracted to his new way of living the Christian life—a way characterized by simplicity, poverty, fraternity with all human beings, and joy. After some time, enemies opposed to Francis's radical way of life attack his followers and burn their chapel. Francis is devastated. He resolves to seek guidance for his new movement from the pope.

When he arrives in Rome with his small band of barefoot followers, a bishop arranges for him to meet with Innocent III, the most powerful of all medieval popes. The bishop carefully crafts an address for Francis to read to the pope, seeking approval for his new religious community.

---

1. Thomas of Celano, *The Legend of the Three Companions*, in *Francis of Assisi: Early Documents*, ed. Regis J. Armstrong, OFM, J. A. Wayne Hellmann, OFM, and William J. Short, OFM, 3 vols. (Hyde Park, NY: New City Press, 1999), 2:80.

As Francis enters the audience hall, filled with cardinals and Vatican officials, he walks toward the pope (brilliantly played by Alec Guinness), seated on a high throne. Francis becomes deeply disturbed as he observes the opulence and pomp of the papal court. Standing below the papal throne, he tosses his prepared text to the ground and begins to proclaim the same Gospel passage that I read to M.A. on the banks of the River Seine just two days before:

> Therefore I tell you, do not worry about your life, what you will eat or drink, or about your body, what you will wear. Is life not more than food and the body more than clothing? Look at the birds in the sky.... Learn from the way the wild flowers grow.... But seek first the kingdom of God and his righteousness, and all these things will be given you besides. (Matthew 6:25–26, 28, 33)

The courtiers around Pope Innocent erupt with indignation: "How dare he preach to the Pope!," they cry out. The pope appears to be dazed by Francis's words. Meanwhile, Vatican guards drag Francis and his brothers out of the audience hall. When the pope regains consciousness he calls out, "Where is he? Bring him here!" Francis and his little band are brought back into the hall. The pope dramatically rises from his throne and descends a long flight of steps to greet Francis. He begins speaking to Francis as a loving father would speak to his son. He recalls his days as a young priest when he was full of evangelical zeal. He thanks Francis for his witness to the Gospel and gives him permission to preach everywhere. Then he kneels down and kisses Francis's feet. The courtiers are shocked.

At this point I became completely unglued. Tears streamed down my face. I was overwhelmed by the coincidence of the film ending with Francis proclaiming my "go-to" Gospel passage. I was also profoundly disturbed by the contrast I felt between Francis and myself. The film presented him as unreservedly devoted to Jesus and committed to living radically and joyfully the life of Jesus and his teachings. At that point in my life, I viewed myself as a mediocre Christian and a confused, self-preoccupied young man who didn't know what to do with his life.

As soon as the film ended, I dashed to the bathroom to wash my face and compose myself. I didn't want to upset M.A. I met her in front of the theater where we encountered a group of young evangelicals who held signs that said, "Long live the truth of Brother Sun" and "You too can be like Francis of Assisi." I broke down again, and told a bewildered M.A., "I have to be alone. I'll meet you in a couple of hours." She knew that I was terribly troubled, and she gave me her moral support.

I headed to Hyde Park, where I walked and cried for an hour. Spontaneously, I began to invoke out loud the name of Jesus—over and over. I continued to weep but, unexpectedly, the tears of anguish changed into tears of joy. I felt a very deep and rare consolation welling up inside me. After about an hour of walking and repeating his holy name, I had a strong desire to pray in the presence of the Blessed Sacrament. I ran to Westminster Cathedral, which was only a few blocks away, darted up a side aisle to the Blessed Sacrament chapel, fell on my knees and burst into tears again—tears of extreme joy. I remained in that blessed state for about fifteen minutes, pouring out my heart in prayer, until a sacristan informed me that the church was closing.

I boarded the "Tube" (the London underground transit), sat down, and looked at my reflection in the glass. I realized that the intense fear that had been overwhelming me the previous couple of days was gone. Why? How? I had not taken any measures to overcome the fear beyond reading the Lilies of the Field Gospel after the Mass in Notre Dame two days earlier. Even so, the fear returned with full force the next morning. Psalm 34 provided me with illumination on what caused the dramatic change:

> I sought the Lord, and he answered me
>   delivered me from all my fears.
> Look to him and be radiant,
>   and your faces may not blush for shame.
> This poor one cried out and the Lord heard,
>   and from all his distress he saved him. . . .
> Taste and see that the Lord is good;
>   blessed is the stalwart one who takes refuge in him. (Psalm 34:5–7, 9)

I returned to the B & B where M.A. and I were staying, and I invited her out to a pub. I shared with her what had happened to me the previous few hours and tried to interpret the experience. I told her that something exploded within me during the film. When we arrived in Paris, I felt a deep void. The darkness led to a moment of truth while watching *Brother Sun, Sister Moon*. After breaking down during the film and weeping for an hour while praying intensely, I came to realize how I had changed over the previous few months.

The Transcendental Meditation teacher-training in Spain had stimulated me intellectually and spiritually, but it triggered in me unwanted side-effects. Even though Maharishi taught us to "be simple and natural," we were made very conscious of our new status as teachers of a "path to enlightenment," and I began to be careful of showing weakness. As a devoted TM apologist, I wouldn't even admit to feeling occasionally tired and stressed. My artificiality had a lot to do with the tensions that developed between me and M.A. and Dennis while traveling together.

The most adverse change in me was a gradual redirecting of my spiritual attention away from the person of Jesus. Maharishi never tried to convert us to his religion, and he encouraged us to follow our own faith traditions. Nevertheless, the TM culture was so all-inclusive that the time and energy that I had formerly dedicated to my Christian spiritual practices were replaced by long hours of TM and Vedic studies. The redirecting of my attention led me to much confusion regarding my spiritual path. I didn't have sufficient emotional maturity and spiritual/theological depth to adequately evaluate and integrate the new Eastern knowledge and practices with my Christian identity and convictions. As I adopted my new role as a teacher of meditation, I fell into one of the most serious sins: spiritual pride—the belief that I was superior, more spiritual, and more enlightened than others. God, in his mercy and love, then humbled me.

> My son, do not disdain the discipline of the Lord
> or lose heart when reproved by him;
> for whom the Lord loves, he disciplines.
> He scourges every son he acknowledges.
> Endure your trials as "discipline"; God treats you as sons. For what "son" is there whom his father does not discipline? (Hebrews 12:5–7)

After offering M.A. my initial analysis of what led to my spiritual crisis, I went on to explain how the story of St. Francis revealed to me a young man who acknowledged his pretensions and self-centeredness and fell in love with the person and message of Jesus. I ached to attain the same integrity of life and intimacy with Christ.

I explained to M.A. that something major was unfolding within me, and I needed significant time for prayer and reflection in order to discern how to proceed. She understood and offered me the time and space I needed to make a decision regarding next steps.

Throughout my life I have periodically observed that the readings of the daily Mass often help me to interpret significant events that are happening to me at the time. At such moments the workings of Divine Providence become clear to me. Readers will recall in chapter 10 my experience of attending Mass for the first time in La Antilla. The Gospel of the Last Judgment (Matthew 25) proclaimed at that Mass was the same Gospel that had come to my awareness in meditation a few days prior as a key to understanding the uniqueness of Christianity. The day I underwent the powerful conversion after watching *Brother Sun, Sister Moon*, I did not attend Mass. While writing this chapter, I wondered what the readings were that were proclaimed at Mass that day? Reviewing my 1973 journal, I realized that the conversion experience occurred on May 10, 1973, which was Friday of the third week of Easter. I looked up the Mass readings for that day and discovered that the first reading was Acts of the Apostles 9:1–20—the dramatic account of the conversion of St. Paul! The conversion of St. Paul from being a fanatical persecutor of early Christians to becoming the most dynamic evangelizer of the first century a.d. is the archetypical example of the power of "Amazing Grace" to transform lost souls: "I once was lost, but now am found, was blind, but now I see." Discovering the coincidence fifty years after the event was another moving validation of the action of Divine Providence in my life, especially, in my darkest moments of the void.

For the next few days, I spent much time walking the streets of London and entering churches to pray with my pocket *New Testament and Psalms*. I kept asking the Lord, "What do you want me to do?" Finally the intuition came: "Return to Taizé." When M.A. and I said farewell to Leo, he told us that he intended to remain at the monastery for a week, so I knew I would find him there if I left soon. He would understand what I was undergoing. He had noticed my spiritual pride and inflation during our travels together, although he kept his observations to himself. I needed a spiritual brother and mentor. Leo was both.

I shared my plan with M.A. Since our mutual friend, Maureen, was just about to arrive in London, M.A. would have a companion, so I didn't feel too guilty about leaving her. She understood my need to return to the monastery, and she graciously loaned me money for a flight to Paris (I was almost broke). It wasn't easy for M.A. to accompany me during my crisis. She was a true friend.

Before flying to Paris, we attended Mass at Westminster Cathedral. Before Mass we noticed that a priest was in the confessional at the rear of the huge, Byzantine-style cathedral. I had not confessed my sins to a priest since my departure from the seminary. Because I had been thinking so deeply about the state of my soul in recent days, I was acutely aware of my need to make a thorough confession of my sins and weaknesses. I entered the confessional without hesitation and opened my heart to the priest. He was gracious and kind. After the confession, I felt light and free. I realized what I had been missing by staying away from this healing sacrament.

Some non-Catholics ask, "Why confess your sins to a priest?" I think the answer is very simple. We human beings regularly betray our deepest values. We cause suffering for ourselves and others through egocentric attitudes and behavior. We need a very human way of receiving forgiveness and reconciliation. After his resurrection, Jesus sent his disciples into the world to continue his mission to forgive sins. He could have said, "Tell people to confess their sins to God in the silence of their own hearts." Instead, he gave instructions that are more down-to-earth, more "human." The night of his resurrection from the dead, he appeared to the apostles and said:

> Peace be with you. As the Father has sent me, so I send you." And when he had said this, he breathed on them and said to them, "Receive the holy Spirit. Whose sins you forgive are forgiven them, and whose sins you retain are retained." (John 20:21–23)

These apostles, who were themselves weak and sinful (they had abandoned Jesus during his crucifixion), were given the power and mission to forgive sins. They, in turn, passed on the same power and mission to their successors, the bishops and priests of the Church.[2] On that Sunday

---

2. See Acts 14:23; Titus 1:5; 2 Timothy 1:6.

in Westminster Cathedral, I thanked God for the sacrament that communicated to me such peace of mind and tranquility of conscience.

Return to Taizé ▶

I took a short flight from London to Paris, where I caught a train to Taizé. As the train headed south, I gazed at the miles of countryside in full spring bloom, fields ablaze with wild mustard. I found myself suffused in a deep peace and joyful expectation of what lay ahead at the monastery. I was convinced that the decision to make a long retreat in Taizé with Leo was divine inspiration.

The sun was setting as I arrived at the monastic church. I waited at the front door for Leo as hundreds of young people exited after Evening Prayer. Leo had no idea that I would return to Taizé, and I looked forward to shocking him just as he had shocked me at the Rome train station and at St. Peter's Square. I was not disappointed. When he finally emerged from the church in a very quiet, contemplative state of mind, he looked at me with a stunned expression and kept saying, "I don't believe it! I don't believe it!"

Leo was as excited to see me as I was to see him. After briefly recounting how and why I returned to the monastery, we found a monk who was able to provide me with a room in the same cabin as Leo. Since it was late and I was quite tired from the trip, we agreed to retire early that evening and have a long talk the next morning.

I slept like a rock and woke up early enough to join the community for 7:30 A.M. Morning Prayer. As we walked to the monastic church, the enormous Taizé bells started ringing, and hundreds of young people started filing out of their tents and cabins to join in the prayer service. The Taizé style of prayer is highly meditative. Singing and silence play a large part. Hymns are sung in different languages, and the structure of prayer is similar to the Divine Office (the "Liturgy of the Hours") from the Catholic monastic tradition with a hymn, psalms, a scripture reading, and intercessions. It was awesome to pray and sing in the huge church with close to a thousand young people sitting on the floor surrounding the monastic community of about one hundred monks. The church contained no seats or benches. Everyone knelt or sat on the floor.

After breakfast, I joined other new arrivals in an orientation session led by a few monks and young adult leaders. They explained that throughout the summer months, thousands of young people, aged seventeen to thirty, come to Taizé to explore or rediscover their Christian faith. They will typically camp in the fields around the church and monastery, joining in the community's worship three times a day. Daily Mass is available for Catholics and others who desire to participate. Throughout the day, the youth spend time studying the Bible, reflecting in silence, and meeting in discussion groups.

Leo and I were not interested in group activity except for the daily prayer and Mass. The rest of each day we walked and talked through the stunning French countryside, and spent a couple of hours in personal prayer and meditation in the exquisite Romanesque adoration chapel that had been the village church since the eleventh century. Peace and a sense of God's presence continued to grow within me.

The Universal Value of Monasticism ▸

Immersion in the monastic rhythm for a week reminded me of a talk given by an Episcopalian priest at my high school seminary during the annual week of prayer for Christian unity (the "Octave for Christian Unity"). I didn't understand one of his messages, but I filed it away for future reflection. He said, "What keeps the world from being blown up are oases of prayer like the Trappist monastery in Vina, California." Maharishi used the same peculiar phrase as he made the identical point during my TM teacher-training course in La Antilla: "What has kept the world from being blown up are oases of *satva* (Sanskrit for "purity") like the Himalayan hermits and the monks of Mount Athos."

Monastic life has pride of place in most of the great world religions. Early in the history of Christianity, large numbers of people sought a deep experience of God and spiritual enlightenment by fleeing the cities of the decaying Roman Empire and forming monastic communities in the Egyptian and Syrian deserts, often around a wise elder who was called "Abbot" ("Abba" in Aramaic). Soon the movement became institutionalized under St. Benedict of Nursia (b. A.D. 480) in the West and St. Basil (b. A.D. 330) in the Christian East. In Hinduism, Shankara's monastic order ("Sannyasi") can be seen as a natural institutional embodiment of his teachings on *Advaita Vedanta* whereby one seeks a master for guidance toward enlightenment and lives a life of poverty, celibacy, and obedience—the same vows taken by Christian monastics. In Theravada Buddhism, the central religious institution has been the monastery.[3]

I suspect that most people who spend time in a monastery—whether as a monk/nun or as a layperson on retreat—sense the spiritual power generated by the monastic community. It is no accident that, for millennia, monasteries have often been places where people have sought spiritual guidance.

Monasteries have been places not only for individual spiritual regeneration, but for societal renewal and rebirth as well. A compelling example would be how Benedictine monasticism enabled Western civilization to survive the devastating fall of the Roman Empire in the fifth century.

> Europe was in shambles. Roman law and order and civilization had crumbled. In their wake, robber-bands and barbarian tribes roamed up and down the continent, pillaging, destroying, making civilized life impossible. Educated Christians and unlettered ones were of the same mind: it looked like the end of the world.
>
> It wasn't.... Instead, God sent one of His greatest saints—and the West lived on.[4]

In the midst of such war and chaos, Benedict of Nursia was born. He was "concerned only with the inner moral struggle of his spiritual enterprise,"[5] but his monasteries that began to sprout up all over Europe and beyond became missionary centers, not only of the Christian faith but also of the fundamental arts of civilization—agriculture, architecture, Greek and Latin classical learning, and the arts and sciences.[6]

Since the first monks of Taizé took their vows in 1949, their monastic movement has served to draw hundreds of thousands of seekers to

---

3. D. K. Swearer and G. A. Zinn, "Monasticism, East and West," *The Perennial Dictionary of World Religions*, ed. Keith Crim et al. (San Francisco: Harper & Row, 1989), 489.

4. Abbot Justin McCann, O.S.B., *Saint Benedict: The Story of the Man and His Work* (Garden City, NY: Image Books, 1958), Back Cover.

5. Ibid., 26.

6. Ibid., 76.

God and to the highest ideals of humanity. It has also served as a unifying center for Catholic, Protestant, and Orthodox Christians and has provided an oasis of spirituality for untold numbers of non-Christians as well. Leo and I witnessed this phenomenon firsthand throughout our week at Taizé. I had already experienced the transforming power of monastic life at the Trappist Abbey of New Clairvaux in Vina and at the New Camaldoli Hermitage in Big Sur. Soon I would encounter another Benedictine monastic community, where the ideals of St. Benedict continue to transform individuals and society, and where I would undergo the final breakthrough of the European "odyssey."

14

The Final Weeks of the Odyssey

The Monastery of la Pierre-qui-Vire ▶

AFTER AN IDYLLIC WEEK AT TAIZÉ, THE NUMBER OF NEW arrivals increased considerably, prompting Leo to suggest we travel to another monastery where we could find more solitude and silence, the Benedictine Abbaye Sainte-Marie-de-la-Pierre-qui-Vire. The monastery was founded in 1850, deep in the Morvan Forest, about a ninety-minute drive west from Dijon. Nestled in a wild and verdant environment, the place's name, *la Pierre-qui-Vire* ("the rock that turns"), is a reference to an enormous balanced stone, which now has a statue of the Virgin Mary on top of it. In earlier days, before it was sealed, the rock could be moved by just pressing on it with your hand.

With grateful hearts, Leo and I said good-bye to Taizé, caught a train to Dijon, and then took a bus to Saint-Léger-Vauban. From there, the only transportation available for the ten-kilometer trip to the monastery was a taxi, which we could not afford. So, we began the long walk along a country road, carrying our heavy suitcases (without wheels) and winter coats. After about three kilometers, we were sweating profusely, despite a light rain. We came upon a small inn and decided to treat ourselves to a gin and tonic at the bar. However, the bartender did not know how to mix drinks, American-style. I noticed a bottle of gin and some tonic water tucked away on a shelf, so I asked him if I could go behind the bar and mix the drinks. He responded with a slightly annoyed look, probably thinking to himself "*Qui pensent ces Américains!*" ("Who do these Americans think they are!"). But apparently he wanted our business because he invited me behind the bar, where I looked for some LARGE glasses, and prepared the best gin and tonics ever served in the history of France.

The respite refreshed us greatly, and we undertook the remaining seven kilometers happy as larks, laughing our way down the road. Soon a pickup truck passed us by, but then stopped and returned to offer us a ride. The cab of the truck was full, but we were happy to sit in the truck bed, on top of a pile of garden cuttings. We reached the monastery, rang the bell, and the guest master opened the door introducing himself as Father Sebastian. He asked us if we had reservations. We responded that we had no reservations, very little money, but wished to make a week's retreat. He opened his arms and said, "*Bienvenue, mes frères!*" ("Welcome, my brothers"). That hospitable welcome embodied the type of monastic community we were about to encounter for the next eight days.

Father Sebastian led us to sparse but comfortable guest rooms and gave us a tour of the large, picturesque, nineteenth-century monastery, which housed about eighty monks. He also showed us the dairy, where the monks raised cows and made an exceptionally delicious Camembert cheese. When we arrived at the small guest breakfast room the next morning, we found a good-sized loaf of this cheese on the table along with the customary *café au lait*, croissants, butter, and jam. I had never eaten strong-smelling French cheeses and was not attracted to the cheese's pungent aroma, but Leo encouraged me to give it a try. One bite of that amazing monastic creation converted me, and we polished off the entire loaf. This experience was repeated each morning throughout our eight-day retreat. On the last day, we went to the monastic gift shop to buy a loaf to take with us for the next leg of our journey, and then discovered what a financial liability we had been to those poor monks. We calculated that we had eaten hundreds of dollars' worth of their precious cheese!

We also consumed a fair amount of their wine. A high-end local winery provided the monks with fine red wine at reasonable cost. Leo and I joined the monks in their monastic refectory for the noon meal each day at which the fine wine was served. Having been on a very low-budget European journey for two months during which we usually drank *vin ordinaire*, we were overcome by the luscious vintages and failed to follow the monastic custom of moderate drinking. The monks seemed amused at our enthusiasm for their wine, so they regularly passed an extra bottle in our direction.

Lest readers think that our week at the monastery was all about wine and cheese, I assure you that we were more enthusiastic about the opportunities for prayer, meditation, and fellowship with the monks.

Leo and I followed the prayer rhythm of the monks: Morning Prayer, Mass, Midday Prayer, and Evening Prayer. I maintained my daily practice of Transcendental Meditation, and I continued to ponder the relationship between the spiritual teachings of the Far East and Christianity. I did not doubt the value of Eastern meditation for settling mind and body, for release of stress, and as a vehicle for entering into interior silence. At the same time, the six months of long meditations during the TM teacher-training course followed by the recent breakthroughs in London and Taizé convinced me that what I most wanted in life was intimacy with God. The experience of Jesus flooding my soul after watching *Brother Sun, Sister Moon*, and my renewed daily practice of *Lectio Divina* meditation in London and Taizé filled me with a type of joy and fulfillment that was beyond what I had experienced through Eastern philosophy and meditation. I still had many unanswered questions that intrigued me with regard to the relationship between the two traditions. I knew that eventually I would engage in an in-depth academic study of these issues. That opportunity would present itself a few years later.

Revelations ▸

The quiet and solitude of la Pierre-qui-Vire afforded me the opportunity to process the tumultuous life-changing events of the previous months. I began to practice *Lectio Divina* in a way I had never done before. The monastery had a small, secluded adoration chapel where I would sit on my heels in front of the Blessed Sacrament meditating on the scriptures, especially the psalms. Instead of ending the meditation in thirty or sixty minutes, I felt inclined to continue for two hours at a time. I experienced deeper peace and joy each day. One scripture passage that especially touched my heart was Psalm 25, verses 4–5:

> Make me to know thy ways, O Lord;
> > teach me thy paths.
> Lead me in thy truth, and teach me,
> > for thou art the God of my salvation;
> > for thee I wait all the day long.[1]

What most touched me in this psalm was the promise that God was going to make known his ways to me. My future still seemed completely unknown. I had no job prospects back in California, no money, and no sense of a vocation. Yet the more I prayed, the more the fear and anxiety lessened. Each day during the two-hour prayer period, I asked the Lord, "What do you want me to do with my life?" Then I would meditate on the scriptures seeking light and wisdom. After six days of this practice, out of the blue came an answer to my prayer—but not what I expected. Instead of gaining some guidance regarding a career or vocation, I heard in my heart of hearts these words: "God is my future." That unanticipated message brought me enormous peace and a quiet joy. At that moment I believed firmly that my future was in God's hands—that God *was* my future. The more I reflected on this message, the more excited I became because I realized that God had plans for me that were far greater than what I could imagine. Over time I have come to believe this to be true for every serious seeker of God.

I connected the message with verses from Psalm 16:

> Preserve me, God, I take refuge in you.
> I say to the Lord: "You are my God.
> My happiness lies in you alone."
> . . . .
> O Lord, it is you who are my portion and cup;
> it is you yourself who are my prize. (Psalm 16:1–2, 5)

The next day after my two-hour prayer period—a beautiful spring day that coincided with my twenty-fourth birthday—I walked along a country road outside the monastery, meditating on the scriptures. I experienced a blessedness so profound and so complete, that I couldn't imagine any greater pleasure or satisfaction. There I was, a twenty-four-year-old young man, out of money, no job, no discernible future, and I

---

1. Revised Standard Version (RSV)

felt extraordinarily joyful. Another verse from Psalm 16 reflects my experience:

> You will show me the path of life,
> the fullness of joy in your presence,
> at your right hand happiness for ever. (Psalm 16: 11)[2]

Then another surprising insight came to me. "Now I understand how a fulfilled life as a celibate is possible."

When I was in the seminary preparing for the celibate priesthood, I had not seriously grappled with celibacy on a spiritual level. My understanding of celibacy had primarily been a matter of sexual abstinence and renunciation of marriage as a requirement for priestly ministry. One of the principal reasons I left the seminary was that I longed for romance and eros in a loving marital relationship. But as I walked down that country road, I said to myself, "I have never experienced anything in this world that has made me as happy as I am at this moment. Now I understand how a fulfilled life as a celibate is possible."

I relate this experience to what happened to me after watching the film *Brother Sun, Sister Moon*. Christ flooded my soul. This may sound like mystical mumbo-jumbo to some, but such experiences are common in the history of Christianity and are simply the fulfillment of promises Jesus made in the Gospels:

> Whoever has my commandments and observes them is the one who loves me. And whoever loves me will be loved by my Father, and I will love him and reveal myself to him. (John 14:21)

> Whoever loves me will keep my word, and my Father will love him, and we will come to him and make our dwelling with him. (John 14:23)

Perhaps some readers may think that my reflections on celibacy may have led me to revisit a possible priestly vocation. The question of priesthood did not enter my mind at that time. The insight had to do specifically with the possibility of living a fulfilled, happy life as a celibate. Jesus speaks about this way of life in Matthew 19:12:

---

2. The Grail Translation: Psalms (London: Collins, 1963).

Some are incapable of marriage because they were born so; some, because they were made so by others; some, because they have renounced marriage for the sake of the kingdom of heaven. Whoever can accept this ought to accept it.

I reflected on the fact that not only does the Christian tradition value celibacy, but also the Hindu and Buddhist traditions. I recalled reading in Maharishi's *Commentary on the Bhagavad-Gita* his definition of celibacy: "a state of the individual where the life force is always found directed upwards towards supreme consciousness."[3]

Farewell to Pierre-qui-Vire and Leo ▸

Later that day, Leo and a few of the monks prepared a delightful twenty-fourth birthday party for me. Throughout the week, I had grown very fond of Father Sebastian, Brother Fernando from Colombia, and Father Ghislain Lafont, a renowned theologian who taught half the year in Rome. For me they became examples of how monastic life can transform people into Christlike individuals. Leo and I bade farewell to them a couple of days later when we hooked a ride to Paris from another guest.

By this time in our journey, Leo had been away from Rome for three weeks, with the understanding that the archbishop of Calcutta would send documents authorizing a bishop in Rome to ordain Leo a deacon. Ordination would automatically incorporate Leo into the clergy of the Archdiocese of Calcutta, making it easier for him to obtain a visa. Leo's plan was to take a train from Paris to Rome the evening of our departure from la Pierre-qui-Vire. My plan was to celebrate the great feast of Pentecost at Solesme, a Benedictine monastery famous for its Gregorian chant, and then to return to Paris for a reunion with M.A. a week before our return to California.

Upon arrival in Paris, Leo and I had our farewell supper prior to going our separate ways. The weeks of traveling with Leo had been momentous and transformative for both of us. We had bonded as spiritual brothers,

---

3. Maharishi Mahesh Yogi, *Maharishi Mahesh Yogi on the Bhagavad-gita: A New Translation and Commentary with Sanskrit Text*, chapters 1 to 6 (Baltimore, MD: Penguin Books, 1969; reprint, 1973), 484.

and I knew that I was going to miss him very much. We did not know if we would see each other again, since his intention was to spend the rest of his life serving as a priest in Calcutta. We arrived at a Metro station, from which Leo would go in one direction and I in another. We said a warm good-bye, and off we went to pursue our separate destinies.

A Surprise Trip to Mont Saint-Michel ▸

After parting from Leo, I took the Metro to the Montparnasse-Nantes train station. From there my plan was to board a train to Le Mans, which is close to Solesme. When I reached the station, however, I discovered that I had missed the last train of the day and would have to spend the night in the station waiting for an early morning departure. The waiting room was almost full, and I dreaded the thought of trying to sleep amid a noisy crowd on a wooden seat. Then I remembered that an American couple, the Ceases, whom I had met at my convent pensione in Rome, had invited me to contact them when I arrived in Paris. They were renting a Parisian apartment for a couple of months. I phoned them several times over the next couple of hours, but there was no answer.

Finally, around 10:00 P.M. I gave up and tried to sleep. After about an hour a woman who had probably not bathed for days sat down in the only empty seat in the waiting room—the seat next to me. I try to be compassionate in such situations, but I was almost gagging because of the smell. In complete desperation, I begged the Lord for help, and tried once more to reach the Cease family. Wondrously, they answered! They had just returned from an all-day outing. I apologized for calling so late, but they were happy to hear from me and told me to come right over.

I marveled at my good fortune. I headed to the Metro station, and as I descended the stairs to the train platform, I saw graffiti sprayed on the arch over the entrance in big, bold letters: "*J E S U S.*" I got the message.

When I arrived at the Ceases' attractive Parisian flat, they welcomed me warmly and had a tasty supper waiting for me. During the meal they presented me with a proposal. They had been traveling with their three young children for over a month and could use some help with childcare for a few days. Would I be interested in joining the family on a trip to

Mont Saint-Michel and serve as an "*au pair?*" I was thrilled with the idea of visiting Mont Saint-Michel, and I liked the kids, so I gladly accepted.

The next morning, we drove a couple of hours to reach Mont Saint-Michel, a small island on the Normandy coast, just a few hundred yards from land. The Mont has a circumference of about 3,100 feet, and its highest point is 300 feet above sea level. In the eleventh century, Richard II, duke of Normandy, hired an Italian architect to build a Romanesque abbey at the top of the mount. The island's position made it accessible at low tide to the many pilgrims who came to the abbey, but defensible as an incoming tide stranded, drove off, or drowned would-be assailants. Over sixty buildings on the monastic island are protected in France as *monuments historiques*.

Our three-day excursion gave me further appreciation for the marvels of French history, geography, and Benedictine monasticism. We all returned refreshed and relaxed to Paris. The parents had a break from parenting, the children had a reprieve from being parented, and I had the opportunity of letting my inner child have a field day.

The World-Famous Monastery of Solesmes ▸

Throughout my years in the seminary, I had come to love Gregorian chant, the original "soul music" of Catholicism. The chants sung during the Mass and at appointed times during the day (the Divine Office) have their roots in the early fourth century when desert monks, following St. Antony of the Desert, introduced the practice of singing the complete cycle of 150 psalms each week.

Around the year 520, St. Benedict of Nursia established his *Rule* for monks, in which the protocol of the Divine Office for monastic use was laid down. Pope Gregory the Great (540–604) established a more uniform standard in church services, gathering chants from among the regional traditions.[4]

---

4. Of those liturgical traditions, Pope Gregory retained what he could, revised where necessary, and assigned particular chants to the various services. His goal was to organize the bodies of chants from diverse traditions into a uniform and orderly whole for use by the entire western region of the Church. These significant steps account for why the chants of the Church came to be called "Gregorian" chant. (See "Gregorian chant" in *Wikipedia*.)

Gregorian chant has in its long history been subjected to a series of redactions in response to changing tastes and practice. The most influential redaction in the nineteenth and twentieth centuries was undertaken in the Benedictine Abbey of Saint-Pierre de Solesmes. In 1903, Pope Pius X accepted as authoritative the extensive research and proposed revisions of the Solesmes monks, compiled as the *Liber Usualis*.

When I entered the high school seminary in 1963, each member of the community had a copy of the *Liber*, from which we sang every Sunday and Feast day. We learned to sing the chant in classes offered by the seminary's musical director, Father John Olivier, S.S., who would often demonstrate chant by playing recordings of the monks of Solesmes, which "enchanted" me. Father Olivier was a world-class musician. He communicated great enthusiasm, expertise, and appreciation for chant in his teaching. Since that time, I had wanted to make a pilgrimage to Solesmes and experience firsthand what Father Olivier considered to be the best rendition of Gregorian chant in the world.

The morning I said good-bye to the Cease family, I boarded an early train to Solesmes and arrived, as I had arrived at la Pierre-qui-Vire, without a reservation and without sufficient money to pay for accommodations. The Abbey of Saint-Pierre de Solesmes is located adjacent to the River Sarthe, halfway between Le Mans and Angers. I checked in with the guest master, Father Jean Claire, who was also choirmaster of the monastery. When I told him that I wished to make a five-day retreat in preparation for the great feast of Pentecost, he expressed regret that all the guest rooms were occupied. I appealed to his compassionate heart by stating that I had longed to make a retreat at Solesmes ever since I fell in love with Gregorian chant as a high school seminarian. He was sympathetic to my supplication and asked me if I would be willing to sleep on a pile of hay in the monastic barn until a room became available. I was on a pilgrimage, and pilgrimages traditionally involve some hardship and penance, so the thought of sleeping in a barn appealed to me.

Throughout my five days at the monastery, Father Jean Claire took me under his wing. He was especially responsive to my interest in Gregorian chant and arranged for me to examine their remarkable collection of ancient chant manuscripts. When he learned that I was an organist, he allowed me to play the magnificent organ in the monastic church. When a room finally became available, he liberated me from my haystack in the barn. He also put me to work in the monastic garden so I wouldn't feel like a freeloader.

The high point of my stay was the daily Liturgy of the Hours and Mass, chanted beautifully by the hundred or so monks. It is easy to understand why people of all religions and of no religion purchase millions of Gregorian chant CD's each year. As spiritual music that touches the soul, it's hard to beat. In 2015, a new Gregorian chant CD sung by a community of Benedictine monks in Norcia, Italy, debuted at number 1 on *Billboard*'s classical music chart. The album, *Benedicta*, was also the top overall seller at Barnes & Noble, was number 1 on Amazon, and made iTunes' Top 40.[5]

Despite the prominence of Gregorian chant in the monastic daily routine, the monks make it clear that chant is not the center of their life. The Solesmes website states:

> The Abbey of Saint-Pierre de Solesmes is steeped in 1,000 years of history and is a leading centre for Gregorian chant. Above all, however, it is a living community of Benedictine monks searching for God. Since our monastery is a place of silence and recollection, we invite you to share in our spirituality, liturgical prayer, community life, heritage, and the central presence of Christ in our life.[6]

When I arrived at Solesmes, I hoped that the spiritual consolations I had been experiencing since my breakthrough in London would continue. "Spiritual consolation" is a term that St. Ignatius of Loyola (the sixteenth-century founder of the Jesuits) employed to describe our interior life when "we find ourselves so on fire with the love of God that neither anything nor anyone presents itself in competition with a total gift of self to God in love. Rather we begin to see everything and everyone in the context of God."[7] Spiritual consolation also manifests as sadness "for our infidelity to God but at the same time thankful to know God as Savior." When in a state of spiritual consolation, we find our life

---

5. Leslie Miller, "Churches may be in decline, but Gregorian chant beats secular competition," *National Catholic Reporter* (online), June 16, 2015.

6. www.solesmes.com

7. David L. Fleming, S.J., "Guidelines for the Discernment of Spirits, Week One, Third Rule," *The Spiritual Exercises of St. Ignatius: A Literal Translation and a Contemporary Reading* (St. Louis, MO: The Institute of Jesuit Sources, 1978), 206–7.

of faith, hope, and love strengthened and emboldened, and we sense a deep-down peace in God.[8]

St. Ignatius's description of spiritual consolation had been my experience the previous three weeks. The joy and peace were so great that I thought I would never lose them. However, if I had been trained in his "Rules of Discernment," I would have been preparing myself for the inevitable return to a more ordinary state of consciousness.

My first couple of days at Solesmes, I continued with the prayer routine that I had followed at la Pierre-qui-Vire. Prayer and meditation continued to be effortless and deep. Then, on the third day, I remained in the monastic church after Vespers and intended to spend time in silent *Lectio Divina* as I had been doing the previous days. To my utter surprise and dismay, the spiritual consolation suddenly disappeared. My prayer was dry as a bone. I tried to recapture the feeling of devotion and peace to no avail. "What happened?" I asked myself. "What have I done wrong?"

If I had posed those questions to an experienced spiritual master, he or she would have probably said, "You are encountering the same dryness as does every neophyte seeker of God after a period of spiritual consolation." In his "Guidelines for the Discernment of Spirits," St. Ignatius writes,

> When we are enjoying a consolation period, we should use foresight and savor the strength of such a period against the time when we may no longer find ourselves in consolation.
>
> A time of consolation should provide the opportunity for a growth in true humility. We can acknowledge with gratitude the gifts we have received and recognize the full gratuity of God's favor. It may be well to take stock of how poorly we fare when such consolation is withdrawn.
>
> On the other hand, if we are afflicted by desolation, we should take some consolation in knowing that God's grace is always sufficient to follow the way of the Lord.[9]

Another great spiritual master, the sixteenth-century mystic and poet St. John of the Cross, explains that spiritual consolations can lead

---

8. Ibid.
9. Ibid., "Tenth and Eleventh Rule," 210–11.

beginners to "spiritual gluttony," self-centered attachment to the pleasure and peace that often accompany prayer and meditation rather than attachment to the One offering the peace and joy.

> These people incur many other imperfections because of this spiritual gluttony, of which the Lord in time will cure them through temptations, aridities, and other trials, which are all a part of the dark night.[10]

"Dark Night" is the term St. John of the Cross uses to refer to the experience of privation or void. The soul has to be emptied of what is not God in order to be filled with God. St. John employed this term to designate the painful purifications we usually undergo before reaching union with God.

Having been on a spiritual "high" for three weeks, I did feel a letdown when I returned to earth. But thanks be to God, I didn't lose faith in Divine Providence. I still had a sense that God was leading and guiding me.

The Last Week in Paris ▸

When M.A. and I parted in London before my departure for Taizé, we agreed that we would meet up in Paris in front of Notre Dame Cathedral at noon a week before our return flight to California. She had made arrangements for us to stay with friends that week. On the appointed day, I said good-bye with deep gratitude to the monastic community of Solesmes and boarded a train for Paris.

M.A. was waiting for me in front of Notre Dame. We were overjoyed to see each other. We found a bistro on the Left Bank and began sharing our adventures of the previous three weeks. During our time apart, M.A. had traveled around England with Maureen for a week. Maureen was completely unfamiliar with making travel arrangements. She relied on M.A. to organize the entire trip. When Maureen returned home after a week, M.A. was exhausted. She knocked on the door of a convent and asked the nuns if she could stay with them for a few days

---

10. St. John of the Cross, *The Dark Night*, in *The Collected Works of St. John of the Cross*, translated by Kieran Kavanaugh, O.C.D. and Otilio Rodriguez, O.C.D. (Washington, D.C.: ICS Publications . 1991), book 1, chapter 6, para. 8, p. 373.

and make a retreat. Although she had no reservations (following the Leo and Kevin playbook), the nuns welcomed her warmly and took care of her like a daughter. I took pleasure in her story, sensing that the Holy Spirit had led both of us in similar directions during our time apart.

After our lunch, we headed to the home of the Arrez family, who lived in an attractive Parisian suburb. Madame Arrez greeted us warmly but expressed embarrassment because she did not know M.A. would be arriving with a friend. There was no extra bedroom. I told her that I had just spent the previous several days sleeping on a haystack in a monastic barn and that I would be very content simply to sleep on the floor of the living room. Madame Arrez was amused by my story, and we sealed the deal.

Once we settled in at the Arrez residence, my priority was to see again the renowned north rose window in Notre Dame Cathedral that I had been unable to appreciate during my first stay in Paris because of my severe depression. As I noted in chapter 12, photos of that window had fascinated me ever since I had read about it in *National Geographic*. M.A. and I headed to Notre Dame, entered the cathedral, and walked directly to view the rose window. This time, I completely resonated with Bishop Robert Barron's experience of the window on the first day of his doctoral studies in Paris:

> I entered the cathedral . . . and then stood fixed and mesmerized for twenty minutes by the sheer beauty of that window. . . .
>
> The great wheel of the north rose window, with its myriad parts in harmonious interconnection and with the sunlight shining through it, certainly qualifies as a beautiful thing. But its beauty is in service of a higher good, for it is meant to be a foretaste of the beauty of the beatific vision. One is supposed, even while looking at it, to look beyond it and say, "Oh heavenly God."[11]

In the Catholic and Orthodox traditions, authentic religious art is meant to be "iconic"—instruments for communicating the spiritual realities represented by the images. That magnificent iconic window with Christ in the middle surrounded by eighty-eight images of angels, prophets, and saints expresses dramatically the Christian convictions about Christ

---

11. Robert Barron, *Catholicism: A Journey to the Heart of the Faith* (New York: Image Books, 2011), 272–73.

and his central place in the universe. The sheer beauty and complexity of the multicolored, jewel-like rose window has likely led many nonbelievers to doubt their unbelief over the past eight centuries.

After being dazzled by the windows and architecture of Notre Dame, M.A. said something that I found difficult to believe. "As splendid as this cathedral is, the cathedral in Chartres is even more spectacular." She began to explain to me that the cathedral of Notre-Dame de Chartres, located in the Centre-Val-de-Loire region, is probably the most authentic and complete work of religious architecture of the early thirteenth century. It was the destination of pilgrimages dedicated to the Virgin Mary and was built by the rich and poor who labored alongside each other for decades, bonded by a common love for the Mother of God. The incomparable stained-glass ensemble, monumental statuary, and the painted decorations miraculously preserved from the ravages of time, make Chartres one of the most loved and best-preserved churches in the entire world.

After that superlative tribute, I was ready to take the next train to Chartres. We decided to go the next morning. When we awakened, however, clouds had descended on the entire region, and we needed a sunny day to fully appreciate the stunning stained glass. We were sorely disappointed. Since our flight to California was seven days hence, we assumed we would have ample opportunity to travel to Chartres on a clear day. Yet the clouds remained for five days. On the fifth night, we knew that our only option was to travel the next morning, rain or shine.

The Last Day: Chartres Cathedral ▸

We rose early to a brilliant, sunny morning. We thanked God for our good fortune and took an early train to Chartres—an hour-and-a-half journey. We arrived about 8:30 A.M. and walked toward the cathedral through the empty cobblestone streets of the famed medieval town. Surprisingly, the immense processional doors of the cathedral were wide open. Within the dark interior, we could see multicolored flickers of light darting everywhere. The moment we entered the massive, largely empty cathedral, the great organ and a trumpet began playing a splendid march. We could hardly believe the timing. It was as if the musicians were waiting for us! That was the beginning of an extraordinary day. We spent the morning on the southeast side of the church, slowly following the sun as it moved from window to window. We reveled in the astonishing beauty of the 178 windows—probably the finest ever created. The windows tell the story of the Bible from Genesis to the Book of Revelation and represent a great number of saints up through the Middle Ages.

We broke for lunch and then spent the afternoon following the sun from window to window on the northwest side of the church. Midway through the afternoon, we discovered that the great scholar of Chartres Cathedral, Malcolm Miller, was on site offering guided tours. One of his superb guidebooks to the cathedral ends with a description of the purpose of the stained glass and of the cathedral itself:

> The stained-glass, like the sculpture with which it is programmed outside, first was intended to teach medieval man how to conduct himself in this world, so that he might hope, at the end of time, to transcend death into an eternal life. The second purpose was to beautify, so that the diaphanous walls breathing with the changing light might create an atmosphere of awesome mystery. Thirdly, just as the resplendent painted and gilded porches outside symbolize the Gates of Heaven, so the walls inside, set as with a myriad of glittering jewels, recreate in physical form John's vision of the walls of the Heavenly Jerusalem, "garnished," he wrote, "with all manner of precious stones, jasper, sapphire, chalcedony, emerald, topaz, jacinth and amethyst"(Rev. 21:19, 20).[12]

We returned to Paris immensely grateful and thrilled to have ended our three-month sojourn through Europe at one of the most exquisite and spiritually inspiring churches in the entire world.

---

12. Malcolm Miller, *Chartres Cathedral: The Medieval Stained Glass and Sculpture* (London: Pitkin Pictorials LTD, 1980), 32.

15

Forging a New Path in California

The morning after our exhilarating day in Chartres, the Arrez family gave M.A. and me a warm send-off. We then headed to the Paris airport for our flight to Oakland. It was mid-June of 1973. Once on the plane, I spent a few hours journaling about my life-changing nine months in Europe. Those nine months confirmed and reinforced the Christ-centered direction of my life that emerged with my First Communion and was reignited at the Monastery of New Clairvaux when I was nineteen. The fundamental message I received through the several crises and breakthroughs was "Trust in Divine Providence." This is how I interpreted the saying of Jesus that repeatedly came through to me during the latter part of the European odyssey: "Seek first the kingdom of God and his righteousness, and all these [other] things will be given you besides" (Matthew 6:33).

I still had no concrete plans for the future, no job, no money, no sense of vocation except the desire to marry and raise a family. But I was not worried. I knew that God had a plan for my life just as he has a plan for everyone who seeks his will. The witness of a host of saints testifies to the truth that such faith is never in vain.

The nine months also deepened my conviction that daily meditation is of great value in one's spiritual growth. The big unanswered question for me was the relationship between Eastern meditation, which leads to interior silence, and Christian meditation, which focuses on the Word of God and union with the Word made flesh. How one responds to this question can significantly impact one's spiritual path.

Back with Family in Alameda

My parents, brother, and grandmother picked me up at Oakland Airport and gave me an extremely warm homecoming. We had deeply missed one another. One of the greatest gifts in my life story has been the loving relationships with my immediate family. Even when my brother and I underwent a period of painful estrangement a few years later, the profound bonding we had established as children was always latent within us.

As we excitedly shared news of our respective recent happenings, my mom shared some startling news: "Leo has returned home!" I was flabbergasted! I had thought we wouldn't see each other again for many years—if ever! I immediately phoned him and asked him the same question I posed to him when he shockingly appeared at the Rome Airport and at St. Peter's Square: "Leo, what are you doing here?!!" He replied, "I'll be right over."

Twenty minutes later Leo arrived and told us why he returned to California. After we had said farewell three weeks earlier at the Paris Metro station, he had taken a train to Rome, expecting that the authorization would have arrived from the archbishop of Calcutta for a bishop in Rome to ordain him as a deacon. The authorization had not arrived. Leo phoned the archbishop, who told him that there were visa difficulties and Leo should return to California, where the bishop of Oakland would receive the papers and perform the ordination. Then Leo could travel to Calcutta and be ordained priest soon thereafter. As it turned out, a year would pass before the papers arrived. In the meantime, Leo lived with his mother and pursued a master's degree in theology at the Graduate Theological Union in Berkeley.

I stayed with my family throughout the summer, unsure what to do next. When I had considered possible career options while in Europe, I had thought of teaching theology at a Catholic high school and directing choirs. Since the age of eight I had played the piano. In high school I had studied organ and served as choir director. I knew that the best choral director in California, Dr. Charlene Archibeque, taught at San Jose State University (SJSU). I was attracted by the possibility of studying with her, but I was uneasy about starting a new life in San Jose without money or connections with the university.

My father encouraged me to pursue the SJSU option. Both he and my mother were very supportive despite not understanding many of my decisions. I knew that they were deeply disappointed that I had left the seminary. Soon after I returned from Europe my mom asked me, "Have you ever thought about returning to the seminary?" I replied, "No. I'm on a different path now." She didn't bring up the question again, but I sensed that she still believed I had a vocation to the priesthood. She and my dad had nothing against TM, but they could not see me devoting my life to teaching Eastern meditation. They and my grandmother kept praying for me, and I know that their prayers greatly helped me to gradually discover God's will for my life.

I put off making a decision regarding SJSU as long as possible. Meanwhile I enjoyed quality time with my family, taught a few TM courses, and sang in a superb choir at St. Francis de Sales Cathedral in Oakland.

As the fall semester approached, I still had no clarity about what to do. Then an inspiration hit me. I remembered how my fears about the future dissolved as a result of engaging in two hours of daily prayer in front of the Blessed Sacrament at the monastery of la Pierre-qui-Vire. I decided to take my New Testament and Psalms and repeat the same practice at our family parish church until I received an answer to my question: "Lord, what do you want me to do?"

For six nights I knelt in prayer before the tabernacle for two hours, meditated on the scriptures, and asked the Lord for light. No light appeared. On the seventh night, despite all the insecurities, a gut feeling emerged from within me: "Go. Don't be afraid." The message brought me peace, which I interpreted as divine confirmation.

Full Time at the School of Music ▸

Shortly before the beginning of the 1973–74 fall semester, I registered at the university, packed my bike and other earthly possessions in my 1953 Oldsmobile "Rocket 88," and headed to San Jose. I located temporary housing at the Catholic Campus Ministry Center, was offered part-time employment as music director of Sacred Heart Church in San Jose and began full-time music studies at the university. I passed the auditions for

Dr. Archibeque's Concert Choir and her smaller Chamber Choir. I felt as if I were in a musical Disneyland.

Dr. Archibeque exceeded my expectations. From the first Concert Choir rehearsal, I realized that I was in the presence of a musical genius. She knew how to pull together the one hundred choir members into a coherent, enthusiastic ensemble. She chose challenging, inspiring repertoire—mostly religious: a Bach Cantata, Brahms's *Requiem*, Stravinsky's *Symphony of Psalms*, and Handel's *Messiah* in collaboration with the San Jose Symphony under the baton of George Cleve. Singing Handel's *Messiah* to a packed house at the Civic Auditorium was the most thrilling musical experience of my life. The SJSU School of Music attracted excellent musicians from around the state and beyond. I had not participated in such a stimulating musical environment since singing Gregorian chant with four hundred seminarians under the direction of Father John Olivier in high school.

Most of the ducks were in a row for a productive, fulfilling year except for a residence. No permanent housing was available at the Campus Ministry Center. I had insufficient funds to pay for student housing. I shared my dilemma with Father Moriarty, the pastor of Sacred Heart Parish. The next Sunday after the parish Mass, long-time parishioners Bob and Terry Johnston approached me and invited me to stay with them. They had several children, but a room was available. I liked the Johnstons a lot and was delighted with their generous offer. They housed and fed me the entire first semester, and they never asked me for a dime.

Meanwhile, I was saving up a bit of money from my small salary. As the semester neared an end, I felt that I should not continue to rely on the Johnston's generosity. Shortly after the new year of 1974, I offered a TM introductory lecture at a city library. After my presentation, two of the attendees, Rudy and Sharon Carino, approached me, motivated to take the four-day TM course, along with their four children. In the course of our conversation, I mentioned that I was looking for housing. They told me they lived on three acres of an old ranch in the San Jose foothills near Alum Rock Park. They had two small cabins on the property, one of which was available. They said that it needed some fixing up, but I was welcome to move in. As rent, they asked me to buy milk for the family (the four kids drank a lot of milk).

The next day I drove up to their property and discovered that "needed some fixing up" was an understatement. The small two-roomed L-shaped cabin originally was a stable for the ranch. It had neither running water nor insulation. Most of the windows were broken. Despite the primitive nature of the dwelling, I was rather excited by the prospects of living in such a rustic place. For years I had admired St. Francis of Assisi's commitment to simplicity of life, and I periodically longed to imitate him. So, I invited my parents, Dennis Stradford, and a carpenter friend to help me make the place livable.

When my parents arrived for the fix-up party, they were horrified by the sight of my new digs. But I assured them that I would be just fine in my new Spartan dwelling. We got to work repairing the roof and painting the walls. We installed a thick carpet to cover the cement floor, donated by Louise Benson,[1] a legendary woman in San Jose who operated a community services center out of her garage. We bought windows salvaged from an old house and moved in furniture my parents had brought from the family home: a bed, an easy chair, and a small oak round dining room table and chairs that my maternal grandparents bought after their wedding in 1919. Ma's oak table has traveled with me since that day.

I lived in what my parents called "Kevvy's Cabin" for a year. The Carino family lived fifty yards away in the original ranch house. They gave me full access to their kitchen and bathroom. The only discomfort occurred during cold winter nights when I had to get up in the middle of the night to relieve my bladder. I didn't want to disturb the family, so I simply did my business in the open field next to the cabin.

A Spiritual Experiment That Failed ▸

During my final weeks in Europe, I had followed a rich daily spiritual routine: Mass, thirty-minute sessions of Transcendental Meditation twice a day, and an hour meditating on the Word of God (*Lectio Divina*). When I returned to California, I was still on a spiritual high, and I

---

1. Louise Benson, assisted by Rex and Lee Lindsay, was the founder of what later came to be called "Sacred Heart Community Services" in San Jose.

assumed that the closeness I felt to God would continue almost automatically.

Because of my presumption, I became sloppy in my spiritual practices. While staying with my family in Alameda I attended Mass on Sundays and occasionally on weekdays. I practiced TM twice a day, but I neglected to practice *Lectio Divina* with any regularity, except for the seven days when I sought divine guidance regarding my SJSU decision.

I missed *Lectio Divina*. Once I was settled in my cabin, I tried to resume the practice. The first morning I rose early, knelt on the floor in front of my Bible, and started meditating on the Word of God. Soon I fell asleep. I was so exhausted after days of fixing up my new home that my body just wouldn't cooperate. "The spirit is willing but the flesh is weak" (Matthew 26:41). I decided that I would wait a few days until I caught up with my sleep before practicing *Lectio Divina*. However, I became so overextended with my classes, part-time job at the church, and two long bike rides each day to and from the university, that I kept making excuses for not resuming my practice. One justification was that I was practicing Transcendental Meditation twice a day. It provided me with a settled mind and refreshed body. However, it failed to nourish my conscious connection with God. Maharishi had taught us in La Antilla that TM is an excellent preparation for prayer, but it is not prayer. Failing to resume *Lectio Divina* proved to be a big mistake.

In what sense was failing to establish a daily prayer practice a big mistake? In my daily routine I gave precedence to intense activity rather than to conscious contact with God. This is the perennial delusion of people who have misplaced priorities, of people who believe that worldly pursuits will give them all the fulfillment they need. My gradual fall into that delusion not only was a sin of omission. It was irrational. My failure to continue with significant daily prayer progressively desensitized me to the will of God. It was also irrational because I knew from my European experiences that the highest and only enduring joy is to be found in a conscious, faithful relationship with the Lord.

As I look back on that period in my life, which began only a few months after the remarkable encounters I had had with God in London, Taizé, and la Pierre-qui-Vire, I am stunned by how soon I began to ignore certain life lessons learned from those encounters. Without realizing it I was conducting an experiment regarding the question: "What is the source of enduring joy?" I thought that the combination of an Eastern meditation practice that facilitates interior silence and the intense pursuit of worthwhile activities would make me happy. I also assumed that my connection with God would continue to be nourished by the powerful religious transformation I had experienced in the monasteries of Taizé and la Pierre-qui-Vire. I ignored the common danger of "backsliding." I forgot what Father Dunstan had told me when I excitedly shared with him my spiritual high that followed the month I spent meditating at Humboldt State University in 1971: "It's the long haul that counts." We can't rest on our laurels. We can't depend on previous spiritual experiences to sustain us on our journey through life, no matter how exalted.

We all want to be fully alive. Well-known atheists such as Richard Dawkins, Christopher Hitchens, and Sam Harris argue that belief in God destroys human freedom and self-realization. The great second-century Christian theologian St. Irenaeus of Lyon learned through abundant personal experience that the exact opposite is true. He famously said, "The glory of God is a human being fully alive."[2] This is the experience of every Christian saint since the time of the apostles.

I certainly was not adopting the beliefs of atheists, but I was unconsciously living according to one of their tenets: "I create my own life and destiny." I was on the common slippery slope toward minimizing the importance of conscious contact with God because of excessive activity and failure to devote significant time to meditative prayer each day. Without conscious contact, we easily fail to receive divine guidance because we don't ask the all-important question each day: "What do you want me to do, Lord?"

Fortunately, there remained in my life one important Catholic spiritual practice. I was very connected with the Sacred Heart parish community where I found inspiring worship and warm fellowship. My

---

2. "*Gloria Dei est vivens homo*," which is to say God receives glory when humans are truly alive, alive in God. St. Irenaeus (A.D. 130–202) was a Greek bishop noted for his role in leading Christian communities in what is now the south of France and, more widely, for the development of Christian theology by combating heresy and defining orthodoxy. See Irenaeus of Lyon, *Against Heresies* 4.20.5–7 (*Contre les hérésies*, Sources chrétiennes 100 [Paris: Cerf, 2002], 640–42, 644–48).

professional responsibilities at the parish included playing the organ at three Sunday Masses and directing the parish choir.

When I arrived at the parish in the fall there was no choir, so I recruited singers and began to train them as Dr. Archibeque was training me. Soon we had about twenty-five members, some of whom were excellent singers. I challenged them to learn difficult choral works. The weekly choir rehearsals were exciting. Not only did we sing inspiring sacred music from across the centuries, but the choir also became a close-knit Christian community. Our music and our transparent camaraderie became infectious. More and more people began attending Mass at Sacred Heart. My years at the parish demonstrated to me the power of well-prepared and properly celebrated Sacred Liturgy to bind together a worshiping community and to nourish souls.

That parish community became the center of my social life. I had friendly interactions with fellow students at the SJSU School of Music, but no significant relationships developed. I dated a couple of young women who sang with me in the Concert Choir, but we didn't have much in common. With the members of my parish choir, I felt more of a bond, especially with M.A. and her family. They often invited me over to dinner and treated me like a member of the family.

A Prophetic Dream ▸

Ever since attending the TM teacher-training course at Humboldt State University in 1971, I had been preoccupied with the relationship between Far Eastern and Christian spirituality and practices. A few months after I moved into my cabin, I had a dream that struck me as revelatory regarding that preoccupation. Having learned from my Jungian studies the value of dream analysis to reveal what's happening in one's unconscious, I was in the habit of recording in my journal dreams that struck me as significant. Upon awakening the morning of May 9, 1974, I knew that I had just had a "big" dream which I immediately recorded:

> Leo and I went on a long, marvelous trip through many lands in search of the source of the Ganges River. At one point we traveled through a dark jungle where dangers lurked. We came upon a party of Westerners who were being entertained by a tribe of primitive people. We dis-

covered that the people were cannibals and were about to eat the Westerners. So, we made a quick getaway, pursued by some members of the tribe.

After a long journey, we ascended the Himalayas and finally arrived at the source of the Ganges. The scene was incredibly powerful and beautiful. We stood on sheer cliffs overlooking torrents of water gushing out of the ground into the air and cascading into the river.

After some more adventures we said, "Now we can head home to Rome." We levitated and began flying through the air. Someone had told us to simply follow point sixty-four on our compass. The trip was gorgeous. We traveled through lush green valleys, above wooded mountains, and finally over the Mediterranean. We landed safely in Rome. Leo and I were elated and ready to undertake another journey.[3]

The meaning of the dream seemed clear to me. An important stage in my spiritual journey would involve a long and serious search for the wisdom of the East, as symbolized by the source of the Ganges River, the most sacred river of Hinduism.[4] My journey would include challenges and dangers along the way as I investigated Indian spirituality. Eventually I would reach my goal of discovering the "source," the core teachings of Vedanta. I would appropriate what I found to be true and valuable and then "return home to Rome," my original spiritual home (Roman Catholic Christianity). However, I was still in the early stages of my Eastern journey. Several more years would pass before I would be able to bring my investigations to a conclusion.

Withdrawing from the SJSU School of Music ▶

Sometimes the only way to discover whether a particular vocational goal is the right one is to pursue it without reservation and see what happens. While in Spain, Maharishi told us, "We often grow by fulfilling desires,

---

3. From my *Journal*, vol. 3 (December 1972–October 1974), 93–94.

4. The River <u>Ganges </u>flows 2,700 km from the Himalaya mountains to the Bay of Bengal in northern India and Bangladesh. Regarded as sacred by Hindus, the river is personified as the goddess Ganga in ancient texts and art. Ritual bathing in the Ganges is an important part of Hindu pilgrimages and the ashes of the cremated are often spread across her waters.

not by denying them. In that way we raise our level of desiring." He was referring to desires that are healthy and life-supporting. When I was trying to decide what to do after returning from Europe, the possibility of taking up a career in music attracted me. But I was not certain. When I sought divine guidance by means of a seven-day prayer campaign, I sensed that God was inspiring me to seriously check out the possibility.

I enjoyed my year of full-time music study immensely. I deepened my knowledge of music theory. I sang in two first-class choirs directed by one of the best choral conductors in the state. I mastered the art of forming and directing a large parish choir. I became skilled at playing a wide variety of advanced organ repertoire. At the end of the year, I felt a deep sense of satisfaction. I had worked hard and achieved my musical goals. At the same time, I arrived at the conclusion that music was to be only an accompaniment to my life. It would not be my life. "Now what?" I asked myself.

During my year at the School of Music, I had a tangential relationship with the San Jose TM Center. Occasionally I would give introductory lectures at community centers and schools and teach the four-day course of meditation instruction. I felt some desire to continue teaching TM, but TM teachers don't make much money and I needed income. I decided to continue with my part-time position as music director of Sacred Heart and look for a full-time job.

At that time Leo found himself in similar circumstances. He had decided not to go through with ordination to the priesthood but had no other immediate plans. He had just painted the kitchen of a neighbor and he asked me if I would like to form a temporary painting "company" with him. Neither one of us knew much about painting, but we did have contacts with people whose homes needed painting. I did wonder how two ex-seminarians with almost no experience painting houses were going to succeed in this business proposal. But I had an adventurous spirit, and the time was ripe for a new adventure.

Painting Our Way to Hawaii ➤

Once Leo and I had decided to try our hands at house-painting, we bought a long extension ladder and painting equipment and began contacting family and friends who might be looking for energetic painters. We avoided telling people that we had almost no experience painting houses. Fortunately, people trusted us to do a good job. Frankly, I was surprised by how well the jobs turned out. People were very pleased with our work and impressed by our competitive prices. One satisfied customer after another spread the word and, before we knew it, we had enough work for the entire summer of 1974.

The most enjoyable painting project of the summer was my grandmother's beautiful old Tudor-Revival house in Alameda. She only wanted the woodwork painted. However, for a Tudor-style home, that meant half the house—including fifty windows. We calculated that the job would probably require three weeks, so I moved into my grandmother's house for the duration. Ma would only live four more years, so the opportunity to stay with her during those three weeks and enjoy her loving company was an enormous blessing. Ma insisted on preparing lunch for us daily. She served it in her back yard gazebo, where Leo would have us in stitches with his uproarious sense of humor. It was a summer for which I am immensely thankful.

Our last paint job was on Bay Farm Island just north of the Oakland Airport. The house we were painting in the late summer was near the bay. Mark Twain once said that the coldest winter he ever experienced was summer in San Francisco! The warm summer air from inland meets with the cold air from the northern Pacific Ocean and creates thick fog hovering over San Francisco and its environs. The late summer of 1974 felt like the coldest on record.

One day when Leo and I were on the roof painting the eaves, shivering as if we were in the Arctic Circle, Leo blurted out, "Let's go to Hawaii!" "What a great idea," I responded through my chattering teeth. That ended our illustrious painting career. We finished the job, took some of our earnings, and flew to Oahu for the month of October. Father Gene Konkel, my good friend from St. Joseph's College, oversaw a retreat center on Oahu. He was happy to host us and didn't charge us a penny. We worked for our keep by cooking for a couple of weekend retreats.

I was no cook. But just as my lack of painting skills didn't prevent me from serving as a partner in a painting "company," my lack of cooking skills didn't prevent me from saying "yes" when Father Konkel asked us if we could prepare three meals a day for seventy people on two weekend retreats. I did fear that that the old adage might apply—"fools enter where angels fear to tread." But Leo saved the day. During his early years as a Dominican seminarian, he was assigned periodically to cook for a large seminary community. In true Leo fashion, he didn't cook humdrum, unexciting dishes. He cooked like a French chef. Those attending the retreat couldn't believe the gourmet *coq au vin* (aka "Drunken Chicken") and *boeuf bourguignon* that we produced.

When we weren't cooking, Leo and I enjoyed the splendid beaches of Oahu and went body surfing with the Trask family, old family friends who had migrated to the islands. After a couple of weeks of living the beach life, I needed some intellectual stimulation. I read a book that led me on a new path to the source of the Ganges.

16

Encountering Buddhism in Hawaii

DURING THE MONTH IN HAWAII, I READ *In My Own Way: An Autobiography*, by Alan Watts (d. 1973), a prominent writer in the 1960s known for popularizing Buddhism for a Western audience. The book reawakened my interest in Buddhist teachings and meditation that had begun in college when I read Thomas Merton's *Mystics and Zen Masters* and William Johnston's *Christian Zen*. Johnston's book presents a study of Zen meditation in the light of Christian mysticism.[1] Reading these works on Buddhism by Christians stimulated me later to read books by prominent Buddhists: *The Good Heart: A Buddhist Perspective on the Teachings of Jesus*, by the Dalai Lama (the worldwide leader of Tibetan Buddhism), and *Living Buddha, Living Christ*, by the Vietnamese Buddhist monk, Thich Nhat Hanh.[2]

    I was also inspired to study Buddhism by the significant dream I had had the previous year about traveling to the source of the Ganges. As I reported in the previous chapter, I interpreted the dream to mean that an important stage in my spiritual journey would involve a long and serious search for the wisdom of the East as symbolized by the source of the Ganges River, the most sacred river of India. Along with the Vedic-Hindu

---

    1. Johnston is a Jesuit priest who completed a doctorate in mystical theology at Sophia University, Tokyo. Throughout his forty years living and teaching at the same university, he engaged in Buddhist–Christian dialogue.

    2. Thich Nhat Hanh was nominated for the Nobel Peace Prize by Rev. Martin Luther King Jr. in 1967.

tradition, Buddhism is the other most significant spiritual tradition to have originated in India.

There exists a search on the part of many Westerners for spiritual guidance from Buddhist teachings and practices. People ask me periodically how Christian doctrines regarding the soul, the spiritual path, God, Christ, and the afterlife compare with Buddhist teachings. Before sharing my research and reflections on some of these important questions, I would like to present the Catholic context for interreligious dialogue.

The Catholic Approach to Interreligious Dialogue ▸

The highest teaching authority in the Catholic Church is an Ecumenical Council authorized by the pope.[3] These councils are assemblies of bishops and other ecclesiastical representatives of the whole world, whose decisions on doctrine, worship, and discipline are considered by Catholics to be guided by the Holy Spirit and, thus, authoritative. The most recent Ecumenical Council was the Second Vatican Council, which met in Rome from 1962 to 1965.[4] It spoke directly about the dialogue between Catholicism and the other great world religions in its "Declaration on the Relationship of the Church to Non-Christian Religions" (the Latin title is *Nostra Aetate*). Its opening paragraph presents the spirit of the document:

> In this age of ours, when people are drawing more closely together and the bonds of friendship between different peoples are being strengthened, the Church examines with greater care the relation which she has to non-Christian religions. Ever aware of her duty to foster unity and charity among individuals, and even among nations, she reflects at the outset on what people have in common and what tends to promote fellowship among them.[5]

---

3. "Ecumenical" comes from the Greek *oikoumenē* ("the whole inhabited world").
4. Vatican II was a monumental task. It took four years of preparations and multiple sessions of debates over three years. Almost three thousand bishops, heads of religious orders, and theologians from all over the world participated in the council.
5. "Declaration on the Relationship of the Church to Non-Christian Religions,"

The document proceeds to examine how people look to their religions for answers to the perennial and universal questions and problems that affect them, such as, What is the human person? What is the meaning and purpose of Life? Where does suffering originate? How can genuine happiness be found? What happens at death?[6]

With regard to Hinduism and Buddhism, the Vatican Council's document (*Nostra Aetate*) makes a few brief observations on how these religions respond to some of the fundamental questions:

> ... in Hinduism people explore the divine mystery and express it both in the limitless riches of myth and the accurately defined insights of philosophy. They seek release from the trials of the present life by ascetical practices, profound meditation, and recourse to God in confidence and love.[7]

> Buddhism in its various forms testifies to the essential inadequacy of this changing world. It proposes a way of life by which people can, with confidence and trust, attain a state of perfect liberation and reach supreme illumination either through their own efforts or by the aid of divine help.[8]

In these brief excerpts, we can see that the Catholic Church respects and admires various teachings and practices of Asian religions. *Nostra Aetate* states:

> The Catholic Church rejects nothing of what is true and holy in these religions. She has a high regard for the manner of life and conduct, the precepts and doctrines which, although differing in many ways from her own teaching, nevertheless often reflect a ray of that truth which enlightens all people.[9]

At the same time, the Council invites people of all religions to seriously consider the truth claims Jesus Christ makes about himself and about what he offers humanity:

Vatican Council II: The Conciliar and Postconciliar Documents, ed. Austin P. Flannery, O.P. (1975; repr., Northport, NY: Costello, 1996), 738.
   6. Ibid.
   7. Ibid.
   8. Ibid., 739
   9. Ibid.

Yet [the Church] proclaims and is in duty bound to proclaim without fail, Christ who is the way, the truth and the life (John 14:6). In him, in whom God reconciled all things to himself (2 Corinthians 5:18–19), people find the fullness of their religious life.[10]

Having looked at the official Catholic approach toward dialogue with other religions, I will share some of my reflections regarding Buddhism.

When I began to study Buddhism, I wanted to know why many former Christians have embraced Buddhism during the past few decades. What was missing in their Christian experience? To answer that question, I needed to understand the Buddhist tradition and compare and contrast it with Christianity.

Fundamental Buddhist Teachings ▸

Buddhism is often seen as a reform of the Vedic-Hindu tradition (which I introduced in chapter 7). Buddhism was founded by an Indian prince, Siddhartha Gautama, born in what is now Nepal around 560 B.C. Tradition has it that, in his late twenties, he began to leave his sheltered royal life and encountered much suffering in the world around him. He was overwhelmed by the misery and asked why there was so much suffering. At age twenty-nine he left his wife, children, and home to seek a solution to the problem of suffering. At age thirty-five, through meditation and austere ascetical practices, he claimed to find the solution, became enlightened, and henceforth became known as the Buddha—the "enlightened one."

"Four Noble Truths" constitute the essence of Buddha's teachings.[11] The First Truth identifies the reality of suffering. The Second Truth seeks to determine the cause of suffering. According to the Buddha, desire and ignorance lie at the root of suffering. By desire, Buddhists refer to craving pleasure, material goods, and immortality, all of which are wants that Buddhists believe can never be satisfied. As a result, desiring them can bring only suffering. Ignorance, in comparison, means not

---

10. Ibid.
11. Roy C. Amore, "Four Noble Truths, *The Perennial Dictionary of World Religions*, ed. Keith Crim (Harper & Row, 1989), 264–66.

seeing the world as it actually is. Without the capacity for mental concentration and insight, one's mind is left undeveloped, unable to grasp the true nature of things. Vices, such as greed, envy, hatred, and anger, derive from this ignorance.

The Third Noble Truth claims that suffering can end through achieving Enlightenment, called "Nirvana," the ultimate goal of Buddhism. Nirvana is described in part as a perfectly peaceful and illumined state of consciousness in which passions and ignorance are extinguished.

The Fourth Noble Truth charts the path to Nirvana called the Noble Eightfold Path. The steps of the path are Right Understanding, Right Thought, Right Speech, Right Action, Right Livelihood, Right Effort, Right Mindfulness, and Right Concentration. Moreover, there are three themes into which the Path is divided: good moral conduct, meditation and mental development, and wisdom or insight.

Here we find striking similarities and significant differences between Buddhism and Christianity. Both traditions conclude that much human suffering arises from unhealthy attachments and habits. In the teachings of early Christian spiritual masters, the Desert Fathers and Mothers (the "Desert Monks") of the third to fifth centuries, we find deep and detailed analyses of nine afflictions of the soul—mental and emotional habits that sabotage human happiness and relationships: gluttony, unchastity, greed, anger, melancholy, acedia (spiritual laziness), envy, thirst for esteem, and spiritual pride. One of the greatest masters, St. John Cassian (b. A.D. 360), explains in his seminal work *The Conferences* how to reach liberation from the afflictions.[12] Two helpful contemporary presentations of the teachings are found in *Thoughts Matter: The Practice of the Spiritual Life*, by a Benedictine nun, Margaret Mary Funk,[13] and in *Heaven Begins within You: Wisdom from the Desert Fathers*, by a monk-psychologist Anselm Gruen.[14]

---

12. Note especially "Fifth Conference—The Conference of Abba Serapion: On the Eight Principal Vices," in John Cassian, *The Conferences*, trans. Boniface Ramsey, O.P. (Ancient Christian Writers 57; New York: Newman Press, 1997), 177–209.

13. Mary Margaret Funk, *Thoughts Matter: The Practice of the Spiritual Life* (New York: Continuum, 2002).

14. Anselm Gruen, *Heaven Begins within You: Wisdom from the Desert Fathers* (New York: Crossroad, 1999).

Salvation in Buddhism and Christianity

The teachings of the Desert Monks embrace much of what is contained in the Buddhist Noble Eightfold Path. The three themes of the Eightfold Path are prominent in the lives and sayings of the Desert Monks: good moral conduct, meditation and mental development, and wisdom.

The fundamental difference between the Buddhist and Christian approaches to liberation from afflictions of the soul has to do with the question, Where do we find the power to change our unhealthy desires and habits? The Buddha taught that no one saves us but ourselves:

> By oneself the evil is done, and it is oneself who suffers. By oneself the evil is not done, and by oneself one becomes pure. The pure and the impure come from oneself: no man can purify another.[15]

In this saying, Buddha taught that we can only depend on our own efforts and spiritual practices to achieve liberation. He does not speak about a "Higher Power." Christianity teaches something quite different. The Desert Monks discovered through the Bible and from personal experience that they could not save themselves. They could not find liberation from unhealthy desires and habits through their own efforts alone. On the one hand, they knew that they had to do their part in seeking liberation and healing from the afflictions. They had to engage in spiritual disciplines such as the sacraments, fasting, meditation, vigilance over their thoughts, obeying the commandments, and apprenticing with a master. On the other hand, they knew that the ultimate purpose of each one of these spiritual disciplines can be realized only with the help of God.

St. Paul called the divine gift that leads to liberation and salvation "grace." Grace is the self-communication of God to a human being.[16]

---

15. *The Dhammapada: the Path of Perfection*, trans. Juan Mascaró (Harmondsworth: Penguin Books, 1973), Saying 165, p. 59.
16. Catholic theology describes "grace" as God's personal condescension and absolutely gratuitous clemency to human beings; but grace also signifies the effect of this clemency, in which God communicates himself to human beings. See Karl Rahner and Herbert Vorgrimler, "Grace," *Dictionary of Theology* (2nd ed.; New York: Crossroad, 1990), 196.

> For by grace you have been saved through faith, and this is not from you; it is the gift of God; it is not from works, so no one may boast. (Ephesians 2:8–9)

Christian experience and teaching assert that human beings reach liberation from unhealthy thoughts and habits through the grace of God that is accessed by faith in Jesus Christ. In the widest sense, faith means "freely accepting what a person says because of one's confidence in that person. This is to say that faith always entails a relationship between persons which stands or falls with the credibility of the person who is believed."[17] The Christian experience of faith in Christ finds a foreshadowing in the Hebrew Scriptures, in which faith is presented as a personal relationship between God and a human being who believes in what God has revealed and in his promises. The primordial example is Abraham, who, as an old man, believed the divine promise that he would have descendants as numerous as the "stars of the sky" (Genesis 15:6), and so it happened.

St. Paul struggled mightily with certain sinful inclinations and habits. In chapter 7 of his Letter to the Romans he presents his struggles with extreme realism:

> What I do I do not understand. For I do not do what I want, but I do what I hate.... The willing is ready at hand, but doing the good is not. For I do not do the good I want, but I do the evil I do not want. Now if I do what I do not want, it is no longer I who do it, but sin that dwells in me.... For I take delight in the law of God in my inner self, but I see in my members another principle at war with the law of my mind, taking me captive to the law of sin that dwells in my members. Miserable one that I am! Who will deliver me from this mortal body? (Romans 7:15–24)

All of us who have struggled with an obsession, compulsion, or addiction can identify with this passage. St. Paul also invites us to identify with the marvelous breakthrough that led him to liberation and healing. In the verse immediately following his description of the struggles he exclaims, "Thanks be to God through Jesus Christ our Lord." Paul came to realize through his own experience the power of Jesus Christ to save human beings.

---

17. Rahner and Vorgrimler, "Faith," *Dictionary of Theology*, 167.

"To save" in the New Testament refers to the saving not only of one's soul after death but also to the thousand and one ways Jesus Christ saves and heals his disciples in their daily struggles and dysfunctions.[18] The key to accessing that saving power is *faith* in its full biblical meaning.

St. Paul's struggles and breakthrough are echoed in the first three steps of the Twelve-Step program developed by Alcoholics Anonymous:

Step One: We admitted we were powerless over alcohol—that our lives had become unmanageable.
Step Two: Came to believe that a Power greater than ourselves could restore us to sanity.
Step Three: Made a decision to turn our will and our lives over to the care of God *as we understood Him.*[19]

Millions of people have entered into recovery through the Twelve-Step program when they came to realize that they could not save themselves. They needed a higher power. They needed a saving God. People can practice meditation for years and find calmness of mind and release of stress, but still be under the influence of unhealthy attractions, aversions, and addictions. The Twelve-Step programs testify through abundant experience that, with the help of the Higher Power, people can enter and remain in recovery. This is the promise of the New Testament. Having experienced liberation, St. Paul writes:

> . . . put away the old self of your former way of life, corrupted through deceitful desires, and be renewed in the spirit of your minds, and put on the new self, created in God's way in righteousness and holiness of truth. (Ephesians 4:22–24)

Understandings of Jesus Christ ▸

Buddhism does not admit in its teachings the existence of God or that of a Savior. With regard to who Jesus Christ is, the Dalai Lama says,

---

18. "Salvation" comes from the Latin *salvare*, "to make safe, secure." The English "salve" comes from the Latin *salvus*, "uninjured, in good health, safe." This is from the root *sol-* "whole."

19. *Twelve Steps and Twelve Traditions* (New York: Alcoholics Anonymous World Services, Inc., 2003), 5.

"For me, as a Buddhist, my attitude toward Jesus Christ is that he was either a fully enlightened being or a bodhisattva of a very high spiritual realization."[20]

The Dalai Lama is a great and wise sage. Christians who listen to him can find much to admire and accept. But his perception of Jesus differs radically from Jesus's own self-perception. Jesus had clarity about his identity. In his lifetime some wanted him to be a political leader or a revolutionary Messiah to free the Jews from Roman oppression, but he refused. Some saw him as a great teacher and sage, but he claimed to be much more. He spoke words that had never before been spoken in Israel: "Before Abraham was, I am" (John 8:58); "The Father and I are one" (John 10:30). The religious leaders who heard him speak these words picked up rocks to stone him saying, "You, a man, are making yourself God" (John 10:33).

Directly and indirectly throughout his life Jesus said he was God. In the Gospels he referred to himself as the "Son of Man" eighty times.[21] The Book of the great Jewish prophet Daniel presents a vision concerning a coming "Son of Man" who will exercise dominion, glory, and kingship:

> As the visions during the night continued, I saw coming with the clouds of heaven One like a son of man. When he reached the Ancient of Days and was presented before him, He received dominion, splendor, and kingship; all nations, peoples and tongues will serve him. His dominion is an everlasting dominion that shall not pass away, his kingship, one that shall not be destroyed. (Daniel 7:13–14)

In claiming to be the fulfillment of Daniel's prophecy, Jesus was proclaiming: "Every nation will worship me. . . . People of every language will serve me. . . . My dominion is divine." At his trial before the chief priests and Sanhedrin,[22] the high priest asked Jesus: "Are you the Messiah, the son of the Blessed One?" Then Jesus answered:

---

20. His Holiness the Dalai Lama, *The Good Heart: A Buddhist Perspective on the Teachings of Jesus* (Boston: Wisdom Publications, 1996), 83. Buddhists consider a "bodhisattva" to be a liberated soul who chooses to come back after death in order to serve humanity.
21. Matthew Kelly, *Rediscover Jesus: An Invitation* (Boston: Beacon, 2015), 32.
22. The Sanhedrin was the supreme council of the Jews.

> I am;
> and you will see the Son of Man
> seated at the right hand of the Power
> and coming with the clouds of heaven.
>
>   At that the high priest tore his garments and said, "What further need have we of witnesses? You have heard the blasphemy. What do you think?" They all condemned him as deserving to die. (Mark 14:61–64)

Jesus was crucified because he claimed to be the fulfillment of Daniel's vision. He claimed to be the incarnation of the God of Israel, the one God who created and maintains the universe.

C. S. Lewis, the renowned twentieth-century author of *The Chronicles of Narnia*, maintains that there are only three reasonable interpretations of Jesus's claims. In his book, *Mere Christianity*, he writes:

> A man who was merely a man and said the sort of things Jesus said would not be a great moral teacher. He would either be a lunatic—on the level with a man who says he is a poached egg—or he would be the devil of hell. You must take your choice. Either this was, and is, the Son of God, or else a madman or something worse. You can shut him up for a fool or you can fall at his feet and call him Lord and God. But let us not come with any patronizing nonsense about his being a great human teacher. He has not left that open to us. He did not intend to.[23]

The three possible interpretations of Jesus's claims according to C. S. Lewis are "liar, lunatic, or Lord." Lewis and all the great saints and theologians throughout Christian history are convinced: Jesus *is* who he claimed to be.

God and the Afterlife ▸

The claim of Jesus to be God would have no meaning unless God exists. As I read the literature about Buddhism, I appreciated the mental training it offers in the process of moving toward liberation from afflictions of the soul. I was surprised, however, that the Buddha and

---

23. C. S. Lewis, *Mere Christianity* (1955; repr., Westwood, NJ: Barbour, 1985), 45.

his tradition failed to recognize the most powerful element in the liberation process: the power of God. The Dalai Lama states explicitly, "Buddhism [is] a nontheistic religion."[24] He affirms that Christians and Buddhists must "part company" with regard to the existence of a Creator God:

> The entire Buddhist worldview is based on a philosophical standpoint in which the central thought is the principle of interdependence, how all things and events come into being purely as a result of interactions between causes and conditions. Within that philosophical worldview it is almost impossible to have any room for an atemporal, eternal, absolute truth. Nor is it possible to accommodate the concept of a divine Creation. Similarly, for a Christian whose entire metaphysical worldview is based on a belief in the Creation and a divine Creator, the idea that all things and events arise out of mere interaction between causes and conditions has no place within that worldview. So, in the realm of metaphysics, it becomes problematic at a certain point, and the two traditions must diverge.[25]

In response to the Dalai Lama's contention that "all things and events come into being purely as a result of interactions between causes and conditions," the Christian tradition—and many scientists—would ask, what is the source of the "causes and conditions"? Astrophysicists generally agree that time and space must find their origin in something beyond time and space. Their conviction echoes philosophical arguments for the existence of God laid out by Thomas Aquinas, the greatest Catholic theologian of the thirteenth century. The arguments point to a sourceless source for all created reality. The eminent contemporary theologian Bishop Robert Barron explains:

> God is not a being in the world, one object, however supreme, among many. The maker of the entire universe cannot be, himself, an item within the universe, and the one who is responsible for the nexus of causal relations in its entirety could never be a missing link in an ordinary scientific schema. Thomas Aquinas makes the decisive point when he says that God is not *ens summum* (highest being) but rather *ipsum esse* (the sheer act of Being itself). God is neither a thing in the

---

24. The Dalai Lama, *Good Heart*, 74.
25. Ibid., 82.

world, nor the sum total of existing things; he is instead the unconditioned cause of the conditioned universe, the reason why there is something rather than nothing. Accordingly, God is not some good thing but Goodness itself; not some true object, but Truth itself; not some beautiful reality, but Beauty itself.[26]

Barron explains that God cannot be some being in the universe like a mountain, or a human being, or a star. If he were one being among other beings, then the universe plus God would be more than God. Whereas God is the sourceless source of everything that exists.[27]

Buddhist practices that contribute to liberation from attachments would be considered by Christians as representative of "natural mysticism" as would the experience of enlightenment. The ultimate liberation goes beyond enlightenment to union between the human person and God. This is a gift received through the grace of God—a state of spiritual development possible only through "supernatural mysticism" (a gift from God). After death, the liberated soul enters into the Beatific Vision of God in the kingdom of heaven. The soul then lives eternally in a personal, blissful communion with God and all the angels and saints. St. Paul writes,

> Our citizenship is in heaven, whence we long for the Lord Jesus Christ, our Savior, who will come to transform our lowly body into a likeness of His glorious body, by the power that enables Him to subject the entire universe to Himself. (Philippians 3:20)[28]

From reading the Buddhist literature I concluded that it coincides with Christianity in its analysis of one of the main sources of suffering, namely, unhealthy desires and attachments, while it departs from Christianity in its presentation of the cure and in its understanding of the ultimate state of transformation. Christian saints unanimously report that the highest state of the spiritual journey is union with God, whereas

---

26. Robert Barron, *Seeds of the Word: Finding God in the Culture* (Park Ridge, IL: Word on Fire Catholic Ministries, 2017), 233–34.

27. See Barron's exposition regarding the existence of God in his book *To Light a Fire on the Earth: Proclaiming the Gospel in a Secular Age* (New York: Image, 2017), 191–96.

28. See Xavier Léon-Dufour, "Heaven," *Dictionary of Biblical Theology*, 2nd ed. (New York: Crossroad, 1973), 229–32.

Buddhists believe that the highest state is Nirvana ("enlightenment"), a state of illumined consciousness and freedom from attachments. Buddhists teach that "anyone who has not achieved enlightenment will be reborn as a god, a human, an animal, a ghost, or a denizen of hell."[29] This rebirth in a new body is called "reincarnation."

Belief in reincarnation is prominent in Buddhism and Hinduism. Reincarnation is described as "the process by which the soul of a dead person enters another body in order to continue its existence."[30] According to this teaching, the body is not an essential part of the human person. The person goes from life to life assuming a new body in each life.

In contrast, Christians believe that the body is essential. Christians firmly believe in the *resurrection of the body*. Christ rose from the dead in the very body that had died on the cross. The New Testament affirms that the bodies of all human beings will also be resurrected on the last day and rejoined to their souls for the final judgment and then go on to their eternal destination. This resurrected body, like that of the risen Christ, will be different from our earthly bodies in that it will be more refined and more like the angelic nature. However, it will still be the body of the same human being, miraculously restored and made fit by God for eternal life. In heaven the redeemed will recognize each other and rejoice eternally in a loving fellowship with Christ and all the angels and saints. The body is an essential part of the whole person who will live forever.

Meditation Practices ▸

An area where Buddhists and Christians can find some common ground has to do with meditation practices. Two Buddhist methods have become popular in the West: Zazen and the practice of Mindfulness.

---

29. Charles R. Taber, "Reincarnation," *Perennial Dictionary of World Religions*, 609.
30. Ibid., 608. Buddhism teaches that the "aggregates," not a soul, is reincarnated. According to Buddhist thought, the person is composed of five aggregates (*Skandas*): matter, sensation, perception, predisposition, and consciousness, "every one of which is constantly arising. At every moment in our life, we are a temporary combination of the five aggregates." See Kenneth K. S. Ch'en, "Buddhism," *Perennial Dictionary of World Religions*, 127.

Zazen (literally, "sitting cross-legged in meditation") is the basic discipline of the Zen school of Buddhism, in which the body is immobilized in the traditional Lotus posture, breathing is regulated, and one attempts to unify the mind in a profound concentration.[31]

Mindfulness is the psychological process of purposely bringing one's attention to experiences occurring in the present moment without judgment.[32] One practice is to sit erect, close one's eyes and bring attention to either the sensations of breathing in the proximity of one's nostrils or to the movements of the abdomen when breathing in and out.

Another mindfulness practice is body-scan meditation by which the attention is directed at various areas of the body and noting body sensations that happen in the present moment.

The primary Catholic meditation practice in the West is *Lectio Divina* (described at the end of chapter 2). The primary meditation practice of Eastern Christianity (Orthodox and Catholic) is the "Jesus Prayer," a short invocation, designed for mental repetition and addressed to the Savior. A common form among Eastern Christians is "Lord Jesus Christ, have mercy on me."[33]

Teachers of the Jesus Prayer note that Jesus expressed approval of a way of prayer that involves repetition of a sacred phrase in his parable of the Pharisee and the tax collector:

> The tax collector, standing afar off, would not so much as raise his eyes to heaven, but beat his breast, saying: "God, be merciful to me a sinner." (Luke 18:13)

Interpreting this passage, St. Gregory Palamas (1296–1359) notes that the tax collector persisted with his prayer of a single phrase, paying attention only to himself and God. Palamas finds in the parable encouragement to practice meditative prayer that leads to stillness (*hēsychia*) and as the best way to receive mercy from God.

---

31. Clifford W. Edwards, "Zazen," *Perennial Dictionary of World Religions*, 821.

32. Most of the information in this section comes from web articles on "Mindfulness."

33. Kallistos Ware, "Ways of Prayer and Contemplation: Eastern," in *Christian Spirituality: Origins to the Twelfth Century*, ed. Bernard McGinn and John Meyendorff, World Spirituality 16 (New York: Crossroad, 1985), 395–414, here 402.

> It is the most perfect prayer. It is prayer of a single word, it contains deep penitence, the body participates in the prayer since it too will receive the grace of God, and the prayer has an atmosphere of self-reproach.[34]

Jesus taught his disciples to pray in his name (John 14:12-13). Some early Christians began to repeatedly invoke the name of Jesus as a way of prayer, both in the Sacred Liturgy and as a way of personal meditation.

The Jesus Prayer has been called a "Christian mantra," but this is misleading. The great Orthodox scholar of Eastern Christianity Kallistos Ware insists that the Jesus Prayer implies a personal relationship with Jesus and a consciously held belief in the Incarnation. The aim is not simply the suspension of thought and the entering into interior silence, but an encounter with Someone. The prayer is addressed directly to Jesus and embodies an explicit confession of faith in him as the incarnate Son of God. "Without this personal relationship, without this explicit confession of faith, there is no Jesus Prayer."[35]

In the late medieval period, St. Gregory of Sinai (1255–1346) initiated a revitalization of the Jesus Prayer among the monks of Mount Athos.[36] He recommended a faith-filled mental repetition of the simple phrase, "Jesus, have mercy on me."

The noted Jesuit scholar William Johnston found that silent meditation can be a meeting place for people of different religious traditions:

> I find that the silence of mysticism is our best meeting point as followers of different religions. It is here that we can be united; it is here that we can meditate together. Many years ago I joined a group of Buddhists and Christians who meditated together in the shrine city of Kamakura outside Tokyo. We all sat in silence, so what the others were doing interiorly I do not know. But I do know that we

---

34. Metropolitan of Nafpaktos Hierotheos, *Orthodox Psychotherapy: The Science of the Fathers* (Akrefnio, Greece: Birth of the Theotokos Monastery, 2002), 329.

35. Ware, "Ways of Prayer and Contemplation, Eastern, 403.

36. Jean Leclercq, François Vandenbroucke, and Louis Bouyer, *The Spirituality of the Middle Ages*, History of Christian Spirituality 2 (Minneapolis: Seabury Press, 1982), 583. Mount Athos is one of the three peninsulas in Greece; it is populated by about twenty thousand monks in twenty monasteries.

became good friends, and that made it an excellent dialogue. I believe that mystical silence is the best meeting place for the great religions.[37]

Comparing Buddhist with Christian meditation, we find a common emphasis on stillness and silence but a difference in contexts and goals. Christian meditation is practiced in the context of a personal relationship with God, whereas Buddhism is a nontheistic religion. Buddhist meditation is one practice of the Eightfold Path toward Nirvana, while Christians meditate primarily to move toward greater intimacy with the Lord. A secondary consequence is freedom from unhealthy desires and habits.

The Fruit of the Hawaiian Experience ▶

After a month of intense reflection on the Buddhist and Christian experiences of meditation, I felt the need to enter more deeply into my own meditation practice. I decided to attend a six-week advanced meditation course at a TM academy on Cobb Mountain in Northern California. There I would have the opportunity to slow down after a year and a half of non-stop activity and enjoy the silence of long meditations. I didn't realize that the course would also lead me in a new vocational direction.

---

37. William Johnston, "In Mystic Silence: Where East and West Can Meet" *Faith in Focus*, November 19, 2007.

17

Teaching Meditation during the "Boom"

AFTER A YEAR OF INTENSE STUDY AT THE SJSU SCHOOL OF Music, a summer painting houses, a month of bodysurfing and studying Buddhism in Oahu, I longed for a retreat and interior renewal. I also was considering the possibility of teaching meditation full-time. A year and a half had passed since I had completed the TM teacher-training in Spain. I needed some retooling to be an effective TM teacher. The advanced meditation course at the TM academy on Cobb Mountain would be similar to those I attended at Humboldt State University and in Spain, during which we would meditate for a couple of hours in the morning and evening using the advanced meditation practice called "rounding."[1]

The academy on Cobb Mountain had once been Hoberg's Resort, a rural fifty-three-acre mountaintop property in Lake County, California. The TM organization purchased the property in the 1970s and transformed it into a retreat and conference center.[2] The course was offered after the Thanksgiving holiday in 1974.

---

1. "Rounding was explained in chapter 7. A "round" consists of ten minutes of yoga postures (asanas), five minutes of a simple breathing exercise (pranayama), and thirty minutes of the Transcendental Meditation technique.

2. The resort/academy on Cobb Mountain was destroyed in the Valley Fire on September 12, 2015.

Six Weeks on Cobb Mountain ▸

The academy was an ideal place for R & R. It was located far from any city, several miles up a mountain road, nestled within a secluded forest. The facilities were rustic but comfortable. Many course participants had individual cottages. Others lodged in log-cabin motel structures.

Upon arrival, I parked my 1953 Oldsmobile "Rocket 88" next to a Bentley. Comparing my old Rocket 88 to that luxurious automobile, I wondered if I would be out of my league on the course. I soon learned that the Bentley belonged to Mike Love of the Beach Boys.[3] Until that moment I did not know that Mike Love had been trained as a TM teacher. On the course he pretty much kept to himself and was unpretentious despite being a rock star.

After registration, I joined an informal gathering of course participants in the dining room for some snacks and socializing. Most of us were in our mid-twenties or early thirties. About half were female. Since my departure from the university, I hadn't spent much time with women my age and I was interested in correcting that deficit. I found that being a musician helped. During the course, the participants organized a talent show for which I volunteered to play the piano, including Claude Debussy's very romantic *Clair de Lune*. One afternoon when I was practicing the piece in the lodge, a young blond woman approached me from behind, grabbed my face and smothered me with a big kiss. When I came up for air, she made a hasty exit. Later she said that she found my music irresistible. I use this story to encourage young men to learn to play the piano and to practice with passion!

Returning to the account of my first day on the course, after dinner the sixty-five course participants gathered in a conference room. The course leader laid out the daily schedule:

- Two hours of rounding in the morning
- A conference and videotape of Maharishi after lunch

---

3. The Beach Boys rock band formed in California in 1961. The group's original lineup consisted of brothers Brian, Dennis, and Carl Wilson, their cousin Mike Love, and their friend Al Jardine. Distinguished by their vocal harmonies and early surf songs, they are one of the most influential groups of the rock era.

- Two hours of rounding in the afternoon
- A conference and videotape after dinner
- Silence after the conference until breakfast the next morning

I relished the opportunity to catch up on my sleep, to spend several hours a day in meditation and prayer, and to continue studying the teachings of Maharishi. After six weeks, I emerged energized to begin a new chapter in my spiritual journey and vocational quest.

Teaching Meditation ▶

Upon returning to San Jose in January of 1975, I was met with good news from the Carino family (my landlords) that the other cottage on their property had become available. It was the size of a large studio apartment and had running water! Not only water but a kitchen and bathroom. I said farewell to my Franciscan stable-turned-cabin, and moved next door. No longer would I have to make trips to the open field in the middle of a cold night!

Soon I made contact with the San Jose TM center, which was run by two couples out of a rented tract home. It was a small operation. Only ten to twelve people signed up for the weekly four-day course of instruction. The two couples were happy to have me join the operation, but they could not offer me a salary unless more people signed up for the weekly course. At the same time, I was rehired by Sacred Heart Church as part-time music director, which provided me with sufficient funds to cover food and rent.

I began to schedule introductory TM lectures at public libraries, high schools, and colleges. Volunteers and I would go to local businesses and ask the owners for permission to place posters in their windows announcing the lectures. Soon, increasing numbers of people signed up for the weekly courses.

Then an unexpected event occurred that led to an avalanche of interest in TM. Around mid-February word was sent to all the TM centers in the United States that Merv Griffin had invited Maharishi to be a guest on his program in March. His talk show was one of the most popular programs on afternoon TV. Merv's conversational style created an ideal atmosphere for conducting intelligent interviews that could be serious with some guests and light-hearted with others. Rather than interview a guest for only a five- or six-minute segment, Merv preferred lengthy, in-depth discussions with guests. He sometimes dedicated an entire show to a single person or topic, allowing for greater exploration of his guests' personalities and thoughts.

We knew that the nationally televised interview with Maharishi would generate increased interest in TM, so we immediately began to mobilize in order to handle an expected onslaught of telephone inquiries during and after the show. We added an extra phone line in the TM center and reserved facilities around the Santa Clara Valley for introductory lectures following the broadcast.

Our already high expectations were exceeded by what happened. In addition to Maharishi, Merv Griffin had invited his friend Clint Eastwood to appear on the show. Eastwood had been practicing TM for about three years. During the interview, he enthusiastically endorsed its benefits for mind and body. Merv's interview with Maharishi was respectful, serious, and light-hearted at the same time. Merv appeared very impressed by Maharishi and TM.

Shortly after Merv initiated the interview, our phones began ringing off the hook. The next day I offered an introductory lecture at the San Jose Main Library. Hundreds of people showed up. Within a couple of weeks, we were teaching between eighty and one hundred people every weekend. We recruited more TM teachers from around the Bay Area. Within a couple of months our teaching staff had grown from six to about twenty. We convinced the national TM organization to purchase a former dental clinic to be our new center just in the nick of time.

As we were moving into the new center, Maharishi made a second appearance on the Merv Griffin show along with Burt Reynolds and Harold Bloomfield, a psychiatrist who had recently written a book called, *TM: Discovering Inner Energy and Overcoming Stress*. The combination of a second Merv Griffin show devoted to the benefits of TM, the popularity of Bloomfield's book, and the appearance of Maharishi on the cover of *Time* magazine resulted in a second big wave of interest in TM throughout the country.

At the beginning of the second wave, I became the chair of the center, which began to receive requests for interviews from regional TV and radio stations. My colleagues chose me to respond to these requests and

I soon entered into a short-lived stint as a TV and radio personality. Every couple of weeks or so I was appearing on interview shows and news broadcasts.

The high volume of people taking the TM course continued throughout 1975 into 1976. Because of my administrative responsibilities, heavy lecturing schedule, and media appearances, I couldn't keep up with my other position as music director of Sacred Heart Parish. With a heavy heart I resigned my position at the church.

My demanding schedule overseeing the ever-expanding TM center was lightened by the warm relationships that developed among the TM teachers. We were all young and idealistic. Besides working together, many of us began to hang out socially. Romances developed among some of the teachers that ended in marriages.

I still believed that my path included marriage and raising a family. During 1975–77 I entered into close relationships with two fine women. But I was not prepared to make a life commitment at that time.

Despite the satisfying nature of my work and relationships, the administrative and teaching responsibilities became too stressful for me. I burned out in early 1976. How ironic that teaching people how to meditate and release stress wore me out! My burnout was not a reflection on the practice of meditation. Rather, it was a manifestation of perfectionism and workaholism. Meditation does not automatically remove one's unhealthy habits. I turned over my leadership position to a colleague and assumed a lighter teaching load.

A Six-Month Advanced Meditation Course in Switzerland ▸

Around the time I cut back on my work at the TM center, Maharishi developed a six-month program in Switzerland to train TM teachers to help usher in a new "Age of Enlightenment" that he envisioned. We were told that it would be the most transformative program in the history of Maharishi's international movement, involving advanced meditation techniques and ascetical practices.

When I heard of the program, I was strongly motivated to attend. The challenge would be to find $4,000 to cover the course fee, room, board, and transportation. I had $600 in my savings account. I shared the dilemma with my family. My grandmother agreed that I could cash in a $2,000 insurance policy she purchased on my behalf when I was born. My brother offered me $1,400 he had received unexpectedly. Thanks to their generosity I made plans to head for Switzerland.

The buzz among TM teachers was that this course would serve as the breakthrough to enlightenment. "Cosmic consciousness or bust!" was the slogan I heard from some colleagues. I didn't have any idea whether I would reach enlightenment on the course, but I did have the strong intuition that the six months of withdrawal from frenetic activity, engaging in long meditations, prayer, fasting, and study would help me define my path in life.

Ever since leaving the seminary four years earlier I had traveled widely, explored career options, entered a new social world, pursued a couple of serious relationships, engaged in the East–West interreligious dialogue, and tried to deepen my spirituality. But I still did not know what to do with my life. My hope was that the six-month course would catalyze a definitive breakthrough.

My expectations were to be fulfilled, but in a way I never anticipated.

18

Seeking Enlightenment in Switzerland

IN APRIL OF 1976, FIVE HUNDRED TM TEACHERS FROM around the world traveled to Switzerland for the six-month course that would take place in different cities simultaneously. The course was called "Age of Enlightenment Governor Training Course." Each location was led by senior members of Maharishi's staff. Men and women were housed separately. Maharishi would periodically visit each course location.

However, those responsible for arranging the separate course locations had made a major miscalculation. They had reserved only four hundred hotel rooms. Upon arrival in Switzerland, I ended up in the group of one hundred men who had no reserved rooms. We were put on buses that embarked for parts unknown as Maharishi's staff furiously searched for temporary housing. After a few hours of driving through the glorious Swiss countryside, the bus drivers received word that a hotel was found in a small city that could accommodate us for a couple of weeks.

During those two weeks in our temporary residence, we meditated in the morning and again in mid-afternoon preceded by a nap. My nap each day lasted three hours. I awoke barely in time for dinner. I did not realize how much fatigue I had stored up during the previous year of intense teaching activity during the "boom" catalyzed by the Merv Griffin shows.

Finally, a permanent facility was located. My fellow TM teachers and I were amazed when told we would be transported to St. Moritz, a luxury alpine resort town at an elevation of about six thousand feet, where the Winter Olympics were hosted twice. The destination connected me with my Swiss roots. My maternal grandfather, John Thoeni, and his father, Henry, had transported tourists by horse and carriage from Bern to St. Moritz in the late 1890s.

Several of my companions opined that we would probably be housed in a budget hotel since we had paid only a modest amount for the six-month course. I was hoping for a more classic Swiss hotel with a view of Lake St. Moritz.

As our buses entered the pristine nineteenth-century alpine town, I gazed with awe at the mountain that rose high above the town. Halfway up the mountain was an elegant five-story hotel with turrets and balconies. I had an intuition we were headed to that hotel. With excitement I pointed to the hotel and said to my companions, "That's our hotel!" They just laughed in disbelief.

The buses drove through the entire town and then began ascending the mountain. There was only one hotel on that mountain—the one that had originally caught my eye. With self-vindication I told my friends, "I told you so!" Hotel Chantarella looked like a classic five-star Swiss hotel from the 1920s. We excitedly entered the lobby to receive our room assignments. Mine was on the top floor. I had the feeling that my initial hopes would be realized. I walked into my room and encountered a large, well-furnished space with French doors opening up onto a balcony overlooking Lake St. Moritz. It felt like a dream come true. It was only the beginning of the realization of a much bigger dream.

Serious Asceticism in the Alps

We soon learned that life in Hotel Chantarella would be rather monastic. Silence was maintained throughout the hotel from 9:00 P.M. until lunch the following day. We followed an exclusively vegetarian diet and fasted each Thursday until Friday dinner. (Our method of fasting was to eat no solid foods but to drink diluted fresh orange juice several times a day.) We took cold baths every morning, followed by stretching exercises (yoga asanas), and then meditated the rest of the morning. We could speak during lunch or eat in a silent dining room. After lunch we took walks with a buddy and then attended a conference in the hotel ballroom.

Periodically Maharishi would come to the hotel and give a lecture followed by Q & A. We then meditated for a couple of hours, ate dinner, attended another conference, and retired early. The daily conferences were usually video tapes of Maharishi's lectures, beginning with a course that lasted for several weeks called "Vedic Studies." The central theme of the course was the development of higher states of consciousness.

The fasting, cold baths, abstinence from flesh foods, and long periods of silence would be called "austerities" by religious traditions. The Indian tradition calls such practices *tapas*, which are considered aids to enlightenment.[1] Christians call these practices "penance." Those who fast usually find that their mind experiences increased clarity. Cold baths calm the passions and contribute to a more settled mind during meditation.

I certainly was not looking forward to the cold baths. Rising early on a cool morning in the Swiss alps, then immersing myself in very cold water was not my idea of a spiritual experience. However, I soon noticed that the weekly fasting, disciplined daily routine, and cold baths had a strong impact on the quality of my meditations.

In my previous experience of practicing TM, once I began mentally repeating my mantra, I usually experienced a settling of the mind, physical relaxation, and short periods of interior silence interspersed with thoughts. I never meditated longer than thirty minutes except on long meditation courses during which we practiced rounding.

On the St. Moritz course we were instructed to meditate as long as we wanted. For the first time in my six years of practicing TM I meditated for two hours each session. Rarely had I experienced such deep silence. Often the mantra would disappear, thoughts would rarely arise, and I would sense that my conscious awareness was expanding. It was an extraordinarily blissful and clear experience of what Maharishi calls, "transcendental consciousness" or *"samadhi."*

The only time I had consistently experienced similar interior bliss was at the Monastery of la Pierre-qui-vire when I engaged in two hours of daily prayer before the tabernacle in the small Blessed Sacrament chapel.[2] The latter prayer experience was distinctly "I–Thou." As I medi-

---

1. Ishwar C. Sharma, "Tapas," *Perennial Dictionary of World Religions*, ed. Keith Crim et al. (San Francisco: Harper & Row, 1989), 746. Tapas is translated literally as "heat or warmth" usually rendered as "penance or physical and mental austerity."

2. See chapter 14.

tated on the Sacred Scriptures and adored the presence of Christ in the Eucharist, I had a sense of Christ's presence and his love for me. It was a supernatural experience, whereas the meditations in St. Moritz seemed to be a natural (although extraordinary) entering the depths of myself. Comparing and contrasting the two experiences seemed to validate for me the insights of Jacques Maritain regarding the distinction and relationship between natural and supernatural mysticism. "Grace builds on nature."[3] He observes that grace does not destroy nature but fulfills its potential. Grace (God's self-offering) elevates the incomplete natural notion that human beings have of God.

Throughout the course I engaged in many philosophical and theological conversations with my companions. Among the hundred course participants, some were Christian or lapsed Christians, several were Jews, and a handful had Buddhist sympathies. The majority had no formal religion. Their worldview and spirituality were based on the Vedic tradition, and their spiritual leader was Maharishi. My interaction with most of them was friendly and mutually respectful. They often questioned me about Christ and Christianity, but I still could not find satisfactory answers regarding the relationship of Christianity and the Vedic tradition, partly because I didn't know enough about the *Christian* spiritual masters. I had not encountered a systematic Christian treatment of meditation and the stages of spiritual development. Ironically, it was on the St. Moritz course that I encountered a seminal text on Christian mysticism that provided me with a systematic treatment of supernatural prayer and higher states of spiritual development.

St. Teresa of Avila's *Interior Castle*

A Jewish friend of mine on the course had ordered a box of books by Christian spiritual masters, including St. Teresa of Avila's *The Interior Castle*. St. Teresa, a sixteenth-century Spanish mystic and church reformer, is regarded as the foremost female spiritual master in the Catholic tradi-

---

3. This is one of the principles of Catholic theology developed by St. Thomas Aquinas (1224–1274). See Thomas Aquinas, *Summa Theologiae* (New York: Benziger Bros., 1948), First Part, Question 1 ("The Nature and Extent of Sacred Doctrine"), Eighth Article ("Whether Sacred Doctrine Is a Matter of Argument?"), Reply Obj. 2. The citation is traditionally abbreviated as I, I, 8 ad 2.

tion. As I began reading her text, I felt as if I had encountered a hidden treasure after years of searching. The book is based primarily on her personal spiritual journey. I was immediately fascinated that St. Teresa presents seven stages in the spiritual journey. Some of the stages appeared similar to Maharishi's descriptions of seven states of consciousness while, at the same time, diverging on some significant details.

Reading *The Interior Castle* was thrilling. Finally, after years of wrestling with the two traditions, I found a Christian spiritual master who could equip me with the knowledge I needed to understand, compare, contrast, and evaluate the Christian and Far Eastern spirituality traditions more adequately. I will present an extended introduction to St. Teresa and her teachings in chapter 20.

The Vocation Question

For the previous four years I had been seeking my vocation. I left the seminary in 1972 at the age of twenty-two primarily because I wanted to pursue marriage and develop a career in the world. One of my motivations for attending the course in St. Moritz was to arrive at some clarity regarding these vocational issues.

After four months of deep meditation and intensive self-scrutiny, I still felt no closer to resolving these questions. I picked up an anthology of writings by mystics from various traditions, *The Soul Afire*, and came upon a passage by Meister Eckhart that provided me with some direction:

> He who would take upon himself a new life and work shall go to his God and ask of Him with great strength and devotion that He should dispose as He thinks best, and as it appears to Him most seemly and proper. But in doing this, he must not think of what he himself wishes, but only of God's will and nothing else. However God may dispose, let him accept it as coming from God and consider it best, and be wholly and ultimately content with it....
>
> Let a man take one good way and remain in it and comprise in this all good ways, and have faith that it comes from God, and do not do one thing today and another tomorrow, and be without care that in going his way he neglect something else. For if one is with God, one neglects nothing....

God in his faithfulness gives each man what is best for him.... For God in His Godhood sees each thing as it is at its best.[4]

On August 9 I began to pray in earnest according to Eckhart's instructions: "Ask of God with great strength and devotion that He should dispose as He thinks best.... But in doing this, you must not think of what you wish, but only of God's will and nothing else." Every day, before meditating and before retiring at night, I would make the same petition: "Lord, what do you want me to do?"

After four weeks, a ray of light emerged. I had been reading sayings from the Desert Fathers in Thomas Merton's *The Wisdom of the Desert*. One saying struck me as particularly relevant to my quest:

> A brother asked one of the elders: What good thing shall I do, and have life thereby? The old man replied: God alone knows what is good. However, I have heard it said that someone inquired of Father Abbot Nisteros the great, the friend of Abbot Anthony, asking: What good work shall I do? And that he replied: Not all works are alike. For Scripture says that Abraham was hospitable, and God was with him. Elias loved solitary prayer, and God was with him. And David was humble, and God was with him. Therefore, whatever you see your soul to desire according to God, do that thing, and you shall keep your heart safe.[5]

I reflected on Abbot Nisteros's counsel, "Whatever you see your soul to desire according to God, do that thing." I asked myself, "Over the past few years, when did I feel that my desires were in accord with God's will? What were the periods of greatest happiness and peace of mind?" In my journal I responded with the following list:

- 1967, summer: I formed and directed a choir at my parish in Alameda and studied music theory at Holy Names College in Oakland. My love for music and for training liturgical musicians brought me much fulfillment and joy.
- 1968, spring: My conversion experience at the Trappist monastery in Vina led me to the most ecstatic experience of my early life.

---

4. Meister Eckhart in *The Soul Afire: Revelations of the Mystics*, ed. H. A. Reinhold (Garden City, NY: Image Books, 1973), 137–38.

5. Thomas Merton, ed. and trans., *The Wisdom of the Desert* (New York: New Directions, 1960), 25–26.

Afterwards, I studied theology at the college seminary, attended daily Mass and engaged in deep spiritual sharing with good friends. The joy remained constant for two months.

- 1971, spring: I learned TM and began the practice of walking-meditation in the hills reading the Gospels. I wrote my senior paper on Jung's theory of the psyche. The practices and intellectual investigations stimulated much spiritual growth in me.
- 1971, fall: I studied theology at St. Patrick's Seminary, attended daily Mass with devotion and grew closer to spiritual friends. I found theological study very fulfilling.
- 1972, winter: The six-month TM meditation course in Spain led me to engage regularly in stimulating conversations regarding the East–West interreligious dialogue. The meditation and the interactions with people of various non-Catholic traditions led me to a deeper discovery and appreciation of Christian spirituality.
- 1973, spring: After a major spiritual crisis in Paris and London, the Lord led me to a powerful breakthrough and deep prayer at two monasteries. Spiritual friendship with Leo was significant during the breakthrough.

After listing the experiences where I followed desires that led to periods of great happiness and fulfillment, I wrote in my journal the following conclusion:

> These experiences point to centering my life around spirituality. Prayer, meditation, Mass, liturgical music, and deep friendships are key to my vocational fulfillment as well as sharing the fruits with others. None of my previous jobs and professional pursuits have inspired me except choir-directing, studying theology and psychology, and teaching meditation.

Something was brewing inside of me. I continued with my daily prayer petition, "What do you want me to do Lord?"

Breakthrough ▶

On September 2, the breakthrough occurred. I was doing my usual afternoon meditation, during which a spontaneous stream of thoughts surfaced regarding vocational options. I thought of business opportunities and making money. An intuition from deep inside responded, "That's not for you." I thought of a career in music. Another intuition emerged: "Music is an accompaniment to your life. It is not your life." Then I thought of marriage and raising a family. That proposal—which had strongly attracted me for five years—was met with "That's not your path."

At that point I became agitated because all the options I had been considering seemed unsuitable for me. Then from that same source of intuition flowed the following thought sequence:

- Kevin, the reason why none of these options seem right for you is because they do not answer the question, "What is your life all about?"
- Well, what is my life all about?
- Seeking, loving, and serving God and bringing everyone along with me.
- Kevin, you are never going to be satisfied unless you are a priest.

That last thought shocked me. Since leaving the seminary, not once had I considered the priesthood as an option. Despite feeling stunned by the thought, it brought me peace and elation—along with confusion. I prayed, "Lord, I don't know if this thought is from you or from my imagination. I need a sign. I am going to open the New Testament at random and I ask you please to direct me to the passage that will reveal your will for me."

I sat on the edge of my bed, held my New Testament in my hands, and thought of the Gospel story of Bartimaeus the blind man. When he heard that Jesus was passing by, he cried out, "Jesus, Son of David, have mercy on me!" Jesus asked him, "What do you want me to do for you?" He said, "Lord, let me receive my sight." That was the prayer on the tip of my tongue as I was about to open the New Testament. I felt as though I were on the edge of a cliff. With faith that the Lord would not abandon me in such a desperate situation, I opened the New Testament without looking and placed my finger on these words:

> "Sell all that you have and distribute to the poor, and you will have treasure in heaven; and come, follow me." (Luke 18:22 RSV)

That verse shook my world.

The following verses gave me further illumination:

> Peter then said, "Lo, we have left our homes and followed you." And Jesus said to them, "Truly, I say to you, there is no man who has left house or wife or brothers or parents or children, for the sake of the kingdom of God who will not receive manifold more in this time, and in the age to come eternal life." (Luke 18:28–30 RSV)

The last section on the page provided the final confirmation. It was the story of Bartimaeus,[6] the Gospel passage that came to me the moment before I opened the New Testament. The final verse on the page was: "Receive your sight; your faith has saved you" (Luke 18:42 RSV).

I was overwhelmed. After five years of vocational exploration and a month intensely seeking guidance from the Lord, a completely unexpected answer was revealed. I closed the New Testament, knowing that my life was going to change dramatically, and asked, "Now what?"

The following few days I walked around in a daze processing what had occurred. Then the thought came to me, "In the past when something significant happened in my life, I would often find a meaningful connection with the readings proclaimed in the Mass that day. I wonder what were the Mass readings on September 2?" I opened my Missal (the book containing the prayers and readings of the Mass for each day of the week) and discovered that the Gospel reading that day was Luke 5:1–11, the account of Jesus calling fishermen to follow him. Jesus said to Simon Peter, "Do not be afraid; from now on you will be catching human beings. When they brought their boats to the shore, they left everything and followed him" (Luke 5:10–11).

Again, I was amazed at the providential ordering of events. That Gospel passage is traditionally associated with the call to priesthood in the Catholic tradition. It seemed as if all the details surrounding my experience on September 2 conspired to convince me that the Lord was indeed calling me to the priesthood.

Up until that moment I had not shared my experience with anyone. But, with the final confirmation, I was filled with such certainty and

---

6. Mark's account of the story provides the name of the blind man, Bartimaeus (Mark 10:46).

exhilaration that I had to share the experience with some close friends in the hotel.

I first shared my story with Rick Meisenbach, who had become a close friend during the course. We would often take walks together in the mountains around the hotel and share our personal stories, spiritual journeys, and romantic dramas. When I related what had happened on September 2, I was astonished that Rick was not surprised by my story. He said that I so often spoke about Christ and the Catholic Church that it seemed natural that I would become a priest. During the previous five years I had not once suspected that I had a calling to the priesthood. It seemed that some friends had more insight into my vocation than I.

I decided to wait until I returned from Switzerland to California to share the news face-to-face with my family and friends. I did write a letter to Fr. Jerry Coleman, who had become academic dean at St. Patrick's Seminary in Menlo Park asking if I could be admitted to the seminary for the spring semester. He replied that I would be welcome to return the following January (1977).

Because I had been studying with Maharishi and was most grateful for all that I had received from him, I wanted to inform him of my decision. A week or so later, he came to speak in our hotel. After his talk, I entered a long line of course participants who wished to meet with him. After half an hour, he rose from his chair and prepared to leave the hotel. My heart sank when I realized that I would not be able to speak with him. At that moment, one of the course leaders who knew of my desire came up to me and said, "Quickly, get into the elevator with Maharishi." Before I knew it, Maharishi and I were alone in the elevator. I had never been in such close quarters with this world-famous monk whom we meditators considered to be a spiritual master. He was short of stature and dressed in the traditional Indian *dhoti* (a long white robe). He carried a large bouquet of flowers offered by course participants. I felt awe in his presence. I rapidly told him of my plans to become a priest and to write a master's thesis on "higher states of consciousness in the writings of Christian saints and mystics." He responded warmly and offered me words of encouragement at which point we reached the ground floor of the hotel and exited the elevator. As I watched him head to an awaiting car, I felt deeply moved by his heartfelt support.

A couple weeks later the course ended and we all headed back to our countries of origin. I couldn't wait to inform my family and friends of my decision and to return to the seminary. The six months of long meditations and remarkable rediscovery of my vocation made me feel as though I was in a higher state of consciousness. At that time, I could not imagine the trial that awaited me in the seminary.

19

A Rough Landing Back in the Seminary

VERY FEW PEOPLE BACK IN CALIFORNIA SUSPECTED THE NEWS I was about to reveal. During the previous five years, someone would occasionally ask me if I ever thought of returning to the seminary. I always responded with a firm negative: "I gave eight years to seminary formation. The priesthood is not for me."

Upon arrival in California in October of 1976, I returned to my family home and was greeted with a long-awaited intimate family dinner with my mom, dad, and brother. During the meal I told the story of what happened to me in Hotel Chantarella on September 2. My family was stunned by the news that I was going to return to the seminary. My dad expressed great pleasure, my mother cried tears of joy, and Brian silently processed the news. (Later I learned that he had ambivalent feelings about my decision.) During the meal, my parents confided that they always believed I had a vocation to the priesthood but had respected my decision to seek a different path. For the first time I realized how painful my five years of vocational confusion had been for them. They had watched me pursue one new venture after another without coming to any vocational decision. I was deeply touched by my parents' respect for my journey even when they did not agree with some of my decisions. They never tried to push me in one direction or another.

After dinner, I walked to my grandmother's house to share the news with her. We sat in her backyard gazebo on a balmy Indian summer evening. Ma listened intently as I narrated the

St. Moritz story. When I finished the long account, she expressed delight and said, "Kevin, I hope I live long enough to attend your ordination!"

Throughout the previous five years I had remained close to Ma. I particularly appreciated the three weeks I lived with her during the house-painting project. During those five years we spoke often about spiritual matters. She always expressed interest in my stream of new undertakings, and even accepted my offer to teach her Transcendental Meditation, hoping that it would help lower her blood pressure. Even though Ma was a strong Catholic and had looked forward to my future life as a priest, she did not express disapproval when I had announced to her five years earlier that I was leaving the seminary. I remember word-for-word what she told me that evening, "Kevin, I have never prayed that you would become a priest. I have always prayed that you would follow the guidance of the Holy Spirit and I shall continue praying for that."

The next day I paid a visit to our pastor, Father Patrick O'Brien. Father O'Brien was among the best of the old school Irish pastors who had left their homeland to serve the Church in America. He had been pastor of St. Philip Neri parish for over twenty years and had known me since I was seven years old when he gave me my First Holy Communion. I had served as his altar boy throughout middle school. When I left the seminary, I knew he was very disappointed, but he did not try to talk me out of my decision. He respected my desire to explore the world and pursue new dreams. Throughout the ensuing five years I remained close to him, visiting him each time I returned to Alameda. He did not understand my fascination with Eastern meditation, but he always expressed interest in my philosophical musings and latest adventures.

After I recounted the story of my breakthrough in St. Moritz, Father O'Brien expressed his pleasure and encouragement. However, he did not express surprise. Some days later in a conversation with my mother, she told me of a chat she had had with him in 1972 shortly after I had announced I was leaving the seminary. He told her with an Irish twinkle in his eye, "He'll be back."

Father O'Brien was disappointed with one detail of my story. I told him that, because I lived in San Jose throughout most of the previous five years and had served as Director of Music at Sacred Heart Church in San Jose during those years, I had developed good relationships with a great number of parishioners and several priests. I told him I felt more connected to the church in San Jose, which then was part of the Archdiocese of San Francisco. Consequently, I decided to apply to the archdiocese rather than to the Diocese of Oakland. Despite his desire that I return to the Oakland Diocese, he gave me his strong support. His primary concern was that I be happy as a priest.

Deflation ▸

As I communicated my St. Moritz story to family and friends, I received a great deal of support and admiration. People would make comments like, "You must be very special to have received such divine intervention." The truth is that the intervention was a sign of God's mercy for a confused young man.

After receiving so much affirmation and admiration from family and friends, I entered into a psychological state that Carl Jung labels "inflation." It is a perilous condition characterized as "pride goeth before a fall."[1] My ego was becoming puffed up. I felt intoxicated by all the positive regard and unconsciously began to consider myself as spiritually superior to others. If I had looked to the Gospels for guidance, I would have concluded exactly the opposite. Jesus tells the story about a Pharisee (a leading religious figure in Jewish society) and a tax collector (usually regarded as a crook by observant Jews) who went up to the temple area to pray.

> The Pharisee took up his position and spoke this prayer to himself, "O God, I thank you that I am not like the rest of humanity—greedy, dishonest, adulterous—or even like this tax collector. I fast twice a week, and I pay tithes on my whole income." But the tax collector stood off at a distance and would not even raise his eyes to heaven but beat his breast and prayed, "O God, be merciful to me a sinner." I tell you, the latter went home justified, not the former; for everyone who exalts himself will be humbled, and the one who humbles himself will be exalted. (Luke 18:11–14)

---

1. C. G. Jung, *Aion: Researches into the Phenomenology of the Self*, vol. 9, part 2 of *The Collected Works of C. G. Jung* (Princeton, NJ: Princeton University Press, 1968), 23–24.

After spending two months with my family and old friends, the date arrived for my return to St. Patrick's Seminary. I felt excited and almost inebriated by the conviction that God had orchestrated my return to seminary formation. I assumed that the happiness and exhilaration that I experienced since the St. Moritz revelation would continue.

On that cold January evening my parents drove me to the seminary. I had been assigned to what was then called the Deacon House, a wing behind the main seminary building that had originally served as a convent for the French-Canadian sisters who had cooked for the seminary community since 1903 (in the 1970s they moved into a new convent). That grand brick building with about twenty-five bedrooms was constructed in the classic Romanesque style.

As we carried my belongings to the room assigned to me, we did not see other seminarians. My parents bade me an affectionate farewell and drove off. At that moment, I experienced something completely unforeseen. It was as if a balloon had been punctured and its air was being sucked out. The elation and excitement that I had known for three months disappeared in a matter of minutes. I was shocked and completely confused by the mysterious depression that suddenly descended upon me. "What is happening to me?" I asked myself. "I know the Lord sent me back here. Where did this sudden darkness and emptiness come from? Just a few months ago I discovered my path and have felt joyful ever since. Here I am following the path the Lord revealed to me. How could I enter suddenly into a deep depression?"

I went to the small chapel in the Deacon House with my Breviary (the official prayer book of the Church) and opened to a psalm assigned for the day:

> Why are you cast down, my soul,
> Why groan within me?
> Hope in God; I will praise him still,
> My savior and my God. (Psalm 42:6 Grail translation)

With my mind I believed the message, but my emotions were completely overwhelmed by the reemergence of the void.

The next morning, I rose early to join the seminary community for morning prayer and Mass. I had always loved the splendid nineteenth-century chapel with its exquisite stained-glass windows that depict the passion and glorification of Jesus. But the beauty failed to touch me that morning. I continued to feel inexplicably despondent and alone. Several students and faculty welcomed me warmly. I tried not to show my dejected state. I entered into the seminary routine of classes, prayer, meals, and recreation but the depression and confusion did not lift. Only months later did I finally discern the cause:

> Everyone who exalts himself will be humbled, and the one who humbles himself will be exalted. (Luke 18:14)

As strange as it may seem to some readers, the cause of my depression was the mercy of God. When we attempt to turn over our life and will to the care of God, he takes us at our word. If we stray from the path of righteousness, we suffer the consequences:

> My son, do not disdain the discipline of the Lord
> or lose heart when reproved by him;
> for whom the Lord loves, he disciplines;
>   he scourges every son he acknowledges.
> Endure your trials as "discipline." (Hebrews 12:5–7)

Why did I need disciplining? What was my sin? Unwittingly, I had begun to feel impressed with myself over the extraordinary illumination that I received in St. Moritz. The sin was spiritual pride that gave rise to a state of psychological inflation. In the well-known canticle of the Blessed Virgin Mary, the "Magnificat," we perceive how God deals with the proud:

> The Almighty has mercy on those who fear him
>   in every generation.
> He has shown the strength of his arm,
>   he has scattered the proud in their conceit.
> He has cast down the mighty from their thrones
>   and has lifted up the lowly. (Luke 1:50–52)

However, this realization did not occur until a few months passed. In the meantime, I tried to hide my emotional distress–partly because I had internalized the persona of a TM teacher. In the TM movement, meditation teachers were expected to act as "exponents of enlightenment"—to always portray a positive impression of the TM program. Teachers were supposed to dress formally in public. They were to avoid going out in public when "unstressing." Unstressing is Maharishi's way of describing emotional disturbances that may accompany purification of the mind.

Even though I was no longer working as a TM teacher and had begun a new life as a candidate for the priesthood, I remained strongly influenced by the TM-teacher culture. I continued to wear a suit each day, whereas the other seminarians dressed in casual civilian clothing except on weekends when they wore clerical shirts. Many probably considered me pretentious. Few seminarians warmed up to me. My sense of isolation deepened. During those days of interior void and darkness, two members of my class did reach out to me—Manuel Sousa and Tim Stier. They were intrigued by my unusual background and interest in Eastern spirituality.

Tim had lived out "in the world" for several years after graduating from a university in Washington, D.C., and serving in the Army before entering the seminary. We quickly became spiritual brothers and confidants. Tim was one of the most generous friends I had ever known. He regularly bailed me out financially. I had arrived at the seminary with minimal financial resources. Besides that, my 1953 Oldsmobile "Rocket 88" was a gas-guzzler. When Tim and I would go out to dinner or a weekend road trip, he would insist on driving and paying most of the expenses without making me feel like a freeloader. We began to share our stories, including our romances and how we gradually came to the conviction that we were called to be priests. Even though I had made very good friends in the TM movement, I could never fully share my spiritual life with them. With Tim I could share everything.

Manuel Sousa was the other great friend I made upon return to the seminary. Manuel began to come to my room in the evenings to pray Night Prayer (Compline) with me. Compline begins with a short examination of conscience. Instead of doing it in silence, we began to share our examen with each other. Opening up in such a vulnerable way led us to develop a close bond with each other—a bond that has persisted to the present. However, I did not fully reveal my depression to Manuel or Tim because I did not yet understand it and was embarrassed by it.

A Supernatural Intervention ➤

Although I greatly enjoyed my theological studies and some budding friendships, I could not shake the depression. One morning in early May, my despondency got the better of me. I began to doubt my decision to return to the seminary. I said to myself, "Maybe I misinterpreted the experience at St. Moritz; perhaps I was undergoing some delusion." At that moment, the phone rang. It was a dear friend who was a devout Catholic. She asked me, "Kevin, how are you?" I had not told anyone how unhappy I was. I decided to hide my feelings from her. "I'm okay," I answered. She then began to recount an extraordinary experience she had just undergone on a long retreat. She later transcribed what she told me:

> I was going through some painful experiences with my boyfriend. During my evening meditation, I was weeping and suddenly became aware of the presence of Jesus. I heard him say, "Woman, why do you weep?" I poured out my troubles to him, first about my boyfriend, but He interrupted saying, "Are you arguing with Me about My choice of a husband for you?" "No, but . . . ," I started. Then He told me that He had sent me to [the boyfriend] and, that by loving and serving him, I'd be loving and serving the Lord. . . . I felt relieved and satisfied that I was on the right path after all.
>
> My mind turned to Kevin, and Jesus said, "Kevin is badly in need of encouragement right now. He is very discouraged and is having doubts. You must call him and tell him that I say it is very important that he remain in the seminary and become a priest. . . . His calling is to the priesthood. Be sure to call him. Uplift and inspire him. . . ." Jesus' voice was strong, emphatic, and loving.

I was flabbergasted by what she shared with me. I had given her no indication during the previous few months that I was depressed. As far as she knew, I was still excited and enthusiastic about my return to the seminary.

The Catholic tradition is very skeptical about supernormal phenomena such as visions and supernatural messages (locutions). Whether or not my friend's vision of Jesus was from him or was a product of deep intuition, I do not know. What I do know is that she knew nothing about my depression or the doubts that had arisen within me just a few minutes before her phone call. I knew in my heart of hearts that, somehow, the Lord was speaking to me through her.

After she finished relating the vision, I acknowledged to her that I was deeply depressed and had considered leaving the seminary only moments before she called. Having listened to her narration of the vision, my conviction of having been called to the priesthood was reawakened.

The depression soon lifted, and I began connecting with more students and faculty. I stopped wearing my suit and tie and gradually faced my grandiosity and pride with the help of Father Bob Gavin, a wise spiritual director on the seminary faculty. A couple of verses from Psalm 119 helped me process the origins and meaning of my dejection:

> Before I was afflicted, I strayed
>   but now I keep your word.
> You are good and your deeds are good.
>   Teach me your commandments.
> . . . .
> It was good for me to be afflicted, to learn your will.
> The law from your mouth means more to me than silver and gold.
> (Psalm 119:67–68, 71–72 Grail translation)

When the spring semester ended, I got a job at Libby's Cannery in Sunnyvale, heaving boxes of canned fruit from conveyor belts onto pallets for eight hours a day. That exhausting, mindless job helped me to continue in the chastening process that had occurred throughout the previous several months.

When classes resumed in September, I felt on a more level playing field with my classmates. Tim Stier, Manuel Sousa, Dick Hoenisch, and Rudy Ruiz and I formed a small fraternity, following a model promoted by an international organization of diocesan priests called "Jesus Caritas." We would gather once or twice a month for a day of fellowship and spiritual exercises. Together we meditated on a Gospel passage for an hour, spent another hour in silent adoration of the Blessed Sacrament, and engaged in a "review of life" during which each would share some event or struggle to seek discernment and guidance from the others. The day ended with a good dinner and bottle of wine.

I threw myself into seminary life largely unburdened by the inflation and depression that had plagued me the previous semester. In addition to my academic responsibilities, I became involved with music ministry. Ordinarily a faculty member would serve as seminary music director, but no musician served on the faculty at that time. Because of my many years working as a liturgical musician, the seminary president-rector,

Father Howard Bleichner, hired me to serve as organist and choir director. I began to recruit students to sing in the choir. About twenty signed up including several accomplished musicians. We developed a terrific liturgical music program.

Serving as choir director helped me enter more deeply into seminary life. After choir rehearsals several of us would go out for pizza and beer. A lively fellowship developed among us. As I made new friends and shared my love for music, I recaptured the joy that I had lost the previous semester.

Ma's Death

In the midst of my newfound joy occurred one of the saddest experiences of my life. In previous chapters I described the close relationship I had with my maternal grandmother, Ma. From my earliest years we bonded deeply. To me she was not only my beloved grandmother. She was one of my most significant spiritual mentors and models.

A few months after my return to the seminary in January of 1977, Ma came to my family home for dinner during one of my breaks from the seminary. As my mother was preparing the meal, Ma and I chatted in the living room. Out of the blue Ma said, "I swear I see God smiling." Then she went on to say, "You know, I have no fear of death. Of course, I'm glad to be here; but the Lord has given me so much and one day He's going to say to me, 'Mabel, now I want something from you. I want you to give me your life.'"

I felt so choked up at the impact of her words that I could barely hold back my tears. The thought of Ma's death filled me with dread.

In September of the same year Ma came down with a serious case of the flu. By early October she needed twenty-four-hour care. My mom and my Aunt Jeanne (Sister Catherine Irene) moved into Ma's house to care for her. As she approached death, Ma remained her radiant, loving self. The evening before her death, my mother and aunt heard her praying softly over and over, "Holy Mary, Mother of God, pray for us sinners now and at the hour of our death."

Early the next morning I arrived at the house and walked into Ma's bedroom. She was close to death. I was overwhelmed with wrenching fear and sorrow. I left the room, grabbed my Bible, and asked the Lord to direct me to a passage in response to my desperation. I opened the Bible randomly and put my finger on the opened page. The passage was John 16:16, a verse Jesus spoke to his disciples during the Last Supper: "A little while and you will no longer see me, and again a little while later and you will see me."

I felt in my heart of hearts that the Lord directed me to that verse. The context of the passage was Jesus preparing his disciples for his death. I believed that the passage also applied to me. In a little while I would no longer see my grandmother, but later I would see her again. Shortly thereafter my mom came to me in tears announcing that Ma had died. I walked into Ma's bedroom overcome with sadness but also consoled by the message of John 16:16. We prayed around her body, giving thanks for such a beautiful life.

I began phoning friends, including Leo. A few hours later Leo came to my house with a parchment on which he had written in handsome calligraphy: *Modicum et iam non videbitis me et iterum modicum*—the Latin text of John 16:16 quoted above. I framed the parchment and have displayed it ever since next to a beautiful photo of Ma and my mother.

Three days later we celebrated Ma's funeral at our parish church of St. Philip Neri in Alameda, where she had worshiped since 1934. The church was packed. Even though I was not yet ordained, Father O'Brien invited me to preach the homily, in which I noted that in psychological and spiritual literature we often find the concept of living a "holistic" spirituality. Holistic described Ma's way of life. She loved learning and read a variety of secular and religious literature daily. She never let us get away with grammatical errors in our speech, and she kept her mind nimble by daily crosswords—regularly hunting up words in her many dictionaries and reference books. On the walls of her breakfast room were maps of the world and the heavens. She loved to point out the heavenly constellations to us. Sometimes during the day, she would phone and tell us to look outside in a certain direction at some cloud formations. Her garden was central to her life. In her letters to me she would give the latest report on what flowers were blooming. She would often say, "I swear I see God smiling."

After God, family was the center of her life. The times we saw Ma the happiest would be at a family dinner. She would usually end the meal by saying "It's so wonderful to have the gang together. Let's get together soon again." I look forward with all my heart to the next get-together.

A Master's Thesis and a Ph.D. Dissertation

In the course of my grieving, I undertook a project that elicited much creative energy: a Master of Arts degree in theology. Throughout previous chapters, I have often returned to questions regarding the relationship between Christian spirituality and that of India. Graduate studies at St. Patrick's Seminary (1977–1980) afforded me the opportunity to enter deeply into the East–West dialogue through rigorous academic study of the Christian and Vedic spiritual paths and the writing of a master's thesis. In 1988–1992, I completed a Ph.D. program at The Catholic University of America in Washington, D.C., where I expanded my East–West research significantly. I wrote a dissertation comparing the stages of spiritual development as described by both traditions using St. Teresa of Avila and Maharishi Mahesh Yogi as representatives of their respective traditions.

In previous chapters of this book I have shared preliminary analysis and conclusions regarding the relationship between the Christian and Vedic spiritual paths. In chapter 5 I presented an introduction to Transcendental Meditation. In chapter 7 I introduced the teachings of Maharishi Mahesh Yogi and the Vedic tradition. In the next chapter I will examine the life and teachings of St. Teresa.

20

St. Teresa of Avila, Spiritual Master

It is no exaggeration to say that St. Teresa of Avila is one of most influential women in the history of Christianity. Prior to St. Teresa, no one had described the spiritual journey in such a systematic manner, nor in such a personal way. In 1970, Pope Paul VI declared St. Teresa one of the first two female "Doctors of the Church" (along with St. Catherine of Siena).

Teresa de Ahumada was born on March 28, 1515, in the Castilian city of Avila during the reign of Ferdinand V and Isabella (1469–1516). By the time of Teresa's birth, Spain was the major power both in Europe and in the Americas.

Teresa's contemporaries perceived her as an extrovert, cheerful, friendly, a good conversationalist, "pleasing to hear as well as to look at."[1] She was known as a woman of courage and passion for spiritual adventure, qualities already foreshadowed in her childhood exploit of attempting to set off with her brother, Rodrigo, to the land of the Moors to offer herself as a martyr for Christ (*Life*, 1,4).

Teresa's childhood piety waned with the onset of adolescence when she grew increasingly interested in reading romantic novels, in cultivating her feminine charms, and in spending time with young men. After her mother's death in 1528, Teresa began

---

1. Kieran Kavanaugh, Introduction to *The Book of Her Life*, by St. Teresa of Avila, in *The Collected Works of St. Teresa of Avila*, trans. Kieran Kavanaugh and Otilio Rodriguez, 3 vols. (Washington, DC: Institute of Carmelite Studies 1976–1985), 1:2 (cited hereafter as *Life*).

to meet with opposition at home because of her affection for some young male cousins. At the age of sixteen she became so involved with an unidentified relative that her father brought her to an Augustinian convent to save her from scandal.[2] There she was influenced by the friendship of a prayerful nun. Teresa's earlier high spiritual ideals were revived, and she began to consider a vocation to the religious life. Finally, at the age of twenty, Teresa joined the Carmelite Monastery of the Incarnation in Avila.

The Carmelites ▸

The origins of the Carmelite "Order of Our Lady of Mount Carmel" can be traced to a religious community living on Mount Carmel in northern Israel during the Crusades in the twelfth century. The early Carmelite men lived as solitaries, bound together by their common Eucharist and by strict obedience to their rule, which was one of extreme asceticism, prescribing absolute poverty, total abstinence from meat, and solitude. A prominent place was given to contemplation in their spirituality.

Because of Islamic persecution, many of the Carmelites fled to Europe after 1218, where, under the generalship of St. Simon Stock, the order was reorganized in 1247 along the lines of the Franciscan and Dominican friars. The original strictness of the Rule was in many ways mitigated as a concession to the harsher climatic conditions of Europe. The hermit ("eremitic") character of the order gave way in some practices to a communitarian ("cenobitic") way of life, and the order took on two new endeavors: preaching and academic study.

The fifteenth century saw the first major mitigation of the "Primitive Rule" of 1247. In the same century, women were admitted into the order. During the sixteenth century, the discipline among friars as well as among nuns relaxed considerably, especially in Spain, where many new Carmelite convents became homes not only for committed women religious, but also for widows and spinsters of social standing. It was into such a convent, the Incarnation in Avila, that Teresa entered in 1535 and

---

2. Victoria Lincoln, *Teresa, A Woman: A Biography of Teresa of Avila*, SUNY Series in Cultural Perspectives (Albany: State University of New York Press, 1984), 14–15.

where she remained for twenty-seven years until she received the inspiration to undertake a reform of the order according to the Primitive Rule.

St. Teresa's Life as a Carmelite

After two years of monastic life, Teresa's health deteriorated, perhaps due to the stress caused by continuing interior conflicts. She withdrew from the monastery and underwent treatment at the hands of a charlatan. The harsh and ineffective procedure aggravated her condition so badly that she returned to Avila an invalid and a paralytic for three years until she experienced a cure at the age of twenty-seven that she attributed to the intercession of St. Joseph. As a consequence of her illness, Teresa experienced a variety of ailments for the rest of her life.

Teresa made little progress in prayer until the age of twenty-three when she read *The Third Spiritual Alphabet* by a renowned Franciscan spiritual writer, Francisco de Osuna. The book's instructions regarding the practice of mental prayer inspired Teresa to undertake meditation, and she began to experience occasional moments of deep interior peace and silence that she recognized as the beginnings of contemplation (*Life*, 47). Yet she continued to struggle with prayer for over a dozen years, especially because of her inability to control the spontaneous flow of thoughts during her periods of prayer. Concerning those years, she writes:

> And very often, for some years, I was more anxious that the hour I had determined to spend in prayer be over than I was to remain there, . . . and so unbearable was the sadness I felt on entering the oratory, that I had to muster all my courage. (*Life*, 8,7)

Little is known about this period of Teresa's life (1542–1554) except that she found herself in a prolonged struggle between God and the world. She writes:

> Neither did I enjoy God, nor did I find happiness in the world. When I was experiencing the enjoyments of the world, I felt sorrow when I recalled what I owed to God. When I was with God, my attachments to the world disturbed me. (*Life*, 8,2)

In 1554 at the age of thirty-nine, Teresa underwent what she called her "second conversion," which was catalyzed by a cathartic prayer experience that was inspired by a statue of the wounded Christ (*Life*, 9). The experience left her sorrowful over her own mediocrity and determined to follow Christ unreservedly from then on. Within a short time, she discovered the principles governing all her later teachings on spiritual practices, and she began to experience contemplation regularly.

From 1554 until her death in 1582 at the age of sixty-seven, Teresa grew rapidly in the higher "dwelling places." In *The Interior Castle*, St. Teresa classifies the stages of spiritual development as "dwelling places" (*moradas*) of the soul. She regards the human person as a spiritual castle composed of series of dwelling places arranged concentrically and in several tiers about the center.[3] The outermost series gives access to the next inner series, and this series in turn to the next, until the seventh and central dwelling places are reached wherein dwells the King, the Triune God. The path of spiritual development consists of entering progressively into the more interior series of dwelling places until the center is reached.

The first three groups of dwelling places refer to what people can do through their own efforts as they begin the spiritual journey—such as growing in self-knowledge, obeying the commandments, listening to sermons, conversing with spiritual persons, detaching oneself from worldly distractions, and praying. These initial chapters of *The Interior Castle* also deal with trials and temptations that afflict the spiritual seeker, such as dryness in prayer and discouragement.

The remaining four groups of dwelling places deal with the supernatural or mystical elements of the spiritual life, elements that are passively received as gifts from God and cannot be achieved by human efforts. There is much that people can do to prepare for these gifts, disposing themselves for the action of God in their lives, but no one can compel God to bestow mystical experiences.

In the fourth dwelling places, Teresa describes specific spiritual experiences that unfold more systematically than those depicted in the

---

3. St. Teresa of Avila, *The Interior Castle*, "The First Dwelling Places," chapter 1, paragraph 1 (abbreviated I:1,1). See also I:2,8.

first three dwelling places. The central experience of the fourth dwelling places is the first degree of contemplation called the "Prayer of Quiet," which Teresa considers to be a "shortcut" to the seventh dwelling places[4] (we will examine the Prayer of Quiet below). Once Teresa began experiencing the Prayer of Quiet regularly, her contemplative experience deepened so quickly that within two years she had passed from the fourth dwelling places to the most mature contemplation, the "Prayer of Union" of the fifth dwelling places. In 1556 she entered the "Spiritual Betrothal" of the sixth dwelling places, the point at which Jesus prepares the soul for complete union with God. Teresa entered the final stage of the spiritual journey, the "Spiritual Marriage" of the seventh dwelling places, in 1572 at the age of fifty-seven.

Teresa wrote *The Interior Castle* in 1577, five years after she had reached the Spiritual Marriage. She based the book on her own experiences and what she had discovered in the Bible and in teachings of spiritual masters before her, including St. Jerome, St. Augustine, and St. Ignatius of Loyola, founder of the Jesuits.

St. Teresa's Method of Meditation ▸

Because St. Teresa considered meditation and the Prayer of Quiet to be so central in the journey to union with God, we will examine now in detail what she teaches about the Christian practice of meditation.

St. Teresa explains that meditation practiced with simplicity and faith disposes the soul to the Prayer of Quiet, the first stage of contemplation, a gift that God wants to offer everyone who prepares for it. Teresa taught people to practice "active recollection" as a way to be drawn into meditation (also known as "mental prayer"). Teresa writes, "Mental Prayer is nothing else than an intimate sharing between friends; it means taking time frequently to be alone with Him who we know loves us" (*Life*, 8,5). Teresa's active recollection is not a precise technique but is rather an approach toward meditation guided by a few simple principles.

---

4. St. Teresa of Avila, *The Interior Castle*, V:3,4. See also St. Teresa, *The Way of Perfection*, in *Collected Works*, vol. 2 (1980), chapter 28, para. 5 (cited hereafter as *Way*).

The first principle is that one is to collect one's faculties and enter within oneself to be with God who dwells within (*Way*, 28,4). In order to recollect the exterior and interior senses, one must give them something to occupy their attention. There is no value in speaking much. The slow mental recitation of a prayer, simply uttering a few loving words, or devotional spiritual reading (*Lectio Divina*) helps settle the mind (*Way*, 29,6; 26,10; and *IC*, IV:3,7). In the case of spiritual reading, the method involves reading slowly and with frequent pauses, stopping altogether and closing the eyes when one feels drawn to devotion by what one reads—the practice of *Lectio Divina*.

In the *Life*, Teresa recommends an affective way of mental prayer (called by some commentators the "practice of the presence of Christ") that involves imagining Christ within oneself, placing oneself in his presence, directing acts of love to his sacred humanity, and remaining in his presence (*Life*, 12,2–5). In the *Way of Perfection*, Teresa gives similar instructions: one is to imagine the Lord at one's side lovingly and humbly teaching. One should not attempt to form subtle meditations with the understanding but just "look at him," directing one's attention upon the Lord within (*Way*, 26,1–3).

An ancient, simple way of "practicing the presence of Christ" is the "Jesus Prayer," which finds its origins among some of the Desert Fathers of the fourth and fifth centuries. The practice involves mentally repeating the phrase "Jesus, have mercy on me," or a similar formula. I explained the origins and practice of this method of meditation in chapter 16.[5]

Another principle Teresa emphasizes regarding meditation is that one must never try to stop thinking or try to make the mind a blank. Teresa insists that trying to stop thinking will probably awaken more thinking than ever and could even be painful. "In this work of the spirit the one who thinks less and has less desire to act does more. . . . these interior works are all gentle and peaceful" (*IC*, IV:3,5; 3,6).

If one acquires the habit of active recollection, Teresa maintains that the Lord will soon grant the infused Prayer of Quiet when one involun-

---

5. Kallistos Ware, "Ways of Prayer and Contemplation: Eastern," in *Christian Spirituality: Origins to the Twelfth Century*, ed. Bernard McGinn and John Meyendorff, World Spirituality 16 (New York: Crossroad, 2000), 395–414, here 402.

tarily closes the eyes and, without any effort, the senses and all external things gradually lose their hold on one's attention. One becomes markedly conscious of retiring within oneself wherein God is to be found (*IC*, IV:3,1–4).

When the Prayer of Quiet is given, Teresa advises one to stop discursive reasoning but not to try to suspend thinking. If one feels absorbed by the inner quiet and delight, one should simply enjoy it without trying to understand the experience. There is no need for any activity on one's part except perhaps to utter a few loving words (*IC*, IV:3,7).

St. Teresa favors two spiritual terms for interpreting the Prayer of Quiet. She characterizes it as a "foretaste of the Kingdom of God" (*Way*, 30,6; 31,11). She also refers to the Prayer of Quiet as an experience of the "presence of God": "In [this prayer] the Lord puts [the soul] at peace by His presence" (*Way*, 31,2). God is not experienced directly in the Prayer of Quiet; rather, one enters dwelling places that are "closer to where the King is" (*IC*, IV:1,2): "[One] feels so happy merely with being close to the fount that [one] is satisfied even without drinking" (*Way*, 31,3). The nearer one draws toward the indwelling presence of God, the more the effects of God's presence are felt.

When Teresa speaks of experiencing the "presence of God" and "tasting the Kingdom of God" in the fourth dwelling places, she associates this experience with the human will being "absorbed." The operations of the will include desiring, choosing, and loving. Experiencing the "presence of God" is correlated with the suspension of these operations. They are "absorbed," that is, directed inward toward the ground of consciousness—the center of the soul, attracted by the qualities of peace, joy, and delight that are characteristic of the center.

In the fourth dwelling places, Teresa speaks only of experiencing the effects of God's presence, whereas, in the fifth dwelling places, her meditation practice has become so deep that all her faculties (memory, intellect, and will) are completely absorbed in the divine presence during periods of the "Prayer of Union," the most mature stage of contemplation. In the sixth dwelling places she begins to have direct perception of Jesus Christ (through visions and locutions), who gradually leads her to full union with the Blessed Trinity in the seventh dwelling places.

Although she has no direct "perception" of God in the fourth dwelling places, Teresa believes that the interior recollection, peace, and delight are indications of God's presence. She writes that "in this prayer of union or quiet one understands that God is present by the effects that, as I say, He grants to the soul—that is the way His Majesty wants to give the experience of Himself" (*Life*, 27,4). The effects include changes in awareness and behavior. The virtuous disposition and actions that flow from the Prayer of Quiet indicate to Teresa that, in contemplation, the will is "united in some way with the will of God" (*IC*, IV:2,8).

The goal of meditation and contemplation is a new state of consciousness referred to in the Scriptures as the "new self" (Ephesians 4:22–24) and described by St. Teresa in the fifth dwelling places of *The Interior Castle*. Spiritual theologians describe this new relationship with God as "conforming union," that is, the human will fully conformed to the divine will.[6]

According to St. Teresa, the most important practice that will lead us toward union with God, after the Sacred Liturgy and the sacraments, is daily meditation. Following the Rule of Life of the Carmelites, St. Teresa meditated twice a day for an hour each time, once before breakfast and once before dinner. Many teachers of meditation recommend that people living an active life in the world meditate twice a day for twenty to thirty minutes.[7]

St. Teresa's Legacy ▸

As Teresa grew in prayer, she longed for a more simple and uncompromising way of living her Carmelite vocation. At the age of forty-seven (1562) she received permission to found St. Joseph's Monastery in Avila, which would follow the Primitive Carmelite Rule, a way of monastic life characterized by Gospel simplicity, poverty, and deep prayer. Five years later, she began to establish other monasteries. By the time of her death in 1582, she had presided over the founding of seventeen monasteries of the Carmelite Reform for women. With the help of St. John of the Cross,

---

6. Juan G. Arintero, *The Mystical Evolution in the Development and Vitality of the Church*, vol. 2, trans. Jordan Aumann (St. Louis, MO: B. Herder, 1951), 162.

7. Abbot Thomas Keating, M. Basil Pennington, and Thomas E. Clarke, S.J., *Finding Grace at the Center: The Beginning of Centering Prayer* (Still River, MA: St. Bede Publications, 1979), 63.

she also instituted her reform among the men of the order. Their reform of the Carmelites and their spiritual teachings contributed widely to spiritual regeneration of Catholics and Non-Catholics in the past four and a half centuries

The twentieth and twenty-first centuries witnessed a remarkable revival of scholarly and popular interest in Teresa's teachings to the point where her map of spiritual development (the seven dwelling places) is considered axiomatic by many spiritual theologians.[8] Because her insights into the spiritual journey are regarded as so universally applicable, her teachings often form the Christian reference in cross-cultural and inter-religious studies. In writing my M.A. thesis and Ph.D. dissertation, I found that the Teresian body of knowledge is particularly illuminating in a dialogue with the Vedic tradition of India as articulated by Maharishi Mahesh Yogi.

Comparing St. Teresa and Maharishi

St. Teresa and Maharishi describe spiritual development in ways that appear similar at first glance despite the fact that the two traditions have no known historical connection. Teresa classifies the stages of spiritual development as seven "dwelling places" (*moradas*). The first three dwelling places describe the beginnings of the spiritual journey, particularly the crucial role of self-knowledge and prayer. The last four dwelling places are regarded as distinct "supernatural" states: the Prayer of Quiet, Conforming Union, Spiritual Betrothal, and Spiritual Marriage. For Teresa, "supernatural" states of prayer refer to those that are not attainable through human effort.[9] Such states are "infused," that is, passively received by the person.

---

8. Auguste Poulain, S.J., *The Graces of the Interior Prayer: A Treatise on Mystical Theology* (London: Kegan Paul, Trench, Trubner, 1912); Arintero, *Mystical Evolution in the Development and Vitality of the Church*; Réginald Garrigou-Lagrange, O.P., *The Three Ages of the Interior Life: Prelude of Eternal Life* (St. Louis, MO: B. Herder, 1947).

9. St. Teresa of Avila, *The Interior Castle*, in *The Collected Works of St. Teresa of Avila*, trans. Kieran Kavanaugh and Otilio Rodriguez, vol. 2 (Washington D.C.: ICS Publications, 1980), IV:1,4.

Maharishi teaches that there are seven states of consciousness: waking, dreaming, sleeping, and four "higher" states: transcendental consciousness, cosmic consciousness, God consciousness, and unity consciousness. In both Maharishi and Teresa, the first higher state to emerge is the fourth, and the apparent similarities between the two accounts are suggested primarily in the fourth and fifth states.

In my dissertation, I attended to the four higher states of consciousness described by both authors in order to answer some intriguing and significant questions. How are the higher states of spiritual development as described by Teresa and Maharishi related? Do the apparent similarities between Teresa's seven "dwelling places" and Maharishi's seven "states of consciousness" reveal a single spiritual path common to both East and West or, on the contrary, do the differences in doctrines and traditions lead to very different places? One of the most intriguing results that emerged from my research is that there are some striking similarities between the authors' descriptions of the spiritual journey and, at the same time, significant differences. The most striking similarity is found in the fourth state, which, for both authors, marks the transition from active meditation to interior silence. The most significant difference concerns how the two authors describe "union with God" in the seventh state.

I spent three years researching and writing my 326-page dissertation. It is a highly technical and complex study that I cannot adequately summarize in this memoir. In the future, I may rewrite and publish the dissertation in order to address the above questions in a detailed manner.

21

Ordination

ARRIVING AT ST. PATRICK'S SEMINARY IN JANUARY OF 1977 ended one major phase in my life story and gave rise to another. Most of my young adult years were devoted to my spiritual and vocational quests. Once I rediscovered my vocation on the six-month meditation course in Switzerland, my focus became preparation for serving as a priest. A significant part of that preparation was the academic study of Catholic theology: biblical, doctrinal, moral, and spiritual. A second part of the preparation was practical training for the pastoral ministry: courses in pastoral counseling, clinical and pastoral education in a hospital, and fieldwork in parishes, including a year internship in a parish as an ordained deacon in preparation for ordination as a priest.

Once I recovered from the initial depression upon returning to the seminary, I thrived in my new life. I fully engaged in my academic work, new friendships, community life, and spiritual direction. Twice a month I met with my spiritual director, Father Bob Gavin, a loving older member of the faculty who accompanied me throughout my final three years in the seminary and a few years beyond. He helped me recognize and face my struggles with grandiosity and spiritual pride. He served as an inspiring model of a happy, healthy, and holy priest.

I completed my M.A. thesis just in time to prepare for ordination as a deacon. About fifteen members of my class were ordained with me. The celebration took place on April 21, 1979, at St. Mary's Cathedral in San Francisco. About three thousand people attended, including several hundred of my friends and relatives. It was a glorious day. I was particularly happy for my mom and dad. I had put them through much anxiety and confusion during my years of spiritual and vocational exploration. It was such a pleasure for me to see them so joyful and proud of their kid.

The priesthood ordination a year later was even more exhilarating.

Language Study and Reconciliation in Mexico ▸

A couple of months after ordination to the diaconate, about half a dozen of my classmates and I were sent by the archdiocese to take intensive Spanish language classes in Cuernavaca, Mexico. Even though I had studied in Mexico ten years earlier, I had forgotten a great deal and looked forward to the opportunity.

I also hoped to arrange a reconciliation with Antonia.

Cuernavaca is the capital and largest city of the state of Morelos. The city is located about a ninety-minute drive south of Mexico City. It is called *"La ciudad de la primavera eterna"* (City of Eternal Spring). Cuernavaca has long been a vacation destination because of its warm, stable climate and abundant vegetation. I remember as a student in 1969 walking cobblestone streets through neighborhoods of picturesque Spanish colonial homes behind adobe walls covered with bougainvillea.

When we arrived in Cuernavaca, it was just as I remembered: a splendid colonial city teeming with gorgeous, semitropical vegetation. My classmate and fellow deacon, Dick Hoenisch, and I were assigned to live with a family in an attractive middle-class neighborhood. The father of the family was head of the language school, so we assumed that we would have ample opportunity to receive help with our spoken Spanish while at home. However, he and his family were out of the house most of the time, so Dick and I had each other for conversation partners—the blind leading the blind.

Ever since the heartbreaking goodbye to Antonia in Acapulco in 1972, I had carried regret and guilt for the suffering I caused her. While in St. Moritz, I wrote a letter informing her about my rediscovery of my vocation to the priesthood. She responded with a most gracious letter expressing her happiness that I had finally found my calling. Consequently, I wasn't quite as nervous as I might have been with the prospect of an emotional reconciliation after so many years.

I phoned Antonia. She sounded happy to hear from me. What a relief! I told her that Dick and I were going to spend a day off in Mexico City and that we would like to take her to lunch. She accepted the invitation, adding that she would be accompanied by one of her girlfriends.

On the appointed day, Dick and I traveled by bus to Mexico City and took the Metro to an attractive plaza where Antonia and I had agreed to meet. As Dick and I emerged from the Metro station, we saw Antonia and her friend on the opposite side of the plaza. Without thinking, I ran toward her and swooped her up in my arms and twirled her around. The emotion that I had kept bottled up for seven years came bursting out. She seemed just as excited as I. We all introduced ourselves and headed toward a restaurant.

After eating our meal, Antonia said that she would like to speak with me privately for a few minutes. So, Dick engaged Antonia's friend in conversation at one end of the table while Antonia and I chatted at the other end. She proceeded to tell me that she had traveled to England the previous year to study English. During that time, she developed a close friendship with an Englishman named Stan Halse. She described him as a real gentleman who treated her with respect and affection. Eventually, he asked her to marry him. She felt very close to Stan but had not yet made a decision. She sought my advice. It seemed somewhat ironic that she was asking me for such advice. After listening to her description of Stan and their relationship, my counsel was simple: "If you can see yourself having children with him and look forward to growing old with him, I would marry him."

(Fast forward to July, 1980, three months after my priesthood ordination. I received a letter from Antonia informing me that she had decided to marry Stan and then wrote something that stunned me: "I want you to marry us." After all the heartache I had put her through seven years earlier, I was surprised and delighted with her request. Three months later I flew to Mexico City and presided at their splendid wedding.)

Internship ▸

After completing our Spanish language study in Mexico, my fellow deacons and I were assigned to various parishes in the archdiocese to embark on a nine-month internship. The purpose was to initiate us into the variety of ministries and activities of a Catholic parish and to observe the day-to-day lives of parish priests. I was assigned to St. Elizabeth Parish in Milpitas. My mentor and supervisor was the pastor, Father Art Harrison, a native of San Francisco who was ordained a priest in 1956. Prior to becoming pastor, he had served nine-years as chaplain at San Quentin Prison. The associate pastor was Father Francis Cilia, who had just been ordained. We had been students together at St. Patrick's Seminary.

Instead of a traditional parish rectory, the priests and I lived in two tract houses across the street from the church. Father Harrison and I lived in one house and Father Cilia lived next door. We all ate meals together in my house—well prepared by a delightful older woman whose nickname was Freddy.

My first Sunday at the parish, Father Harrison introduced me to the parishioners at all the Masses. Most of them were young Anglo couples and a small number of Hispanics and Filipinos. Very soon I was invited to dinner by the parishioners and learned that one of the needs in the parish was adult faith formation. Most Catholic parishes have a year-long process called "Rite of Christian Initiation for Adults" (RCIA) directed to non-Catholics who are interested in being initiated into Catholic Christianity. St. Elizabeth's had no RCIA, so I asked the pastor if I could develop one. He was all for it.

Fortunately, I had taken a course on the RCIA at the seminary and was prepared to launch it immediately. I decided to open it up to Catholics as well as non-Catholics, since so many parishioners had expressed the need for faith formation. From the pulpit at Sunday Masses, I extended the invitation to everyone. Over forty people, including about fifteen non-Catholics, signed up. Most remained throughout the nine-month process. I dedicated a day each week to preparing the sessions and received invaluable on-the-job training as a teacher. The participants and I formed a close-knit community that became a source of spiritual and intellectual nourishment for all. One of them, Roberta Forem, became one of my closest spiritual sisters and has remained so. The RCIA process established two passions that would remain for the rest of my life: teaching and spiritual formation.

Getting Ready for the Big Day

My life and ministry at St. Elizabeth's brought me much fulfillment and produced in me more enthusiasm for the priesthood than ever. As the date of ordination approached (April 12, 1980), I formed a team of family and friends to help me prepare invitations, receptions, and the Masses of Thanksgiving I would be celebrating the week following ordination.

My mom was my biggest supporter and cheerleader. She volunteered for the huge job of developing a list of invitees—family, friends and teachers from middle school, high school, college, St. Patrick Seminary, friends from my year in Mexico, colleagues in the TM movement, and parishioners from the various parishes where I served. We ended up with about six hundred names. My mother began the challenging task of researching addresses. She was amazing. Within a short period of time, she figured out how to contact most people on the list. She also planned what proved to be a superb reception at the family home following the ordination.

My dear friend from the 1973 European odyssey, Mary Anne Tomacci, her sister Toni, and Roberta helped me address by hand six hundred envelopes. Mary Anne created the invitation card using her beautiful calligraphy.

I wanted to include as many family and friends as possible in the events. My Aunt Jeanne offered to be unofficial photographer. I invited several Sisters of the Holy Names of Jesus and Mary to serve as Communion Ministers. I asked relatives and old friends to serve in other capacities at the Mass of Thanksgiving: my brother Brian as Lector, Nancy Wales as Commentator, Leo as Acolyte, Steve Rickard as Cross-Bearer, Tim Stier as Master of Ceremonies, Manuel Sousa as deacon, and a number of priest-mentors as concelebrants—Fathers O'Brien, Dunstan, Konkel, Chirico, Forster, and my two cousins Pat and Jim Keane. My mother baked a beautiful loaf of bread for the Mass, Aunt Jeanne made the chasuble, the St. Elizabeth young adult choir and some seminarians provided the music ministry. The Italian Catholic Federation of St. Philip Neri Parish and other parishioners prepared gourmet food for the reception, and the pastor, Father Gary Tollner, paid the bill!

They say, "it takes a village to raise a child." From my experience it is also true to say that "it takes a village to prepare a priest."

The Big Day

The eight members of my class from the Archdiocese of San Francisco planned the ordination liturgy together. It was to be a grand celebration. We were even able to find a symphony orchestra from Cañada College to play for the Mass. Sister Suzanne Toolan, a legendary composer of liturgical music, organized and directed a choir of about fifty voices. A fine organist, Father James Alyward, played the massive, world-class Rufatti organ. The Archbishop of San Francisco, John R. Quinn, was to be the main celebrant accompanied by three other bishops and around one hundred priests.

As the Gospel reading, we chose one of my favorite passages from John's Gospel, the "Vine and Branches" section of Jesus's Last Supper Discourse, chapter 15. The first five verses set the theme that I believe directly applies to the ministry of a priest and to all others who minister in his name:

> I am the true vine, and my Father is the vine grower. He takes away every branch in me that does not bear fruit, and everyone that does he prunes so that it bears more fruit.... Remain in me, as I remain in you. Just as a branch cannot bear fruit on its own unless it remains on the vine, so neither can you unless you remain in me. I am the vine, you are the branches. Whoever remains in me and I in him will bear much fruit, because without me you can do nothing. (John 15:1–5)

Since my team sent out about six hundred invitations, I expected a large crowd; so, I arrived early at the cathedral with my parents and brother in order to greet our guests. We were more than excited. We had been preparing for this day since I was fourteen years old—a sixteen-year journey.

Upon arrival, I vested with my alb (a long white robe) and entered the body of the cathedral to find my guests. The massive cathedral accommodates close to four thousand people and each ordinandi had a reserved section. When I reached my section, I was filled with joy to see family and friends from every phase of my life. I worked the crowd of at least six hundred for close to an hour and lost track of time. The Ordination Mass was to begin at 10:00 A.M. At 9:55 all the ordinandi were lined up in the sacristy with the bishops except me. A posse of priests was sent out to find me. They whisked me away from the crowd, took me to the basement to enter a private elevator that goes to the sacristy. When we entered the elevator, a Sister of the Holy Family entered with us. Noticing my alb, she asked "Are you one of the ordinandi?" I answered affirmatively. She then said, "Oh, then you know Kevin Joyce!" I told her I was the man. Then with great emotion she exclaimed, "I have been wanting to meet you for twenty years! I am Sister Monica. Twenty years ago, Sister Austin was on her deathbed and said to me, 'I have been praying for a boy named Kevin Joyce from Alameda whom I prepared for First Holy Communion. I believe he has a vocation to the priesthood. Now that I am about to die, I ask you please to continue praying for him.'"

When I heard this story, I wept. When I was in Sister Austin's First Communion class, I had no idea that she thought I had a call to the priesthood and that she was praying for my vocation. I was so touched that Sister Monica had continued to pray for me after Sister Austin's death. I was overwhelmed by the "coincidence" of meeting Sister Monica five minutes before my ordination Mass.

When the elevator reached the sacristy, I tried to compose myself as I encountered my classmates, our parents, and the bishops who were not too happy with my tardiness. As we formed a procession with the rest of the concelebrating priests, my parents and I could barely contain our excitement.

The ordinandi, with our parents at our sides, joined the procession up the center aisle of the massive cathedral. The organ and fifty-voice choir led the congregation of about four thousand in Ralph Vaughn Williams's splendid setting of St. Francis of Assisi's "All Creatures of Our God and King." My parents and I joined my brother in the front pew of our section. The Mass proceeded with a stirring "Glory to God in the Highest," followed by the biblical readings. After the first reading, the choir sang a four-part setting of Psalm 63 that I had composed. I think my mother was more excited by hearing my music than I was.

After the readings, we ordinandi approached the sanctuary and sat in front of the altar to listen to the archbishop's homily, during which occurred some unexpected drama. One of the members of the orchestra had a seizure and screamed. The archbishop stopped preaching and medical personnel from among the guests quickly made their way toward the afflicted musician. One overly enthusiastic young woman came bounding down the aisle shouting repeatedly "I know CPR!" After the musician was carried outside to an ambulance, the archbishop continued with his homily, a bit shaken up as were we all.

After the homily came the Rite of Ordination, which included another dramatic moment—this one planned, however. The ordinandi lay prostrate on the cathedral floor as a cantor chanted the Litany of the Saints. This is an ancient part of the ordination ritual, during which the entire congregation invokes the intercession of the saints to pray for the young men about to be ordained. Then each ordinandi knelt before the archbishop to profess his priestly promises, after which, the archbishop laid hands in silence upon the head of each young man. Then all one hundred concelebrating priests came forward to also lay their hands on us. The laying on of hands comes directly from the New Testament, a sign of conferral of the Holy Spirit and transmission of the priestly ministry. St. Paul refers to this ritual in 2 Timothy 1:6: "I remind you to stir into flame the gift of God that you have through the imposition of my hands."

After the laying on of hands, each new priest returned to his parents' pew, where priestly vestments were waiting. Two priests then vested the young man. I had requested that my childhood pastor, Father O'Brien, and my diaconate mentor, Father Harrison, vest me. It was a very poignant moment when Father O'Brien placed the chasuble on me, the same priest who had given me my First Holy Communion twenty-three years earlier, and who nurtured my vocation throughout the many twists and turns in my path to the priesthood.

The final ritual in the ordination rite was the "Rite of Peace." The bishops and priests gave an embrace to each of us, signifying our entrance into the "Order of Presbyters."

Presbyter in Greek means "elder." The presbyters and bishops in the New Testament came to be called "priests" before the end of the first century. Protestants sometimes ask why Catholics and Orthodox call their ordained clergy, "priests." The priests of the Old Testament referred to the ministers who offered sacrifices in the temple for the people of Israel. Priests of the New Testament offer the "Holy Sacrifice of the

Mass," the re-presentation of the sacrifice of Jesus on the cross and of his glorious resurrection. A second reason for calling the presbyters "priests," is that their first priority is preaching the Gospel. In Romans 15:16, St. Paul refers to his "service of the gospel of God" as "priestly service."

After the Rite of Ordination, our parents accompanied us one by one to the archbishop and presented to him the chalice and paten that we would be using in our celebration of the Mass.[1] After that ritual, the newly ordained priests joined the archbishop around the altar for the continuation of the Mass. During the distribution of Holy Communion, we each went to the head of the aisle where our family and friends were seated. As they approached me to receive the Eucharist or a blessing, I felt enormously grateful for the love and support of so many people.

At the end of the Mass, the archbishop blessed the congregation. He then knelt and received a blessing from each of the new priests—a humbling gesture for both him and us. We then recessed down the aisle with our parents to greet guests in the piazza.

When I exited the cathedral, the first person to congratulate me caused me great surprise. It was Miguel Mayorga Jr., whom I had known well during my year studying in Mexico. I often joined him, his parents, and his eleven siblings for meals. In my confusion, I asked a very dumb question, "Miguel, what are you doing here?!" I thought that perhaps his job or a vacation had brought him to San Francisco. He responded, "You sent an invitation to my family, remember?!"

I was deeply touched that he had traveled all the way from Mexico for my ordination. He was standing with Steve Rickard, who had joined me often for those memorable meals and parties at the Mayorga home. We had a brief, animated conversation, and then agreed to have a longer chat at the reception to be held at my family home. A few years later, I was privileged to preside over Miguel's marriage in Mexico City and the First Communion Mass of his son, Miguelito. Following a colloquial custom among male youth in Mexico (despite no longer being young), we have always called each other "Miguelazo" and "Kevinazo."

I gave and received hundreds of *abrazos* for about an hour. Long before the ordination, I had decided how I was going to greet each

---

1. A paten is a small metal plate that holds the bread that is transformed into the Body of Christ.

person at the receptions. Over the years I had attended many ordinations and weddings and frequently was disappointed when I approached the new priest or married couple at the reception. They were often overwhelmed and distracted and did not give full attention and eye contact to the guests who were greeting them. I decided that, at my ordination receptions, I would give unwavering attention and eye contact to the person in front of me for at least fifteen seconds. I wouldn't care if the pope or president were waiting to greet me. I would not let my eyes wander from the person in front of me for any reason during that short interaction. People usually have enough common sense not to monopolize time with the person being celebrated. What we all desire on such occasions is a real connection with the person—even if only for fifteen seconds.

My technique worked beautifully. I felt satisfied after each intimate fifteen-second interaction, and the guests seemed to enjoy a fulfilling interface as well. The hour I spent greeting people after the ordination was a good warm-up for multiple celebrations to follow.

22

Celebrations and a Surprise Assignment

First Mass and Reception

AFTER THE ORDINATION ON APRIL 12, 1980, MY MOM AND DAD hosted a lovely reception at our family home for about seventy-five family members and close friends. All six hundred invitees had been invited to a formal reception at St. Philip Neri parish hall after the Mass of Thanksgiving the following day.

Priests tend to remember their first experiences of celebrating the sacraments—their first anointing of the sick, first baptism, first wedding. My first time celebrating the Sacrament of Reconciliation (Confession) was the moment I stepped in the door of the family home after the ordination. My brother asked me to hear his confession. I was very touched by his request.

The reception at our home was extraordinarily joyful. Most of the people who attended had known my family for many years and had witnessed the twists and turns of my long journey to the priesthood. My parents and I were inundated with their affection. One encounter particularly touched me. Our pastor emeritus, Father Pat O'Brien, my lifelong spiritual guide and cheerleader, arrived after most of the other guests. He walked into the entry hall of the house where a large number of people were gathered. As I approached him to offer a warm welcome, he knelt down, kissed my hands and asked for my priestly blessing. Father O'Brien had patiently awaited that blessing for sixteen years.

The next day I arrived early at the church to prepare for the 12:15 P.M. Mass of Thanksgiving. I met for a rehearsal with my two brothers from the seminary, Tim Stier and Manuel Sousa, who were to be emcee and deacon of the Mass. Tim had been ordained the previous year for the Diocese of Oakland, and Manuel would be ordained two months later for the Diocese of Stockton. Soon the church filled up with the six hundred invitees and a few hundred parishioners who regularly attended the 12:15 Mass. As was the case at the ordination, my parents processed into the church with me along with a dozen priest friends and mentors. The joy and excitement that filled the cathedral the previous day was palpably present for the Mass of Thanksgiving.

After the Mass, everyone was invited to the parish hall for the formal reception. Throughout the afternoon, as I personally greeted hundreds of well-wishers, I remembered to employ my fifteen-second greeting technique, which worked just as beautifully as it had the day before.

My parents and I were jubilant throughout the day. In fact, my parents used to say periodically throughout the coming years, that the ordination weekend was the happiest experience of their lives.

More Celebrations ▸

My Aunt Jeanne was another great supporter throughout my life. She had organized two more Masses of Thanksgiving for me: on Tuesday at the convent of Holy Names High School in Oakland, where she was a teacher, and another on Friday at the Holy Names Novitiate and Retirement Center in Los Gatos. Both celebrations were very special to me because of my close relationship with many Sisters of the Holy Names since my earliest years.

I invited Leo to join me on the trip to Los Gatos. He had participated in all the festivities during the ordination weekend. On the way he said, "Kevin, your ordination has affected me more than I can say. I am thinking again about the priesthood." Readers will recall from chapter 11 that Leo had attempted to be ordained for the Archdiocese of Calcutta, met major obstacles, and eventually decided not to pursue ordination. He then became dean of studies at Salesian High School in Berkeley, where he had worked for the past several years. The year following my ordination he decided to join a religious order, the Oblates of Mary Immaculate, and pursue the priesthood. I was overjoyed when he made the decision because I always believed he had a vocation to the priestly ministry.

On Saturday, I celebrated a Mass of Thanksgiving followed by a big reception at St. Elizabeth Parish, where I had been serving as deacon. I had grown close to many people in the parish, especially young couples and the RCIA participants. They came out in large numbers for the celebration and, again, my parents, brother and I felt immersed in waves of love.

Two Weeks in Mexico ▸

During my deacon year, a seminarian from Mexico, Lupillo Moreno, joined the Archdiocese of San Francisco and entered our deacon class. He and I became good friends, frequently spending days off together. He invited me to join him for a two-week trip through Mexico, celebrating Masses of Thanksgiving with parish communities and convents of nuns.

The week following the Mass at St. Elizabeth's, Lupillo and I flew to Mexico City and headed straight for the Basilica of Our Lady of Guadalupe, the central shrine in all of Mexico.

We arrived at the sacristy and told the sacristan that we were newly ordained priests from San Francisco and had come to celebrate a Mass of Thanksgiving at the basilica. The sacristan was delighted to meet two new priests, gave us vestments, and pointed to a door saying, "God bless you as you celebrate your Mass."

The basilica is enormous, accommodating about ten thousand people. It has many side altars for priests' private Masses. I assumed we would be celebrating at one of those altars. When we passed through the door, we found ourselves in the main sanctuary. The basilica was packed. I asked Lupillo if we had gone through the wrong door. He said, "No, we are to celebrate at the main altar, and you will be the main celebrant." I looked at the congregation of ten thousand and responded, "I can't! I have never celebrated Mass in Spanish." He assured me that I would do just fine, and he pushed me ahead of him toward the high altar.

I believe that *La Virgen de Guadalupe* interceded for me, and the Lord gave me the grace I needed to meet the challenge because the Mass turned out beautifully. Lupillo, mercifully, preached the homily.

After Mass, we processed down the central aisle to the plaza to greet people. I had no idea how important ordinations and young priests are to the people of Mexico. Hundreds of people lined up to kiss our hands and to receive blessings. The custom of kissing the newly ordained priests' hands is based on one of the rituals of the ordination ceremony. The new priest's hands are anointed with the Holy Oil of Sacred Chrism by the bishop as a sign that the priest will use his hands to celebrate the Sacred Liturgy, consecrate the bread and wine into the Body and Blood of Christ, forgive sins, and anoint the sick.

After two hours of blessing a few hundred people, we reentered the basilica to remove our vestments and go to dinner. However, some of the people had other plans. Several approached us and requested that we hear their confessions. We sat in pews removed from the crowd and, one-by-one, people came to us for confession. I assumed that once we heard the confessions of the dozen or so people who had made the request, we would be able to leave. Not so. After hearing a half dozen confessions, I looked up and saw that two long lines of people had formed, one next to my pew and one next to Lupillo's. We heard confessions for at least another hour. Prior to that day, I had only heard one confession, that of my brother. Now, on one afternoon, I probably heard a hundred confessions. Good training for my future.

Climbing the Oaxaca Mountains ▸

A few days later, we traveled to Oaxaca in the southern part of the country. Prior to coming to San Francisco, Lupillo had lived for a year in a small village of Zapotec indigenous people in the mountains near the city of Oaxaca, *la Sierra Juarez*. The Sierra Juárez is one of Oaxaca State's wettest areas and richest in forest diversity, with perhaps two thousand of the eight thousand or more plant species that are found in the state. It is mostly covered by montane cloud forest, but includes tropical evergreen forests and forests of pine, pine-oak and oak.[1] Lupillo had been in a Mexican seminary but decided to take a year off and live a quasi-monastic life in the Sierra Juarez mountains.

He chose to live in a small hermitage near the village of Santa Cruz de Yagavila, which has about six hundred inhabitants. Most speak only the native dialect, Zapoteco, rather than Spanish. During the year he became very fond of the villagers and promised them that, if he ever became a priest, he would return to celebrate a Mass with them.

After living in the mountains for a year, Lupillo pursued various options for becoming a priest, and finally chose the Archdiocese of San Francisco because he had heard that many Latinos lived in the city but few Spanish-speaking priests.

From the city of Oaxaca, friends of Lupillo drove us by car up the mountains until the road ended. Then we put on our backpacks and proceeded to hike up a mountain for three hours until we reached the village of Santa Cruz de Yagavila. We stayed in a rustic cottage with a Dutch missionary from the order of the Sacred Heart Fathers, a friend of Lupillo.

The next day, Lupillo led me on a tour of the village, stopping at many of the small homes to greet the people. He knew enough Zapoteco for basic communication. The people were very hospitable and were intrigued to meet an Americano from California.

That night I had a dream about my first assignment as a priest. I saw a small mountain behind a parish church and school and was told that I would be the new associate pastor of the parish. When I awakened, I remembered that I had once been at that parish, St. Catherine's in Morgan Hill. I didn't give much importance to the dream because I had already been assured that I would be sent to a parish in the Mission District of San Francisco. I had asked to be sent there because I wished to be engaged in Spanish-speaking ministry in the city.

After five days in the mountains, Lupillo and I celebrated more Thanksgiving Masses with communities of nuns in Acapulco and Guadalajara, where I left Lupillo with his family. I returned to Mexico City, where I visited old friends—the Mayorgas, the Limon family, and Antonia's family. They all received me like a son. I also traveled to the

---

1. See "Sierra Juarez" in Wikipedia.

outskirts of Mexico City beyond the International Airport to an area called "Los Reyes la Paz" to visit Father Don Hessler. He had become pastor of a very poor barrio called La Ampliación de los Reyes la Paz ("The Extension of the Kings of Peace [Colony]").

I arrived at Father Hessler's church on a Sunday morning just in time for the main Mass of the day. The church was made of corrugated metal—not much to look at from the outside. But the people had created an inviting, devotional worship space within. A youth choir provided spirited music and the packed church rocked! I was impressed and moved by the obvious devotion and enthusiasm of the people. Father Hessler had worked hard to develop lay leadership in the community, and the results were quite evident. For the next several years, I returned to the parish to help Father Hessler each summer for a couple weeks.

A Surprise Assignment ▸

Once Lupillo and I returned to California, we joined the other six San Francisco Archdiocese members of our class for a meeting with the archbishop to receive our letters of assignment. When he handed me my letter, I was looking forward to an assignment in the Mission District. When I read the letter, I was shocked. It said that I would be sent to St. Catherine's Parish in Morgan Hill! My first reaction was profound disappointment. Then I remembered the dream I had in the mountains of Oaxaca. I thought, "The Lord was preparing me for this big surprise."

I knew the pastor of St. Catherine's, Father Joe Milani. He had been my pastoral supervisor when I was a freshman in college and worked in a youth Confirmation program at St. Maria Goretti Parish in San Jose. He was always very good to me. After leaving the archbishop's office, I phoned Father Milani, who already knew about the assignment. He was delighted that I would be working at St. Catherine's. We made plans to meet the next day.

I drove to Morgan Hill, which is about twenty-two miles south of San Jose. When I entered the rectory and met Father Milani in his living room, he opened his arms and said: "Welcome, Kevin! The entire Hispanic community is yours!" He obviously had been informed that I desired to be involved in Spanish-speaking ministry. We proceeded to chat about responsibilities that would be mine in the parish. He explained that he and the other parish priest, Father Leo Rooney, did not speak Spanish. Consequently, he would depend on me to provide leadership for the Spanish-speaking parishioners, who formed about a third of the parish. Total Sunday Mass attendance was around two thousand people. So, I would effectively be pastor of approximately seven hundred parishioners. I would also be an associate pastor for the English-speaking community, and youth minister for both the English- and Spanish-speaking youth.

Being assigned to St. Catherine's enabled me to reconnect with my college aspiration of serving poor and disenfranchised people, a desire further fed by my work with Father Hessler's communities in Mexico. A large percentage of the Hispanic population in Morgan Hill were low-income farmworkers, many of whom lived with the insecurity of having no legal status in the country. My spiritual journey over the previous decade had largely been focused on the interior life and philosophical explorations. My arrival in Morgan Hill as spiritual leader of a largely poor community would afford me the opportunity of integrating the Catholic spirituality tradition with its social justice teachings.

My many years of vocational discernment and seminary formation had convinced me that the Lord had called me to the priesthood, and I was ready to get to work!

23

Divine Providence Is Real

WE HAVE ALMOST ARRIVED AT THE END OF THE BOOK, A MEMOIR of the first thirty years of my life and an introduction to spiritual masters and mentors who guided me through the many twists and turns of my journey. I hope that my account of their lives and teachings will have relevance for others seeking guidance on their spiritual journeys.

As I embarked on my life as a priest, I found myself under a delusion that is common among college graduates, newly married couples, and others who have just accomplished a major life goal—the delusion of believing that we have finally arrived. The truth is, such accomplishments are only the beginning of a new series of challenges and goals. Having reached the goal of my sixteen-year journey to the priesthood, I felt a certain emotional intoxication, believing that I was now a different person, that I had overcome the major obstacles in my spiritual journey. Of course, anyone with sufficient life experience comes to realize that the ongoing process of growth and development is endless. As I began my life as a priest, I had no idea of how many new "agonies and ecstasies" awaited me over the next forty years.

As I conclude this book, I am struck by three prominent themes that have emerged:

> First, the great gift of having family members, masters, mentors, and spiritual friends to support and guide me on my journey.
>
> Second, how the East–West interreligious dialogue impacted my intellectual and spiritual development.

Third, the presence and power of Divine Providence. I will end the book with a story that most powerfully exemplifies this third theme, a story that occurred eighteen years after my ordination.

In chapter 1 I described how close my brother and I were as children. When we reached our twenties, Brian underwent a big change. He became sullen and withdrawn. His lifelong hemophilia had taken a big toll on him. In addition, because of transfusions with tainted blood, he had contracted the AIDS virus. His suffering led to long bouts of depression and anger. His hostility was fostered by the preaching of a firebrand Fundamentalist TV evangelist that led Brian to abandon the Catholic faith.

During his final three years of life, Brian isolated himself from family and friends. The only people he allowed into his apartment were volunteers from the local Catholic AIDS ministry, who brought him food, and nurses, who provided him with blood concentrate for infusions. One of the volunteers informed me and my mom in December 1997 that Brian's condition was critical. We began asking everyone we knew to intensify their prayer for Brian. Since he was closed to all human interventions, I begged God for direct divine intervention as happened in the life of St. Paul, the fanatical persecutor of Christians who became a great saint. I asked St. Paul to be Brian's special intercessor.

On January 17, 1998, an old friend dropped by my rectory with a belated Christmas gift. I apprised him of Brian's grave situation. He recommended that, in our prayer for Brian, we think of the image of Christ the Good Shepherd holding a lost sheep. I remembered that someone had given me a painting of the Good Shepherd. I went looking for it, intending to place it on my prayer table, but could not locate it. Then, glancing at my watch, I realized that I had a wedding awaiting me in five minutes. I ran to the church.

Upon arrival in the sacristy, I discovered that someone had placed a lovely large pencil etching of the Good Shepherd on the vesting table with the inscription "If you wander away, He will always search for you and will gladly welcome you back." I asked the sacristan who had left the etching. He responded that no one had entered the sacristy besides himself. At that moment, I knew that God had somehow sent that etching to confirm what my friend said to me just ten minutes earlier. I felt greatly encouraged to continue the prayer campaign.

On January 25, Brian suddenly and dramatically changed. He called my mother and asked her to come to his apartment. When she arrived, he wept and begged forgiveness for his hostility and hardness of heart. He also said, "I want to see my brother."

When my mom phoned me with the amazing news, I was overjoyed beyond belief. I drove to his apartment and entered his bedroom where he was sitting on the side of his bed appearing very serious. I was shaken by his emaciated body. I sat in front of him. Without greeting me, he said from the depths of his heart, "Kev, please forgive me." I immediately responded from the depths of my heart, "Brian, please forgive me." (I too had harbored anger and resentment toward him because of the way he had treated me and my parents.) At that moment, every negative feeling I had toward my brother instantaneously vanished. Never in my life have I experienced such profound, sudden, and permanent reconciliation with another human being. The sense of deep love we had for each other in our early years immediately resurfaced.

We poured out our souls to each other for several hours. He repented of living in hate, for having blamed others for his pain and suffering. Repeatedly he told me that he loved me and deeply appreciated my presence. Over and over, he said, "Do you love me, Kev? Please don't leave me. You can never imagine how lonely and miserable I have been."

A few days later, I joined my Jesus Caritas priest fraternity for a day of fellowship and retreat. During a quiet hour I journaled about the extraordinary events that had occurred with my brother. As I wrote, I felt immense gratitude to God and to all the people who had been praying for my brother, especially St. Paul. It was then I realized that the amazing change in my brother had occurred on January 25, which is the Feast of the Conversion of St. Paul! The two "coincidences" of seeing the etching of the Good Shepherd on the sacristy vesting table ten minutes after I had been frantically trying to locate an icon of the Good Shepherd, and the stunning change in my brother on the day that celebrates St. Paul's conversion further convinced me of a major theme of this book: Divine Providence is a reality.

For almost three months Brian lay in bed, unable to move without pain, lovingly cared for by my mom and Aunt Jeanne. Throughout those months, a steady stream of visitors came to Brian's bedside including two dear friends who were nurses, Lita and Renee. They stayed for days at a time to help care for Brian along with an exceptional Hospice caregiver. I spent my days off with Mom and Brian, and often brought Antonio Ojeda with me, who would play the guitar and sing with Brian while I took my mom out to dinner so she could relax briefly from caregiving. Brian's room became like a little sanctuary. He would pray throughout the day. We all said that we received more comfort and inspiration from Brian than we gave him.

Mother's love is often used as a way of describing God's unconditional love. In the case of my mother, the analogy is as close as I have ever seen. During Brian's years of estrangement from the family, Mom's love for him never waned. On the contrary, she was always filled with deep compassion and concern for him. When Brian called her unexpectedly on January 25 and apologized to her with tears for several hours, she was ecstatic. She felt no resentment for the years Brian had rejected her. She immediately moved a mattress to the floor of his apartment's living room, moved in, and cared for him 24/7 until the day he died. Her actions did not surprise me in the least. For me she was always the epitome of a mother who would sacrifice her own comfort and desires for the sake of her children.

As we entered Holy Week, we could see that Brian didn't have long to live. I turned over my parish responsibilities to Father Gerardo Menchaca and stayed with Mom and Brian. On Good Friday we read St. John's account of the Lord's passion to Brian, who appeared to be in a semi-coma. On Holy Saturday morning we felt certain that Brian was about to die. We prayed the prayers for the dying, we wept, and we said our good-byes. All day he lay unconscious, barely breathing. That evening we celebrated the Easter Vigil Liturgy of the Word around Brian's body and sang Easter hymns. As we sang the Easter Alleluia, Brian suddenly regained consciousness and exclaimed "Splendid! Splendid!" It was a moment of supreme joy. We felt as if Brian had come back to life. After some brief, sweet conversation, he went back to sleep.

The next morning, Easter Sunday, he was in severe pain. Lita was caring for him. She asked me to bring her Holy Communion. When I arrived with the Eucharist, we celebrated an intimate Communion service around Brian's bed. After giving Lita Holy Communion, I asked Brian, "Would you like to receive the Body of Christ?" (Brian had not attended Mass for ten years.) He replied with great emotion, "Yes, I would! Yes, I would!" After receiving the Eucharist, he said, "Kev, thanks so much for that. Thanks so much for that." Many of us had been praying for months that Brian would return to the Catholic faith and to the sacraments. The prayer was answered that Easter Sunday morning.

Easter night Brian periodically raised his hands in prayer. Very gently he died on Easter Monday morning, April 13, 1998, one day after the tenth anniversary of our father's death.

Brian suffered much throughout his life, yet his last months were often joyful. When news of Brian's death reached my bishop, Pierre DuMaine, he phoned and shared a quotation from Flannery O'Connor that spoke to him of Brian:

> I have never been anywhere but sick. In a sense sickness is a place, more instructive than a long trip to Europe, and it's always a place where there is no company, where nobody can follow. Sickness before death is a very appropriate thing, and I think those who don't have it miss one of God's mercies.

For me, Brian's living and dying embody the truth of St. Paul's poignant teaching in Romans 8:18:

> I consider that the sufferings of this present time are as nothing compared with the glory to be revealed in us.

▸ ───

I am writing this last chapter twenty-five years after my brother's death. His life and his death are as fresh for me today as they were the day he died. For me Brian set the gold standard for brotherly love, and instantiated the power of repentance to transform hearts and relationships. Ending this memoir with the narration of his last months of life brings into vivid relief what I have attempted to explain in this book as the "Providential ordering of events." Even in the most painful happenings of our lives, for those with hearts filled with faith in the God who created us, we can experience the reality of Grace and the invincibility of Love.

About the Author

Kevin Patrick Joyce, Ph.D.

FATHER KEVIN JOYCE, priest of the Diocese of San Jose since 1980, serves as professor and spiritual director at St. Patrick's Seminary & University in Menlo Park, California. He studied at seminaries in the Archdiocese of San Francisco, the University of the Americas in Mexico City, and the Catholic University of America in Washington, D.C., where he received a doctorate in spirituality. He attended courses in Spain and Switzerland on the spirituality and meditation practices of the Far East. As a diocesan priest, Father Kevin served as pastor of large, multicultural parishes and founded and directed SpiritSite, a Catholic Spirituality Center. Father Joyce has a particular interest in the East–West interreligious dialogue and in the spiritual masters of the Christian tradition, especially John of the Cross and Teresa of Avila.

Endorsements for
Kevin Patrick Joyce, *Surprised by Grace:*
A Spiritual Journey from West to East and Back

In the pages of this delightful book, Father Kevin Joyce offers his readers three gifts: a captivating narrative of his journey to the priesthood, a masterful introduction to the mystical life, and a sensitive comparison between Catholicism and Eastern spirituality. In Father Joyce's skillful hands, these three strands form a seamless whole that reflects his joy in the priesthood and his knowledge of divine things. *Surprised by Grace* will appeal to anyone desiring a deeper encounter with God.

Adrian J. Walker
Professor of Theology
Saint Patrick's Seminary and University
Menlo Park, California

Fr. Kevin Joyce has shared a generous story, with humility and humor, that incorporates the personal, the psychological, and the spiritual. His journey, with all its twists and turns, provides spiritual encouragement as well as sophisticated instruction in contemplative practice. In the end it is also a beautiful example that, summoned or not, God is present.

Mario L Starc, Ph.D.
Jungian Psychoanalyst
Dean Emeritus, The Sanville Institute
for Clinical Social Work and Psychotherapy
Berkeley, California

Surprised by Grace recounts an old, familiar tale: a young man sets off to find out who he is and what he's meant to do with his life. What's new here is Kevin Joyce's astonishing dedication to the task. During a far-flung, years-long quest that takes him most of the way around the world, neither disillusionment nor bouts of depression can derail him. At a time when the Church so desperately needs vocations to the priesthood, this exuberant spiritual adventure story could inspire a new generation to answer the call.

Paula Huston
Author of *One Ordinary Sunday*
and *The Hermits of Big Sur*

In the spirit of Thomas Merton's *Seven Storey Mountain*, Fr. Kevin Joyce entices spiritual seekers, non-believers and even skeptics to "gamble on God." After leaving family and friends to pursue the Catholic priesthood in his youth, this lover of old classic cars initiates us into a world of Yoga and Zen, the romance of Mexico, and the contemplative roots of Christian Europe. An epic adventure dancing with the beauty of marriage, the draw of celibacy, the call to ministry, and those voids that only Christ can fill, *Surprised by Grace* is a kind-hearted reason for hope.

Dr. Anthony Lilles
Author of *Fire From Above:*
Christian Contemplation and Mystical Wisdom
Co-founder of the Avila Institute of Spiritual Formation

In *Surprised by Grace*, Fr. Kevin Joyce takes us on an enlightening journey where the spiritual path meets unpredictable twists in life. Seamlessly blending Eastern and Western philosophies, this book transcends religious boundaries. I found solace and comfort in the reminder that a deeper connection with our spirituality can be discovered even in our most challenging moments. For anyone searching for meaning and purpose, *Surprised by Grace* is an invitation to a fuller life beyond labels and ideology. I wholeheartedly recommend it to anyone on their quest for spiritual awakening.

Gerald Gonzales, Ph.D.
Clinical Psychologist
Adjunct Faculty, Santa Clara University